D1615379

REMAINS

Historical and Literary

CONNECTED WITH THE PALATINE COUNTIES OF

Lancaster and Chester

VOLUME XXVIII—THIRD SERIES

MANCHESTER:

Printed for the Chetham Society

1981

THE FINANCIAL ADMINISTRATION
OF THE LORDSHIP AND
COUNTY OF CHESTER

1272-1377

by

P. H. W. Booth

MANCHESTER
Printed for the Chetham Society
1981

Copyright © The Chetham Society 1981

Published for the Society
by Manchester University Press
Oxford Road, Manchester M13 9PL

British Library cataloguing in publication data

Booth, Paul Howson William
   The financial administration of the lordship
  and county of Chester 1272–1377.
  – (Publications/Chetham Society: vol.28).
  1. Chester (Cheshire) – History
  I. Title
  942.7'14   DA690.C5

  ISBN 0–7190–1337–2

Printed in Great Britain
by Willmer Brothers Limited
Rock Ferry, Merseyside

CONTENTS

TABLES

FIGURES

PREFACE

This is the study of one aspect of the government of an English county during a century or so of the later Middle Ages. Cheshire was, however, an unusual county being, to use modern terminology, a 'landed estate' as well as a 'local government unit'. It was subject to the 'royal lordship' of the earl of Chester, who was, in this period, either the king or his eldest son. The earldom of Chester was larger than the county: from 1284 another shire, that of Flint, was annexed to it and became subject to the rule of the earl's chief officials in Chester castle. In 1364 the Black Prince's officials used the term 'lordship and county of Chester' to describe Cheshire, a term which happily unites the modern notions of 'local government' and 'estate'. This book does not deal with the constitutional and administrative complexities of Cheshire's 'palatine' status. Brian E. Harris's section on 'The Palatinate of Chester, 1301–1547' in the recently published volume II of the *Victoria History of Cheshire* provides a good, short outline. It is important to realise, though, that Cheshire's organs of administration were, in the thirteenth and fourteenth centuries, distinct from those of the rest of England. Local officials were responsible for collecting the public revenue which arose from within the county, as well as that which accrued from the earl's estates. (See the map, p. xiii.) This study is mostly concerned with the fiscal activities of these county officials, and the main questions asked relate to how and why they made decisions in the implementation of financial policy. The context for this are the changes in Cheshire's social, political and economic structure which were tending to transform the county's relationship with the rest of England, and which were to promote it to a unique eminence by the end of the fourteenth century.

P.H.W.B.

ACKNOWLEDGEMENTS

For their teaching, advice and encouragement I should like to thank B. W. McManus, David W. Crossley, Edward Miller, E. Margaret Wade, Michael J. Bennett, Ian Kershaw, Anne E. Curry, Denise Kenyon, Robin Studd, P. J. Morgan, S. Rhys Williams, J. Phillip Dodd, O. J. P. Bott, as well as other members of the Liverpool University Medieval Cheshire Seminar. I was fortunate to receive the benefit of criticism of this work, when it was still in typescript, from Brian E. Harris (of chapter three) and Jennifer I. Kermode (of the whole text). I can but reward them with the usual disclaimer of any responsibility for the arguments which I advance in the following pages. W. H. Chaloner and J. S. Roskell, of the Chetham Society, have given considerable help with preparing the monograph for publication. Above all, I am grateful to Dorothea Oschinsky, whose boundless enthusiasm stimulated my interest in the study of medieval estate accounts, and to the late A. R. Myers, who pointed me in the direction of the history of medieval Cheshire, supervised the dissertation on which this monograph is based, and remained constant in giving advice and encouragement.

I also wish to record the help and consideration I have received from the staffs of the Public Record Office, the Department of Manuscripts of the British Museum (now the British Library), the Cheshire Record Office, the Chester City Record Office, the National Library of Wales, the Lancashire Record Office, the Staffordshire Record Office, the National Register of Archives and the Duchy of Cornwall Office. The Keeper of the Records of the Duchy of Cornwall kindly gave me permission to consult the *Jornale* of John Henxteworth, 1355/7.

Financial assistance towards the completion of the research for this monograph has been provided by the University of Liverpool Research Fund and the British Academy's Small Grants Research Fund in the Humanities. The time that was also essential to complete the task was afforded by a term's study leave in the summer of 1979, for which I should like to thank Liverpool University's Leave of Absence Committee, and also several colleagues in the Institute of Extension Studies: Edwin Rhodes, J. Alan Morton, B. M. C. Husain and R. Merfyn Jones.

The Society is grateful to Liverpool University Research Fund and the British Academy for assistance towards the cost of publishing this book.

ABBREVIATIONS

B.I.H.R.	*Bulletin of the Institute of Historical Research*
B.L.	British Library (formerly British Museum)
B.P.R.	*Register of Edward the Black Prince,* 4 vols. (1930–3)
C.A.C.W.	*Calendar of Ancient Correspondence concerning Wales,* ed. J. Goronwy Edwards, Univ. of Wales Board of Celtic Studies, History and Law Series, II (1935).
C. Inq. Misc.	*Calendar of Miscellaneous Inquisitions*
C.Ch.R.	*Calendar of Charter Rolls*
C.C.R.	*Calendar of Close Rolls*
C.C.R.V.	*Calendar of Various Chancery Rolls*
C.C.W.	*Calendar of Chancery Warrants*
C.F.R.	*Calendar of Fine Rolls*
C.M.R.	*Calendar of the Memoranda Rolls, 1326–7*
C.P.R.	*Calendar of Patent Rolls*
Chamb. Acc.	*Accounts of the Chamberlains and other Officers of the County of Chester, 1301–60,* ed. R. Stewart-Brown, Record Society of Lancashire and Cheshire, 59 (1910).
Chet. Soc.	Chetham Society
Ch. Pipe Rolls	*Cheshire in the Pipe Rolls, 1158–1301,* ed. R. Stewart-Brown and M. H. Mills, Record Society of Lancashire and Cheshire, 92 (1938).
D.K.R.	*Report of the Deputy Keeper of the Public Records*
Ec.H.R.	*Economic History Review*
E.H.R.	*English Historical Review*
Q.R.	Queen's Remembrancer
J.C.N.W.A.S.	*Journal of the Chester Archaeological Society* (formerly known as the Chester and North Wales Architectural, Archaeological and Historic Society)
Mich.	Michaelmas
P.R.O.	Public Record Office
Rec. Soc.	*Record Society of Lancashire and Cheshire*
Rot. Parl.	*Rotuli Parliamentorum : the Rolls of Parliament,* 6 vols. (1767); index vol., Record Commission (1832).
T.H.S.L.C.	*Transactions of the Historic Society of Lancashire and Cheshire*

Tout	T. F. Tout, *Chapters in the Administrative History of Mediaeval England*, 6 vols. (1920–33).
T.R.H.S.	*Transactions of the Royal Historical Society*
V.C.H. (Cheshire)	*The Victoria History of Cheshire*

Note. Terminal dates given in the following form—1358-9—should be taken to refer to accounting periods (Michaelmas 1358 to Michaelmas 1359). When this is *not* the case the form 1358/9 is employed.

To my wife Patricia
and our daughters

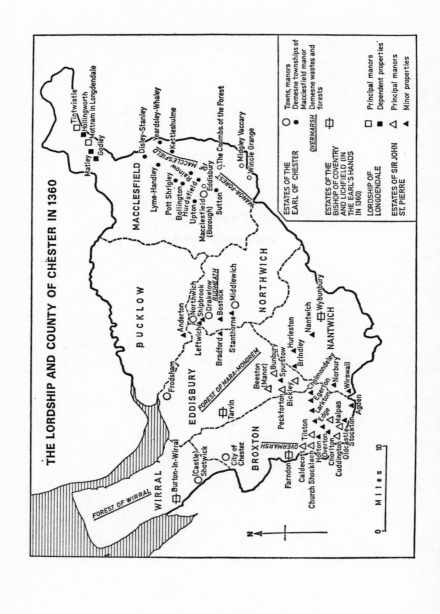

THE LORDSHIP AND COUNTY OF CHESTER IN 1360

ESTATES OF THE EARL OF CHESTER
○ Towns, manors
● Demesne townships of Macclesfield manor
Demesne wastes and forests

ESTATES OF THE BISHOP OF COVENTRY AND LICHFIELD IN THE EARL'S HANDS IN 1360)
□ Principal manors
■ Dependent properties

LORDSHIP OF LONGDENDALE
OVERMARSH

ESTATES OF SIR JOHN ST. PIERRE
△ Principal manors
▲ Minor properties

WIRRAL

FOREST OF WIRRAL

Burton-in-Wirral
(Castle) Shotwick
City of Chester

BROXTON
OVERMARSH
Farndon
Caldecott
Church Shocklach
Tilston
Overton
Horton
Chorlton
Cuddington
Oldcastle
Stockton
Malpas
Egerton
Larkton
Edge
Agden
Wirswall
Norbury
Chalmondeley
Peckforton
Bickley
Bunbury
Spurstow
Beeston (Manor)
Brindley
Hurleston
Brindleston

EDDISBURY
Frodsham
Tarvin
FOREST OF MARA-MONDREM

BUCKLOW
Anderton
Leftwich
Northwich
Shipbrook
Drakelow
RUDHEATH
Bostock
Bradford
Stanthorne
Middlewich

NORTHWICH
Nantwich
NANTWICH
Wybunbury

MACCLESFIELD
Disley-Stanley
Yeardsley-Whaley
Kettleshulme
Lyme-Handley
Pott Shrigley
Bollington
Rainow
Hurdsfield
Upton
Macclesfield (Borough)
Eddisbury
Sutton
MACCLESFIELD FOREST
The Coombs of the Forest
Midgley Vaccary
Wincle Grange

Tiptwistle
Hollingworth
Matley
Godley
Mottram in Longdendale

N

0   10
Miles

CHAPTER I

COUNTY AND COMMUNITIES

No work of administrative history can be written without some conception, either implicit or explicit, of the population being administered. On the other hand, the records which have to be used to throw light on the political, social and economic history of medieval Cheshire are themselves the products of administrative and judicial machinery which needs to be understood in its technical aspects if the resulting evidence is to make sense. Consequently, it is necessary to start with what can be only a provisional account of Cheshire's history in order to set the scene for the investigation of the county's financial institutions.

I THE PEOPLE AND THE LAND

Ever since the serious study of local history began in the seventeenth century, Cheshire's medieval past has compelled students to adopt firmly held views. Such views have often been the product of contemporary needs rather than the result of historical study. Thus, in the so-called 'King's Vale-Royal', which was published in 1656 but compiled earlier in the century, it is said:

So have they [i.e. the Cheshire people] been always true, faithful and obedient to their Superiors; insomuch, that it cannot be said, that they have at any time stirred one spark of Rebellion, either against the Kings Majesty, or against their own peculiar Lord or Governour.[1]

Naturally, such an account must have been calculated to endear the county to the government of King Charles I, although even a cursory search in the abundant and rich fourteenth and fifteenth century records would have shown how false it was. The notion of medieval Cheshire people as being stout-hearted but essentially loyal, of possessing, in other words, the typical virtues of their time, but to a heightened degree, did not finally die until the present century. It was killed off as a result of investigations into the records of the palatinate, the institution whose parts were still in some sort of working order as late as the 1830s and which had long been held to mark out the county as significantly different from the rest of England. By the 1950s an almost complete reversal of the traditional view had been brought about: the county's institutions were no longer thought of as unique, while, in the words of Geoffrey Barraclough's dazzling synthesis, written in 1951, 'Contrary to a widespread belief, the county in the middle ages was sparsely populated, poor and unproductive . . .'. Moreover, he felt that the survival of the palatinate privileges after the wars of Welsh conquest which signalled the end of their useful life resulted in the county administration remaining old-fashioned, inefficient and oppressive, at least until the reforms of the sixteenth century.[2] Barraclough's assessment of Cheshire in the later Middle Ages was heavily influenced by the truly pioneering work of H. J. Hewitt, whose *Medieval Cheshire* told the coherent story of a county which was shamefully abused by the most famous of its earls, the Black Prince. He had adopted, Hewitt maintained, a policy of squeezing the last drop of money from the county in order to finance costly and, in the end, futile wars, and extravagant personal display. This analysis, published in 1929, in its disillusionment with the glamour of medieval warfare, was, once again, very much in accordance with the spirit of the times.[3]

Obviously, any account of Cheshire's administrative history has to try and come to grips with such views. This faces us, immediately, with the most serious difficulty obstructing an assessment of Cheshire's economic and social base in the Middle Ages, namely the lack of firm population data for the period between the twelfth and sixteenth centuries. The recorded population of 1,524 souls at the time of Domesday Book was low, even allowing for omissions and the 'wasting' of holdings as a result of the Conquest. No population at all is recorded for the area covered by the later forest of Macclesfield or the lordship of Longdendale, while virtually no part of the Cheshire plain east of the central ridge had a recorded population density of more than two people to the square mile. Wirral and the south-west were, on the other hand, the two more heavily settled regions.[4] There were, therefore, considerable areas of the county which were still capable of primary settlement, but as there are no late fourteenth century poll tax returns for Cheshire the advances which had been made before the time of the Black Death have to be estimated by the study of those individual manors and forests for which evidence survives. On such a basis there can be little doubt that the county experienced considerable growth of population in old settlements as well as the creation of wholly new ones in the years between 1086 and 1349, and thus participated in the general tendency of the north of England to improve its demographic position relative to the regions of early dense settlement.[5] At least some of this increase may have been brought about as an act of policy by the Norman earls of Chester by employing the local custom of 'avowry' (that is, of offering legal protection to fugitives from other counties) to attract settlers.[6] Changes and movements in population are usually characterised by anonymity, but one example may illuminate this process. Round about the end of the thirteenth century three brothers came to Cheshire from the Isle of Man. They were in the retinue of an unnamed 'great man' and, judging by their surname, were employed in his kitchen. Their master must have been of high rank indeed, because he was given hospitality in the king's castle at Shotwick, which was conveniently situated next to a landing place for vessels coming to the Dee from the Irish Sea. Two of the brothers, Robert and Nik Cook, decided to stay and, in the usual manner of those intending permanent settlement, married local girls, both of whom were unfree tenants of the comital manor of Shotwick. This led to a dispute late in the fourteenth century as to whether the brothers' descendants, as springing from a union of free fathers with unfree mothers, were themselves free or not. It is perhaps indicative of local custom, again tailored to attract immigrants, that their freedom was allowed.[7]

Evidence for the effects of the Black Death on level of population is, of course, fragmentary for England as a whole. Dr. Hewitt's summary of published source material concludes, quite rightly, that the effects of the pestilence on the county's population, although serious, cannot be quantified.[8] There is additional, unpublished, evidence which shows, for example, that at least twenty-one of the county's tenants-in-chief died between the summer and autumn of 1349, but the only instance where a death rate can be hazarded is the 50 per cent which has been tentatively suggested for the tenants of Macclesfield manor.[9] It is feasible to propose, therefore, that the growth of population which Cheshire experienced between 1086 and the early fourteenth century may have been considerably greater than the 360 per cent which has been suggested for Burton-in-Wirral, a manor situated in a region which had been settled relatively early.[10] Changes in the distribution of wealth within the county are even more difficult to document than changes in population levels. There is some suggestion, though, that during the two and a half centuries following Domesday the south central region of the county, largely corresponding with the late thirteenth century hundred of Nantwich, in terms of wealth measurable by both landed and personal property, improved its position markedly, relative to that of Wirral and the Dee valley.[11]

Much more is known about the social structure of the county. In historians' jargon Cheshire was not 'highly manorialised'. This does not mean that estates there were not organised as manors, which they certainly were, but that the ties which bound the typical tenant to his lord were somewhat looser than was the case in the central Midlands of England. There were obviously considerable numbers of free men in the county by the late thirteenth century. They were the largest class in the bishop of Coventry and Lichfield's three manors of Burton, Wybunbury and Tarvin, as they were in the earl's manor of Macclesfield.[12] On the other hand, the abbot of Vale Royal's manors of Gayton, Weaverham and Over seem to have consisted wholly of villein tenants in 1291 when they were surveyed, and bondmen were the largest group on the comital manors of Shotwick and Frodsham in 1280.[13] It is impossible to estimate from such evidence the proportions of free and unfree in the population at any time in the thirteenth or fourteenth centuries. What is clear is that the disabilities of the Cheshire villeins in the half-century or so before the Black Death were largely personal, consisting of controls by their lords over their free disposal of land, and involvement in economic activity, together with the payment of heavy death duties. There is no evidence at all that any Cheshire villein had ever had to work regularly on his lord's demesne lands: that is to perform the 'week-work' which was required from the unfree in highly manorialised areas. Labour services were, it is true, exacted from Cheshire tenants, but they were usually limited and seasonal 'boon services' (for which the lord of the manor had to pay in kind) for which free men were liable as well as villeins. For example, in 1280 every bond-tenant of Shotwick was said to owe two days' free ploughing to the lord every year, one in winter and one in spring, plus three days' help at harvest time.[14] Similar labour services were due, in 1360, from the lords of two east Cheshire manors, Newton and Hattersley, to their overlord, the lord of Longdendale.[15] On the estates of Sir John St. Pierre, which the Black Prince acquired in 1353, and which were scattered over the south-western part of the county, the tenants rendered the minimal labour service of a day's work each at harvest time.[16] Such boon services were obviously regarded as being a typical tenant liability in the county in the mid-fourteenth century because when the new manor of Drakelow was created after 1347 they were imposed on the tenants there.[17] It is indicative of the vagueness of status boundaries that, in the escheators' extents of manors from the 1340s onwards, tenants are not usually classified as 'free' or 'villein' but in accordance with the degree of security of their holding. In 1352–3, for example, the tenants of Newhall and Grappenhall manors were all described as leaseholders (*terminarii*) while in 1349 those of Barthomley, Crewe, Dodleston, Handley and Latchford were called 'tenants-at-will'.[18] This suggests that even before the Black Death there may have been a tendency for free men and 'neifs', as categories, to merge and be reconstituted on an economic basis. Nevertheless, despite the light labour services associated with villein tenure, there is no doubt that the personal and financial liabilities could weigh very heavily. The two bitter and well organised revolts in 1329 and 1336 of the Vale Royal tenants of Darnhall and Over, who appear to have owed no labour services at all, illustrate this fact.[19] On the other hand, these men, who were prepared to go to extreme lengths, were not typical of Cheshire peasant farmers as a whole. They were the victims of the transfer of the ownership of their manorial estates from the crown to a desperately under-endowed religious corporation, which needed to exact every ounce of its rights of lordship to pay its way.[20]

As far as the agrarian organisation of Cheshire manors is concerned, research over the last quarter-century has convincingly demonstrated that open-field systems were widespread in the county, as was the case in all the lowland regions of north-western England.[21] The notion of the dominance of so-called 'Celtic' economic and social institutions in this border region has to be rejected. As most of the evidence is fragmentary, and much of it post-medieval, it is very difficult to say how the open fields were organised. An example of what might be a three-course arable system at Tarvin and Wybunbury in 1297 has been discovered, and the unpublished Shotwick court rolls for 1338/44 demonstrate that communal ploughing was practised on the earl's manor there.[22] It seems, therefore, that the two elements of what has been called the 'Midland' system existed in Cheshire, namely truly common fields (where co-aration was practised) and the three-course rotation. Whether both were ever combined in one manor, and, if so, how frequently, is impossible to say and may well never be known unless records of the early modern enclosure of Cheshire open fields should come to light.

On the whole, therefore, the economic and social history of thirteenth and fourteenth century Cheshire points to an affinity with the north Midlands. The notion of a desperately backward county characterised by a very low level of population and a predominantly pastoral rural economy is not borne out by the evidence. In June 1308 Edward II ordered the justiciar of Chester to provide the following goods for the royal army (the figures relating to requisitions from Staffordshire and Shropshire at that time are given in brackets after those from Cheshire).

500 qr. wheat (300 qr.)
300 qr. barley-malt (300 qr.)
500 qr. oats (300 qr.)
100 tuns of wine (Nil)
400 bacons (200 qr.)
200 qr. salt (Nil)
10,000 horse-shoes[23] (Nil).

The royal government, at least, in its assessment of locally available commodities, was implying a mixed agrarian economy within the county as well as demonstrating the importance of the port of Chester in the trade of the whole region.

II COUNTY INSTITUTIONS

If it is difficult to justify the treatment of Cheshire's socio-economic history in the central Middle Ages as 'exceptional' relative to the English north Midlands, what is left of that other support for the idea of the county's 'separateness' from the mainstream of English historical development, the so-called palatine privileges? From the seventeenth century onwards antiquaries have customarily emphasised the distinctiveness of medieval Cheshire's political and judicial institutions. Barraclough's major achievement was to question the basis on which such notions were formulated and suggest that the palatinate was a relatively late (post-1237) development in the county's constitutional history.[24] The precise nature of what was meant at any particular time by the term 'county palatine', or by the 'royal liberties' which the earl of Chester possessed in the county, is difficult to determine. The question has to be asked here, however: to what extent did the people of Cheshire's unusual relationship with the earl of Chester, together with the self-contained nature of the county's courts of justice, affect the political and social make-up of the county?

In one sense, too much can be made of the county's liberties. Probably the most important tie as far as the vast majority of the population was concerned was that between manorial lord and tenant. The authority which Cheshire landlords wielded in their manor courts, as revealed by *quo warranto* inquiries from the mid-fourteenth century onwards, was no different from that of their contemporaries elsewhere in England.[25] Moreover, one of the main privileges of those of higher social status, namely the limitation of military service due from the feudal tenants-in-chief of the earl to 'within the Lyme', had become meaningless by the end of Edward I's reign, when armies were no longer raised by calling on the service of tenants by knight-service. With the merging of the earl's avowrymen into the rest of the population, it is hard to cite any constitutional abnormality which would have made the purely local communities different from those in neighbouring English counties. As far as the *county* community was concerned, however, the assembly of magnates and free men, in both its political and its judicial aspects, had a cohesion which was unique. This was to have profound effects on the public finances of the county, particularly in the second half of the fourteenth century, since the privileges of the county community (which had developed from those of the earl) were an eminently marketable commodity.

What marked Cheshire out from other counties was this fact

together with the associated phenomenon that there was only one main channel of political power, patronage and judicial favour, namely that which led to the palatine lord of the county and his officials. It was as if in the kingdom of England there was no one in the social scale between the king himself and those of the rank of county knights. The only rival to royal power in Cheshire was the non-resident baron of Halton, whose estates formed part of the earldom of Lincoln until 1311 and then of the earldom and duchy of Lancaster. This barony, with its own private hundred of Halton, serjeanty of the peace and avowries, was an important liberty within Cheshire. On the other hand, it was only during the time of Thomas, earl of Lancaster, that there were two really distinct centres of power as far as Cheshire was concerned, and after his brother Henry's failed attempt at insurrection following the defeat of Boroughbridge Lancastrian politics were for a long time subordinate to royal policy. It is significant that in 1359, by agreement between the Black Prince's council and that of his cousin, Henry of Grosmont, duke of Lancaster, one of the most important privileges of the baron of Halton, the right to have private avowries, was surrendered in the interests of good government.[26]

III CHESHIRE AND ENGLAND

The community of the medieval county of Chester and its history cannot simply be dismissed, therefore, as irrelevant to the history of the rest of England. After all, the county was undeniably part of the kingdom, and was generally subject to both English statute and common law. Its history, after the death of earl John of Scotland in 1237, can be understood only in terms of the policies of the English monarchy. In the 105 year period between 1272 and 1377 Cheshire was under the direct control and lordship of the king of England for about forty years: it was only during the thirty years of the Black Prince's manhood that the earl of Chester had anything like an independent administrative organisation. Even then the prince's career formed a part of the greater plan determined on by his father. On the other hand, there is no doubt that a gap of quite serious dimensions between Cheshire and England opened up in the last three decades of the fourteenth century. The signs appear as early as 1355, when a group of Cheshire men went to poach game in the earl of Arundel's lordship of Bromfield. Two years later a gang with much more criminally serious intentions, led by one Hugh Vernon, invaded Queen Philippa's lordship of High Peak in Derbyshire. The queen's council complained that, as a result, the area was 'on the point of being ruined', and that Vernon and his brothers had behaved in this way because they could not be brought to justice except in Cheshire.[27] This was the beginning of complaints about a series of military-style armed attacks by Cheshire men on other counties which have no parallel even in that violent and lawless age.[28] Successive petitions in parliament between the 1370s and the 1390s reiterated the complaint of the queen's officials in 1357: that the criminals could be brought to justice only in Cheshire and, therefore, could escape scot-free. The conflict culminated at the end of Richard II's reign with the formation of the king's bodyguard of Cheshire archers and the promotion of the county to the rank of principality. By his favouritism the king was attempting to establish a power base in England and restore the authority of the crown, but, as James L. Gillespie has pointed out, in doing so he 'had ceased to be the king of all his people'.[29]

If Richard had not needed to rebuild royal authority, if his father had not required so many soldiers and such large amounts of money for his overseas policy, then it would have been possible to tackle Cheshire's separatist tendencies with firmness and some chance of success. This is not to say that the county's independent-mindedness did not have strong roots. This is where its 'royal liberties' and highly self-conscious county community are important. J. R. Maddicott has recently pointed to the significance of the fourteenth century county community as a grouping whose political consciousness was articulated in its major institution, the county court.[30] Cheshire's county court was a body with much greater power and judicial importance than its namesakes in other counties. There was, therefore, a potent combination of a socially cohesive community with a judicially privileged institution which is best illustrated by an incident which took place on 4 June 1325, the day a newly appointed justiciar of Chester, Sir Richard Amory, presided over the county court for the first time. Amory was a man of considerable importance in national politics and was familiar with English legal forms. As a 'new boy', therefore, he said that he wished to have his somewhat anomalous position in the county court explained to him. It is likely that his ignorance was studied, and that his aim was, in fact, to test the county's privileges. He asked why, although he was termed *justiciarius,* he did not have the right to render judgements (*judicia*) and legal decisions (*consideraciones*) as was the case with justices elsewhere in England. In this county court, he said, it seemed to him that the doomsmen and suitors were setting themselves up as justices, with the implication that they were aspiring above their stations. To this they replied, in their turn, that they were only doing what their ancestors had done before them, and that it was only when one of the earl's officials had been tried for an offence committed either against the earl or the king that the justiciar had been accustomed to pass judgement. They went on to say that their judgements were arrived at by consultation between what were virtually the two 'houses' of doomsmen and suitors, with the provision for a majority decision in cases of disagreement.[31] How big these bodies of county representatives normally were in the fourteenth century is very difficult to determine: in a plea held in 1342 thirty-one doomsmen were present, and it seems that their office was attached to particular pieces of land.[32] On the other hand, the suitors may well have been identical with the whole body of free men of the county (with the exception of Macclesfield hundred), and so the assembly at the county court could have been, at times, a large one.[33]

It is unlikely that the justiciar of Chester was as powerless to influence the course of judicial proceedings as Amory made out, or that the members of the community present in the county court were not liable to be subject to pressure from the magnates of the county. Nevertheless, if only part of what the doomsmen and suitors alleged in 1325 was true, the opportunities for subordinating judicial matters at a high level to the interests of the community and its leaders were certainly there. When the stories begin to be told of gangs fleeing back to the county after committing crimes elsewhere, and, in effect, to evade justice, we may consider that a fair degree of such subordination had already come about. The financial dimension of this political and constitutional development, which has its roots firmly in the last two decades of the thirteenth and the first two of the fourteenth centuries, will be considered in what follows.[34]

NOTES

[1] Daniel King, *The Vale-Royal of England* (1656), p. 19.
[2] Geoffrey Barraclough, 'The Earldom and County Palatine of Chester' *T.H.S.L.C.*, 103 (1951), pp. 30, 40–2.
[3] H. J. Hewitt, *Mediaeval Cheshire: An Economic and Social History of Cheshire in the Reigns of the Three Edwards*, Chet. Soc., New Series, 88 (1929), pp. 6–7.
[4] I. B. Terrett, 'Cheshire', in *The Domesday Geography of Northern England*, (eds) H. C. Darby and I. S. Maxwell (1966), pp. 330–90.
[5] P. H. W. Booth, ' "Farming for profit" in the fourteenth century: the Cheshire estates of the earldom of Chester', *J.C.N.W.A.S.*, 62 (1980), pp. 73–90.
[6] R. Stewart-Brown, 'The Avowries of Cheshire', *E.H.R.*, xxix (1914), pp. 41–5. For the non-military purpose of avowries see Barraclough, 'Earldom', p. 42. In 1311 the avowrymen were described as 'newcomers to Cheshire for felony committed elsewhere, and fugitive bondmen from anyone's villeinage' (Ches. 29/24 m. 6). By offering such people legal protection and a special status (which passed to their heirs) there would be a clear tendency to attract population from neighbouring counties.
[7] S.C. 2 156/13 m. 11.
[8] Hewitt, *Mediaeval Cheshire*, p. 148.
[9] Ches. 3/23 Edward III. For Macclesfield, see below, pp. 89–90.
[10] P. H. W. Booth and R. N. Jones, 'Burton in Wirral: from Domesday to Dormitory, Part Two', *Cheshire History*, 4 (1979), pp. 28–42.
[11] Such a statement depends on two factors: that the assessment list of the 1406 mise book (John Rylands University Library of Manchester, Tatton MS 345), was compiled before 1349, and that the same assessment was based on a combination of landed and movable wealth in the manner of the Tudor subsidies. See below, pp. 124–5.

[12] Staffordshire Record Office D1734/J2268, ff. 30, 31.

[13] J. Brownbill (ed.), *The Ledger-Book of Vale Royal Abbey*, Rec. Soc., 68 (1914), pp. 63–4; C. 145 38(4); R. Stewart-Brown (ed.), 'Extent of the Royal Manor of Shotwick', *T.H.S.L.C.*, 64 (1912), pp. 138–40.

[14] Stewart-Brown, 'Shotwick' pp. 139–40.

[15] P. H. W. Booth and J. H. and S. A. Harrop (eds), *The Extent of Longdendale, 1360*, Cheshire Sheaf, Fifth Series (1976–7), item 83.

[16] S.C.6 783/1.

[17] S.C.6 784/5 m. 12; S.C.6 784/1 m. 10.

[18] Ches. 3/23 Edward III/21, 27.

[19] Brownbill, *Vale Royal*, pp. 31–2, 37–42.

[20] *Ibid.*, pp. 161–3.

[21] G. Elliott, 'Field Systems of Northwest England', in *Studies of Field Systems in ᵗhe British Isles*, (eds) A. R. H. Baker and R. A. Butlin (1973), pp. 41–92.

[22] D. Sylvester, 'A Note on Medieval Three-course Arable Systems in Cheshire', *T.H.S.L.C.*, 100 (1958), pp. 183–6; S.C.2 156/12 m. 2d, 3d.

[23] *C.P.R.*, 1307–13, p. 81. In addition, 100 qr. of beans and peas were required from Staffs. and Salop. In 1306 the purveyance in Chester of 200 oxen, 500 sheep, 52½ qr. oats, 61 bacons, 90 qr. 2 bushels of salt and two tuns of wine was ordered (Ches. 29/17 m. 12d) and in 1309 200 qr. wheat, 500 qr. oats and 200 bacons (Ches. 29/22 m. 9d).

[24] Barraclough, 'Earldom', pp. 34–8. It must be said, however, that his own hypothesis of the malign nature of the palatine privileges in the fourteenth and fifteenth centuries stands up far less well. For a recent contribution to this debate see B. E. Harris, 'The Palatinate 1301–1547', *V.C.H. (Cheshire)*, II, pp. 9–35.

[25] Harris, 'Palatinate', pp. 30–1.

[26] *B.P.R.*, IV, pp. 280–1. In return for the surrender, which was to be only for the duke's life, he was to be paid 100 marks a year. Lancaster's avowries and serjeanty of the peace had been seized at some time before 1355, presumably in the course of the *quo warranto* proceedings which were held in the county court in 1353 (*B.P.R.*, III, pp. 210–11; Ches. 34/1). For his career in royal service see Kenneth Fowler, *The King's Lieutenant* (1969).

[27] *B.P.R.*, III, pp. 202, 267.

[28] P. H. W. Booth, 'Taxation and Public Order: Cheshire in 1353', *Northern History*, xii (1976), p. 20.

[29] James L. Gillespie, 'Richard II's Cheshire Archers', *T.H.S.L.C.*, 125 (1975), pp. 1–2, 31–3.

[30] 'The County Community and the Making of Public Opinion in Fourteenth-century England', *T.R.H.S.*, Fifth Series, 28 (1978), pp. 27–43.

[31] Ches. 29/37 m. 10.

[32] Margaret Sharp, 'Contributions to the History of the Earldom and County of Chester, 1237–1399 . . .', Univ. of Manchester Ph.D. thesis, 1925, p. 178.

[33] In 1298 it appears that suit at the county court ('curia Cestrie') was obligatory by at least five and possibly all of the free tenants of the bishop's manor of Burton-in-Wirral (of whom there were twenty-seven in all), Booth and Jones, 'Burton-in-Wirral', pp. 30–1.

[34] There appear to be strong parallels between Cheshire and the other great palatinate, of Durham, as far as the economic and social history of both counties in the later Middle Ages was concerned. See R. B. Dobson, *Durham Priory, 1400–1450* (1973), pp. 250–96.

CHAPTER II

DOCUMENTARY SOURCES

It might be thought otiose to dwell in detail on the Cheshire financial records now that so many medieval accounts are in print and the work of Dorothea Oschinsky and P. D. A. Harvey on accounting methods is available.[1] However, I hope to demonstrate in this chapter that the Cheshire accounts for the later thirteenth and fourteenth centuries are worth close study because the form which they eventually assumed was rather different from that employed in most contemporary estates, derived as it was from the practices of the (much maligned) royal exchequer. As with any other historical source, the form of an account has to be clearly established if any conclusions based on the records cast in that form are to have validity.

Nearly all the sources for the history of Cheshire financial administration in the Middle Ages are to be found in the Public Record Office. Convenient though this may be from certain points of view, it is an artificial situation, brought about by the Victorian mania for centralisation which led to the removal of records from their existing repositories. After being taken to London, some suffered the further indignity of being forcibly amalgamated with records already there into so-called 'special collections'. So the present-day researcher will find the Cheshire records largely divided between two P.R.O. groups, thus:

1. Palatinate of Chester (now condensed to 'Chester' or 'Ches.').
2. Special Collection: Ministers' and Receivers' Accounts (or S.C.6).[2]

Our first task, then, is to attempt to disentangle the archival origins of the sources before discussing them in some detail. In the following chapter an account will be given of the administrative structure which produced the records, and the workings of which are reflected in them.

In the Middle Ages Cheshire's official records would have been found, to a very great extent, either in Chester itself or in London and Westminster. In 1854 those medieval records still in Chester castle were bundled into railway luggage vans and taken to London, there to be installed in the newly built Public Records Office[3] At the time, all the records of what the civil servants called 'the abolished courts of the principality of Wales and the palatinate of Chester . . .' were being turned out of their various attics and cellars, and so when the Cheshire records reached London they were held to be part of a 'collection' called 'Welsh Records'. Most of them were ink-stamped with this legend after their arrival in the office. It was only about fifty years later that the Cheshire records were removed from this group and reclassified as 'Palatinate of Chester', whereupon the word 'Welsh' was crossed out in many (if not all) of them and 'Chester' stamped over the top. So most of the 'Palatinate of Chester' records are the local records of the Cheshire (and Flintshire) judiciary and administration, although not all the local records now remain in that class.

'Chester' records can be divided into two main sub-groups, one of which relates to the activities of the palatinate exchequer (and the office of chamberlain), the other to the county court (and the office of justiciar). The exchequer was a 'chancery' as well as a financial bureau, and the most important class of records produced in the former capacity were the recognisance rolls (Chester 2). These contain the enrolments of charters and letters patent under the seal of the earldom, as well as recognisances and other memoranda.[4] They start in 1307, and have been calendared in the appendices to three nineteenth century reports of the Deputy Keeper of the Public Records.[5] Many of the fourteenth century rolls are in a poor state of preservation, but they are important for financial administration in that they contain letters of appointment of officials, and also recognisances made in the exchequer by those who took leases of county offices and of the earl's demesnes.[6] Administrative orders coming to Cheshire either from the king or the earl of Chester were not normally enrolled, except as warrants for the issue of charters or letters.[7] It is likely that the chamberlain kept files of all the orders he received, whether enrolled or not, although nearly all have been lost. There are two for our period, a general file for 1344 and 1345, and another relating to escheats for 1374 and 1375.[8] The other part of the chamberlain's duties was concerned with the collection of revenue, and this will be dealt with in the discussion of the accounts.

Cheshire's legal records are of formidable bulk and of great importance for the social history of the county. Foremost among them are the plea rolls of the county court, the first of which dates from 1259 while the regular series begins in 1287.[9] Besides the main business of common and crown pleas 'before the justiciar of Chester', these rolls were used, at various times, for recording general memoranda such as writs, proclamations, inquisitions post mortem, recognisances, petitions, and also property deeds of private persons. Rolls of the early fourteenth century are particularly rich in notes of miscellaneous kinds, and contain records of the farms of offices and lands,[10] purveyance of goods for the Scottish war,[11] orders to levy the arrears of the earl's officials[12] and records of administrative inquiries.[13] Parallel with the formal record of the plea roll, files of writs and memoranda relating to the proceedings of the county court were kept, the first surviving example being for 1342.[14] In addition, there are several classes of subsidiary enrolments relating to the county court and the other principal judicial institutions of the county, none of which survives from before the beginning of Edward III's reign.[15] These records, and especially the county plea rolls, not only throw a great deal of light on the incidental activities of the county's financial administration but are themselves the product of Cheshire's central judicial system, which itself generated a sizable proportion of county revenue.

Records relating to the various central administrative organisations of which Cheshire formed a part in the thirteenth and fourteenth centuries are to be found in both the Public Record Office and the Department of Manuscripts of the British Library. When the county was in the king's hands it came within the purview of the royal chancery and exchequer, and the records of both these departments are important sources for the history of its administration. Of particular value are the chancery enrolments, all of which have been calendared for the period, and the exchequer pipe and memoranda rolls.[16] Comparatively little material from the central administrative records of the three royal earls survives and, indeed, the time of earl Edward of Windsor (1312/27) is an almost complete blank. Some central accounts from Edward of Caernarfon's principate are still extant, together with one of his privy seal rolls.[17] The latter is disappointing from our point of view, since the prince had two seals, and this roll contains little information about the day-to-day running of his estates. Central accounts also survive for the early years of the Black Prince, up to 1345, but none thereafter, all those of his maturity having been lost, together with virtually all other records of his central administration. One exception is a file of petitions to the prince and his council from his tenants of Cornwall and England (1375/6)[18] and another is a group of letters which probably formed part of a file (or files) of his privy seal letters of the 1340s.[19] The third group of survivors completely outweighs in importance any other evidence of this type, namely the four volumes magnificently calendared by the Public Record Office under the title *Black Prince's Register*, volumes I–IV. They are, in fact, registers of the prince's privy seal letters, of which volume I covers all his estates (1346/8) and volumes II, III, and IV cover Cornwall and Devon, Cheshire (including Flintshire and Denbigh marcher lordship) and 'England' for the years 1351 to 1365.[20] The survival of these volumes, and particularly the third, enables a more detailed study to be made of Cheshire financial administration during the decade and a half after the Black Death than at any other time in the county's medieval history. This bias is reinforced by the fact that the vast bulk of so-called Cheshire ministers' accounts (that is, the accounts of the local accounting officials) comes from after the Black Death. These records, which are both 'central' and 'local' in character, form the backbone of this study and are considered in some detail in the remaining sections of this chapter.

I THE CHESHIRE SERIES OF MINISTERS' ACCOUNTS

Nearly all these accounts are now in the P.R.O. class S.C.6. However, their origins are more diverse than this would suggest, since S.C.6 (or Ministers' and Receivers' Accounts) is an artificial collection composed of records of quite different origins. One main source for the Cheshire series is the records which were brought from Chester castle, as described above, in the mid-nineteenth century. Most, if not all, the rest were already in London in the Middle Ages, and formed part of what was once called the 'Ancient Miscellanea of the Queen's Remembrancer of the Exchequer'.[21] Henceforth these two basic sources will be called W.R. and Q.R. The Chester castle (W.R.) accounts comprise almost wholly 'originals', although the survival of three accounts of Macclesfield lordship for 1359–60 suggests that some duplicates (if not a complete set) might also have been kept at Chester.[22] It is not clear whether Q.R. originally formed one collection or not. All of them are 'duplicates', but their transmission to the capital could have been for two reasons: either for the information of the central administrations of the successive royal earls of Chester, or to assist the royal exchequer in its task (from the 1350s onwards) of levying the earl's debts.[23] On balance, the former hypothesis is the more likely, but the possibility cannot be ruled out that Q.R. is two collections, not one, which implies that from the mid-fourteenth century onwards there could have been four series of Cheshire accounts, one of 'originals' and three of 'duplicates'.[24] On the whole, Q.R. is in a much better state of preservation than W.R., several of the latter series being badly damaged at the bottom of the longer membranes, which, of course, lie near the outside when the membranes are rolled up. Although the two collections were merged into S.C.6 after their arrival in the Public Record Office, most of them retain the ink-stamps which they were originally given, and so it is easy to identify the source from which they have come.

It is important, for several reasons, to emphasise the diverse origins of these accounts. The bulk of them come from the years between 1349 and 1376, when it was usual for the Cheshire accounts to be written up by clerks brought to the county by the earl's auditors.

For example, in 1359–60 the chamberlain of Chester (as county receiver) paid £2 expenses to the three clerks who 'wrote and duplicated' his and the other officials' accounts.[25] In February 1357 the auditor William Spridlington was paid various expenses in connection with the audit of the prince's estate accounts for 1355–6, among which was money spent on the employment of his two clerks, whom he had sent to Chester for twenty-four days to write the ministers' accounts there.[26] Thus the duplicates (at least in the first fifteen years or so after the Black Death) were not copies made by the clerks of written accounts submitted by the officials themselves: in fact, they were not 'duplicates' in the sense of being word-for-word reproductions of the 'originals'. The W.R. accounts were obviously written in stages: they exhibit either different hands writing the same account, or the same hand writing at different times, to judge by the ink colours. In the first few years after 1349, at least, they are full of amendments and deletions and contain marginal notes relating both to the audit and to future action to be taken by the officials. Q.R., on the other hand, is a series of fair copies, usually written by one clerk throughout without signs of later additions, which omits or condenses many of the maginalia and other notes present in W.R.

In 1910 the first twenty-three of the Cheshire chamberlains' accounts, together with two sets of accounts of other county officials, were published, in translation, by the Record Society of Lancashire and Cheshire. They were edited by R. Stewart-Brown, under the title *Accounts of the Chamberlains and other Officers of the County of Chester, 1301–1360*.[27] This work, it must be said, has to be used with extreme caution, partly because many of the accounts are presented only as extracts, little or no indication being given of what has been left out, and because the accuracy of the translation is of variable merit. Consequently, many references will be made here to the original accounts rather than to the published volume. Two volumes of the Flintshire portions of the chamberlains' accounts and the corresponding Flint ministers' accounts have been published by the Flintshire Historical Society, and are of a high standard of accuracy.[28] The introduction to the second of these, by D. L. Evans, serves as the best published introduction to the palatinate ministers' accounts as a whole.

II INTERPRETATION OF THE ACCOUNTS

Medieval estate accounts are normally highly formal documents. They have an affinity to plea and court rolls, which, although they are the records of courts of justice, do not pretend to be records of actual proceedings (in the sense of 'what happened') in the modern meaning of the word. Similarly, accounts are records of an occasion— the audit—but they were compiled in accordance with existing forms, and this tends to conceal the reality of what they purport to represent. Few actual descriptions of auditing procedures on English estates survive, and there is none emanating from the government of Cheshire. Nevertheless, there is some circumstantial information from the later years of the Black Prince which can throw light on the practices employed on his estates in the quarter-century after 1350. At that time the audit took place in Chester itself and was conducted by auditors who acted as delegates of the prince's council. The actual place of audit was the exchequer chamber in Chester castle, in essentials a room containing a table abacus—or 'exchequer' proper.[29] When this exchequer was renewed in 1359–60, we are told, it was made of green striped cloth, stretched tightly over an undercloth of canvas, both of which were nailed on to the table.[30] At that time the exchequer also had two coffers, in which were kept the 'rolls and other memoranda of accounts', both of which were double locked.[31] Each year, four large bags of white leather were bought by the chamberlain to keep the year's accounts in, and he had to provide smaller bags for the cash. Up to four dozens of parchment were used in writing the accounts and 'other memoranda', and the list of audit requisites is completed by a supply of red wax which was needed for sealing the letters concerned with the account.[32] Paper began to be regularly used in the exchequer from the early 1370s, for 'entering the chamberlain's receipts', and for making recognisances and letters touching the chamberlain's office.[33]

The time for holding the audit, between 1349 and 1374, ranged from the October to the July *following* the terminating Michaelmas of the accounts being heard.[34] In general, either the spring or early summer was preferred. To take one audit as an example, that of January 1365 was conducted by Richard Stokes and William Cranewell for the accounts of 1363–4.[35] Very likely the clerks retained to write at the audit had been sent to Chester in advance, to help get everything ready. Before the audit started, all the 'accountants' (that is, the accounting officials) of Cheshire and Flintshire had to be summoned to attend, in person, probably by writ under the Chester exchequer seal. Those who defaulted were fined, as happened with the bailiffs of Drakelow and Overmash, who failed to turn up at the audit of 1369. Penalties of 13s. 4d. and 6s. 8d., respectively, were imposed on them but were subsequently cancelled when both officials took an oath to the effect that they had not been forewarned to attend, and their contention was accepted.[36]

By the start of the audit, which could take part of three months to complete (as in 1356), and possibly before the auditors even reached Chester, substantial parts of the accounts had already been written out. Medieval estate accounts were 'conservative' in that they worked on the assumption that each account would be much the same as the one of the year before, unless there was a compelling reason for a particular item to be different. The actual writing and duplicating of the account rolls was a lengthy process: in March 1354 the three clerks were paid for their expenses for nine weeks and two days which they had spent in writing the earldom of Chester's 'accounts and other memoranda'.[37] P. D. A. Harvey suggests that during what he calls 'phase two' of manorial accounting practice, which ended at an uncertain time in the fourteenth century, it was usual for the body of an account to be drawn up before the audit began.[38] This was certainly true of the W.R. ('original') accounts, the sum totals and 'feet' of which were obviously written after the main body of the record. Many of the deletions and amendments of these 'originals' can be accounted for by this practice of pre-writing. Furthermore, an actual pre-written account from the 1365 audit is extant. Why it was left incomplete, and then preserved, is impossible to say. Very likely it was mislaid and then, having been found when a replacement had already been written, was put into the leather bag with the completed accounts. It is the account of the sheriffs of Chester city, and it is structured thus:

1. *Heading* (in the usual form).
2. *Receipts*
   a. Fee farm of the city: nothing (because it is granted to the earl of Arundel).
   b. Chamber rent
   c. Pepper rent
   d. Rent of the Dounfoul lands
   e. Rent of Handbridge
   f. Rent of the city tanners

   Blanks have been left where all the sums should appear

This account has no sum total or discharge at the 'foot', although spaces have been left for them. What suggests that this is a pre-written, rather than merely an abandoned, account is the fact that the parts which were left blank are precisely those which were completed at a later stage in the 'original' account. The city sheriffs' account did not have an expenses side as such, but it is likely that, in those which did, certain fixed expense items could also be pre-written (although their sums were probably left blank, as in the 'receipts' of the above example). In the 1363–4 Frodsham manorial account, for example, an item was originally included in the discharge for 'the stipend of the clerk writing the court rolls' which was, at a later stage, struck out, with the explanatory note 'because the escheator ought to be charged, by ordinance of the lord's council'.[39]

The actual audit, or rendering of account, was conducted by the auditors with each accounting official separately and finishing up with the chamberlain as county receiver. When there were two auditors acting together, as in 1365, it is likely that they divided at least some of the work between them. It can be assumed that the two principal county officials at that time, the lieutenant-justiciar and the chamberlain, would normally be present at the rendering of every account. From 1352 the county escheator acted as steward of the demesne manors and towns of the earldom, and it is likely that he also attended the audit of their accounts. There is no evidence at all that there was any right of general attendance at the exchequer at audit time: the business was a private matter between the prince and his officials, and probably only those connected with the business would be allowed to appear. If the use of an abacus and the actual form of the written accounts are anything to go by, the first task at the audit of each account was to calculate the 'charge' (onus) by laying it out, item by item, on the columns of the exchequer cloth and then making a sum total.[40] Each item had to be checked by reference to subsidiary documents such as court rolls (or estreats), rentals[41] and general lists of receipts called 'particulars' (particule).[42] The most important check of all was the previous year's account (and especially any orders or recommendations that it contained), and the first business of the audit may well have been to read it through. At the bottom of many accounts the phrase 'examinatur' or 'examinatur per totum' is written, and possibly this was put there by the auditors after this initial reading. Another way of checking the accuracy of an official's receipts was to employ the classical medieval device of divided responsibility called 'controlment'. For example, in the case of the perquisites of the county court, one official (the justiciar, or his lieutenant) was responsible for holding the court and for drawing up its plea rolls while another, the county sheriff, was responsible for collecting the resulting revenue. In theory, each official was to act, at the audit, as a check on the other. The major difficulty for the auditors was caused by those types of revenue which were naturally unpredictable, in that any variations in them could be attributed to non-human agency. The best example of this is the yield of corn (as well as the birth—and mortality—rates of stock) on the demesne manors. For such cases the auditors utilised a notional set of reasonable standards of performance derived from the textbooks of husbandry and accounting, which they would use to test the manorial yields. For example, in the case of corn, they examined the previous year's account to see how much seed of each type had actually been sown and then compared it with the amount of corn in the grange before deducting the allowance for the threshers (warranted by a tally) or adding a surcharge based on the assumption that the bailiff or reeve would naturally appropriate to himself the difference between a level and a heaped bushel measure. If the yield, expressed as a multiple of seed, was regarded as unsatisfactory, then the official was required to give good reasons; furthermore, if his story was not convincing, a surcharge could be imposed on his account to bring the yield up to an acceptable standard. In the

Frodsham pea account of 1353–4, for example, to the various amounts of peas received by the bailiff is added

3 qr. 2 bushels 1 peck [of peas] charged on the account so that it [i.e. the pea-harvest] responds twice itself, as in the bailiwick of Drakelow.[43]

Moreover, on the discharge side of the pea account (and in the bailiff's cash receipts) we find 3 qr. 2 bushels 1 peck of peas recorded as a 'sale on the account', at a price of 4d. a bushel.[44] Similarly, in the same bailiff's account there is a surcharge on the yield of oats:

so that it responds three times itself, since the bailiff of Drakelow responds almost to the fourth grain this year.[45]

These fictitious 'sales on the account' could also be employed by the auditors to surcharge the actual sales of corn or livestock if they felt that the prices obtained in the market were suspiciously low. Whether such 'sales' were *always* fictitious,[46] and were not sometimes sales of surplus stock ordered by the auditors when the accounts were balanced, is very difficult to say. The latter possibility certainly cannot be ruled out in the Cheshire accounts.

The use of standards of performance could, on occasions, work in favour of the officials. For example, when the Frodsham manorial account for 1355–6 was audited in June 1357 the bailiff, Henry Torfot, was surcharged for 16½ bushels of wheat (recorded as a 'sale on the account' yielding £5 14s. 6d.) so that the issue should equal twice the seed sown.[47] Torfot resisted this imposition, however, whereupon the auditor and the chamberlain went to Frodsham and held an inquisition by the sworn tenants of the manor on Friday 23 June, which found that

... the said Henry did not receive nor, in any way, could he have received of the same wheat from the issues of the grange more than that with which he freely charges himself, and it is the fault of nobody that the issue is not larger but was the result of the frequent occurrence of bad weather in that same year.

Consequently the 'sale' was largely discharged by an exoneration at the foot of his account for £5 6s. 8d.[48]

It is clear, then, that the sum total of 'receipts', as laid out in the columns of the exchequer cloth, represented not the money the official had actually received during the accounting year but what he was liable for. Some of the revenue may still not have been collected at the time of the audit (although still recorded as 'receipts'). Some of it might never be collected at all, and for perfectly legitimate reasons.[49] After the placing of the 'sum total' on the exchequer cloth it was up to the official to 'discharge' as much of that liability as he could. Very likely, each separate item was put on the cloth and then a total struck which would be placed, in counters, immediately under the piles representing the charge. Discharge was then subtracted from charge, the difference being a debit or (if negative) a *superplusagium*. Each item of the discharge needed firm supporting evidence to be acceptable to the auditors. In most accounts the first item of the discharge is called *decasus redditus* (or fall of rent), which represents that part of the rent roll admitted to be impossible of collection. In most cases this was because the original tenant had died and no one was willing to take up the tenancy.[50] The advantage of such a procedure over the removal of such rents from the rental (and, therefore, from the charged rents) was that the *decasus* served as an annual reminder to the auditors that tenements existed which, although vacant at present, might yield revenue in the future. New rents were put *in decasu* by the auditors only with reluctance, and probably after the holding of a sworn inquisition in the manor or town in question.[51] Next in the account comes the real expenses of the bailiwick, such as wages, repairs to buildings and so on. To receive allowance for these, the accountant had to produce both vouchers and acknowledgements of receipt. Vouchers were writs under the earl's seal, addressed to both the accountant and the auditors, authorising particular items of expenditure. Receipt-acknowledgements were usually in the form of sealed instruments whereby the recipient of the money stated that the authorised expenditure had actually been made on the proper object. In the case of expenditure on repairs to buildings (or 'works') an indenture was usually made between the bailiff or reeve of the particular manor and the county official responsible for works. In the early fourteenth century the chamberlain kept files relating to 'expenses, liveries and letters of allowance' paid on his own account, one of which has survived.[52] Only in cases where the payment made was customary, or was actually mentioned in some other warrant (such as the official's letter of appointment), could the voucher be dispensed with.

At this point the balance was struck, resulting in what should be called the 'net charge', a much less ambiguous term than 'net receipts' or 'net profits'. As the various stages of charge and discharge were approved it is likely that the sums were written in the spaces provided in the pre-written accounts, and either the auditors themselves, or a clerk at their direction, would then write 'probatur' ('it is approved') after each figure. Two categories remain which the 1365 audit has still not touched upon: namely the cash actually paid over by the official (if any) and the arrears (*arreragia*) (if any) of his previous year's account. In medieval accountancy, cash payments are called *liberaciones denariorum* (liveries of money). In the standard estate accounting procedure employed by the late thirteenth century, the so-called 'common' or 'Westminster' form, the liveries were considered to be part of the discharge, the arrears part of the charge, and so both were already included when the balance was struck.[53] Figure 1 shows the structure of such an account.

COMMON FORM ACCOUNT

1. Charge

| *a.* Arrears |
| *b.* Receipts |

2. Discharge

| *a.* *Decasus* |
| *b.* Expenses |
| *c.* Liveries of money |

3. Balance

| Charge *minus* discharge: this becomes the arrears of the following year's account |

The Cheshire accounts, as drawn up at the 1365 audit differed from this structure in two main ways. First, neither the arrears nor the liveries of money, as has been noticed, were included in the balance of charge minus discharge. Secondly, the balance in the Cheshire accounts, which represented the current net charge (as it excluded the liability for arrears), is followed by a 'foot' (*pes*) within which both arrears and liveries are accounted for. After the balance, the remainder (*remanentia*) of the previous year's account is stated, and then added to the balance to form the *summa coniuncta debiti* (joint sum of indebtedness). Then follows each of the liveries of money—the actual payments of cash by the accounting official—which are deducted from the joint sum, item by item. Often the parts of the charge to which the liveries relate will be specified in some detail, and normally the liveries of remainder will come first. After these deductions a further balance is struck which can be followed by any further adjustments to the official's liability in the form of extra charges (for some reason omitted in the body of the account), allowances (*allocaciones*—sums which should have been allowed in the discharge) or exonerations (*exoneraciones*—sums which should not have been included in the charge). Then follows the final balance, prefixed by the words 'et debet . . .', which becomes the remainder (*remanentia*) of the following year's account. Most accounts do not finish here, however, since there is usually some attempt to say who is responsible for the unpaid charge, and why. First the respites (*respectus*) are listed, which are sums for which the auditors acknowledge there is a good reason why they could not have been collected within the year of the account. Also deducted will be any sums which the accounting official can demonstrate someone else is responsible for, and what is then left is the 'clear remainder', which gives the true state of the accountant's indebtedness and which enables the auditors to decide whether legal action needs to be taken to make him pay up more quickly.[54]

It would be rash to assume that each stage of the account as described above was necessarily the record of a discrete action or group of related actions, performed in the same order, in the audit. Accounts are too formal to be related to actuality in such an obvious way. Nevertheless, there can be no doubt that written record and 'occasion' did have a general correspondence. What united them was the operation of the 'adversary principle': the auditors strive to maintain the charge, and the accountant, who was financially guilty until proved innocent, has to reduce it as much as possible. In this battle a great deal of subsidiary documentation was required, apart from the particulars of receipt and the vouchers and acknowledgements of expenditure already mentioned. Tallies were used to record the payments of liveries of money by the lesser officials to the chamberlain, and by the chamberlain to the receiver-general. Accountants sometimes submitted, in writing, petitions to the auditors for items to be respited or allowed on their accounts, possibly in advance of the audit.[55] In the Black Prince's later years it seems that at least some of the officials brought with them locally prepared draft accounts, which were then used to form the basis of the official accounts (both 'original' and 'duplicate') that were made up at the audit. One pointer to this is in the Frodsham account for 1368-9, in which Henry Torfot, the bailiff, was allowed 6s. 8d. 'for the clerk writing his account'.[56] Such drafts relating to the chamberlain's account, which were drawn up by his clerk, survive for Richard II's reign and later,[57] and this practice may account for the fact that the W.R. series, from the 1360s onwards, tends to be written tidily with a minimum of alterations, indicating that they also could well be fair copies although still entitled 'originals'. It always has to be remembered, when attempting to interpret and assess medieval estate accounts such as these, that a great deal of documentation available to contemporaries has usually been lost to us. For example, out of all the court rolls which must have been produced for the demesne manors and towns (excluding Chester) in the years under review only one reasonably full set survives and that is for the Macclesfield manor-hundred complex from 1345 onwards, whereas for the other lordships only six rolls are now extant.[58] Yet they were particularly important, not only as legal records but as subordinate accounting documents: indeed, both the Northwich and Middlewich court rolls for 1328 have accounts relating to the town copied on to them.[59]

In order to see what the structure of the 1365 accounts entails, one of the more straightforward examples from that audit is set out in summary form in Fig. 2. In Pearson's account two very interesting points emerge. First, that sections 5 to 8 constitute what is, virtually, an 'account within the account', in which the reality of cash movements is contrasted with the statement of liability of the first part. Secondly, that *arreragia*, or *remanentia*, should never be equated

FIGURE 2

ACCOUNT OF JOHN PEARSON, BAILIFF OF THE MANOR OF DRAKELOW, MICHAELMAS 1363–MICHAELMAS 1364. (S.C.6 786/3 m. 3d)[60]

1. Charge

	£	s.	d.
a. Rents	£46	6s.	8¾d.
b. Court perquisites	£1	9s.	4d.
c. Turbary and pasture	£2	4s.	0d.
Sum total:	£50	0s.	0¾d.

2. Discharge

	£	s.	d.
a. Rent granted to Chandos	£40	0s.	0d.
b. *Decasus*		12s.	9½d.
c. Bailiff's stipend		10s.	0d.
Sum total:	£41	2s.	9½d.

3. Balance (1 *minus* 2): £8 17s. 3¼d.

4. Joint sum of indebtedness

	£	s.	d.
a. Balance	£8	17s.	3¼d.
b. Remainder of his 1362–3 account	£10	19s.	2d.
Sum total:	£19	16s.	5¼d.

5. Foot of account

	£	s.	d.
a. Liveries to the chamberlain			
i. Of remainder		*Nil*	
ii. Of current issues	£8	9s.	4¼d.
b. Allowance (of rent of lands in hand this year for lack of tenants)		7s.	4d.
Sum total:	£8	16s.	8¼d.

6. Remainder (4 *minus* 5): £10 19s. 9d.

7. Analysis of remainder

	£	s.	d.
a. Rent unpaid by Stephen Merton	£10	15s.	3d.
b. Manor Court amercements unpaid by the abbot of Dieulacres		4s.	6d.
Sum total:	£10	19s.	9d.

8. Clear remainder: *Nil.*

with 'arrears' in the modern sense of that term. At first glance the remainder at the end of his account, of over £10, seems to be an ominously large proportion of a total charge of little more than £50. However, section 7 at the foot shows the matter in a different light, because the whole of the remainder is attributable to two items, by far the largest of which, £10 15s. 3d., is represented by

Stephen Merton's unpaid rent. Examination of earlier Drakelow accounts will show that this rent was an annual charge of 17s. 5½d. on twenty-seven acres of land which Merton claimed as part of his own manor of Lache-in-Rudheath, while the prince's auditors asserted it belonged to their employer's manor of Drakelow. It was thus included in the charged rents in the bailiffs account from 1351–2,[61] on the basis of the revised extent of the manor which had been made in November 1352.[62] It continued to be charged until the account of 1362–3, when the rental was evidently revised, but the accumulated charge was retained in the remainder (representing twelve and a half years' rent, in all).[63] In theory it would have been possible for this annual rent to accumulate in the remainder indefinitely, and it would not have been long before it had become as large as the current charge itself. On their own, therefore, such cumulative remainders or arrears represent a balance of financial obligation and not a judgement of financial viability. Thus when J. A. Raftis, for example, states that the arrears on the estate accounts of Ramsey abbey represent a 'constant burden of debt' which had a deleterious effect on estate administration, the question has to be asked: what factor or factors can they be attributed to, since mere size of arrears (even as a proportion of 'receipts') indicates nothing of significance *by itself*?[64] Moreover, it is not sufficient to repeat the commonly iterated view that arrears represent not the 'balance sheet' of the manor but the personal liability of the official. As Pearson's account shows so clearly, the bailiff himself was not 'in arrears' at all. Admittedly this was an exceptional case, in that the disagreement over Merton's rent involved a decision over complicated interlocking property rights, something which not infrequently in the Middle Ages led to a long delay in reaching a decision. When the last surviving Drakelow account of the Black Prince's time was audited, in June 1375, the arrears of this rent were still included in the bailiff's remainder, awaiting a decision as to whether they should be paid out or not.[65]

One further point to be noticed is that there are no figures, *in the account itself*, which could be called the 'yield' of the manor. This, however, can be easily calculated by adding the £8 9s. 4¼d. (all of which was current charge) which the bailiff paid over to the chamberlain, to the annuity of £40 which was granted to Sir John Chandos out of the manor's issues. This annuity would not have been allowed by the auditors had not Chandos's attorney's acknowledgement of its receipt been produced by the bailiff. Thus three statements can be made about the efficiency of the bailiff in respect of this account:

1. The 'yield' of Drakelow in 1363–4 was £48 9s. 4¼d.
2. The bailiff paid all the 'yield' over within the year of account.
3. The remainder was accounted for by a rent and a court amerce-

ment, and in both cases it was doubtful whether they should be paid or not.

In concluding this discussion of the mechanism of the Cheshire audit in the second half of the fourteenth century it is necessary to pose the question : were the auditors accustomed to take a 'view' (*visus*) of the accounts for the current year in which the audit was taking place? Walter of Henley recommended this practice, but it is not clear whether it was widely adopted in the sense that the interim balance, which was what such a view entailed, was actually written down.[66] Comparatively few 'views' have survived in the records of any medieval estate, but even if they were produced regularly there would have been little point in keeping them after the final account had been drawn up and approved, unless the accountant died (or fled the country) before the audit, when the view could have been kept in place of the missing account. Three Cheshire 'views' are extant, all from between 1356 and 1368,[67] and there is an account for 1315 which may possibly have been a 'view' (but its heading is lost).[68] Of the four, only one can truly be regarded as being the record of an interim 'review', and that is the chamberlain's view for Michaelmas 1356–23 June 1357, which actually runs to the month when the auditors are known to have been in Cheshire, to hear the accounts for 1355–6, and which also has a final account covering the same period.[69]

III THE REFORM OF CHESHIRE ACCOUNTING PROCEDURE, 1347/53

We have seen that the accounting methods employed in the Chester exchequer by the prince of Wales's auditors in the 1360s were different from the 'common form' used on most English estates from the late thirteenth century. It is important to discover, therefore, how and when this method was first developed, and also to ask what is its significance for the history of the county's financial administration. The second question, in particular, is difficult to answer, because comparatively few Cheshire accounts from before 1349 have survived.

With a fair degree of certainty the adoption of the structure of account employed in 1365 can be pinpointed to the audit which was held at Chester in late 1347. Only one account for that audit, that of Hugh Hopwas, the county escheator, for 1345–6, is extant.[70] The years between 1346 and 1348 were a time of great activity and change in the administration of the Black Prince's estates, resulting from his assumption both of adult responsibilities and of direct control of his landed endowment. In Cheshire this meant the final abandonment of farming out the revenues of the county (and

Flintshire) to the justiciar, which entailed, as a consequence, an active and detailed concern with the management of comital finances.[71] In that same year, 1347, all the prince's important estate administrators, led by Peter Gildesburgh, were in Cheshire in order to undertake a thorough overhaul of county government and to organise the transfer of Macclesfield manor and hundred to the prince from his grandmother, Queen Isabella.[72] The audit was held by Nicholas Pynnok, one of the prince's full-time auditors, and John Pirie, who had had wide experience in the prince's service at both the central and regional levels and who, by this time, was probably semi-retired.[73] The clerk who wrote the escheator's account was used to the 'common form' method of accounting, because when he first drafted it he put the *arreragia* as the first item in the charge, immediately after the heading. Having done this, possibly before the audit started, he was instructed to cross this entry out, which he did and then he wrote a note by the cancellation saying that it had been done because the arrears were to be found in the foot ('quod inferius in pede'). True enough, in the foot of that account the arrears have become a remainder, added on to the net charge in the way described above.[74] Unfortunately, this escheator's account has no liveries, but the last one to survive before this, for 1342–3, although it has *arreragia* in the 'common form' position, does have the liveries in the foot, after the balance.[75] There are six other Cheshire ministers' accounts for the years between 1346 and 1350, when the full series starts, and none of them has *arreragia* at the beginning. It took some while, though, for the auditors' clerks to become fully accustomed to the new method of drafting. At the audit of February 1351 the arrears were written in the escheator's account at the beginning and then had to be transferred to the foot.[76] The same mistake was also made in three of the accounts compiled at the November 1353 audit.[77] Doubtless the practice of pre-writing the accounts would have made it easy for the clerks, if they were used to a different method, to make such slips. After 1353 that particular error does not occur again.

This adoption of a new method of accounting made use of a system which already existed: it did not entail 'invention'. In fact, the '1365' type of account is known to have been used in Cheshire at least twice before, in John Paynel's chamberlain's account for 1335–6[78] and John Burnham junior's receiver's account for 1342–3.[79] There can be little doubt that the new method originated in the royal exchequer. When the prince left England to fight in the Crécy campaign, in 1346, his father set up an 'English council' to supervise the government of his estates which was dominated by royal exchequer men. Bishop Edington of Winchester, treasurer of England, was a member, as was Robert Sadington, a baron of the exchequer.[80] Gildesburgh himself had been a royal exchequer official earlier in his career.[81] To be precise, it was the procedure of the exchequer's sub-department of 'foreign accounts' that was taken over, rather than the mechanism of audit of the county sheriffs and others in the 'main-stream' of royal exchequer accounting. The office of the 'auditors of foreign accounts' had first been set up in 1310, and they were subsequently given their own premises on the north-east side of the Exchequer Chamber in the palace of Westminster.[82] It was their task to audit the accounts of the revenue which came outside the control of the English sheriffs (and analogous accountants), including that which arose from the royal manors and towns.[83] Indeed, between 1327 and 1333, when Cheshire was in the king's hands, its financial administration had been the direct responsibility of these 'foreign' auditors. Moreover, there had been, at that time, exchanges of personnel between the department and Chester castle, such as in 1328, when the 'foreign' auditor, Thomas Blaston, became county chamberlain.[84]

FIGURE 3

ACCOUNT OF JOHN PAYNEL, CHAMBERLAIN OF CHESTER,
MICHAELMAS 1327–13 MARCH 1328[85]

1. Charge				
	a. Receipts of Cheshire	£313	1s.	3¼d.
	b. Receipts of Flintshire	£44	19s.	0¾d.
	Sum total:	£358	0s.	4d.

2. Discharge				
	Expenses			
	Sum total:	£130	14s.	6½d.

3. Balance (1 *minus* 2):		£227	5s.	9½d.

4. Joint sum of indebtedness				
	a. Balance	£227	5s.	9½d.
	b. Remainder of 1326–7 account	£1,338	9s.	10¼d.
	Sum total:	£1,565	15s.	7¾d.

5. Foot of account				
	a. Liveries	£1,113	0s.	0d.
	b. Allowances	£289	16s.	4d.
	Sum total:	£1,402	16s.	4d.

6. Remainder (4 *minus* 5)		£162	19s.	3¾d.

The accounts produced by these auditors were enrolled on the 'foreign membranes' which were originally bound up at the end of the pipe roll and later enrolled separately. An examination of the chamberlain's account for Michaelmas 1327–13 March 1328 shows that the method of drawing up such 'foreign accounts' was the same as that employed by the Black Prince's administration after 1347, as Fig. 3 demonstrates. It is not particularly surprising to find the methods of the king's exchequer being employed in the administration of his eldest son. To employ Dr. Sharp's words again:

... though the prince's accounts were not drawn up and passed through the ordinary channels of exchequer procedure, they were, both in the first and the last instance, indirectly subjected to the spirit at least of that department's administration, in the personnel of accountants, receivers and auditors.[86]

Indeed, in 1351 the prince's council went as far as to ordain that the usage of the royal exchequer, both as a court of law and a financial department, was to be the model for the chamberlain's management of the Chester exchequer, although this decree had to be rescinded very soon afterwards.[87]

However, this use of exchequer accounting procedure does not seem to have applied when Edward of Caernarfon was Prince of Wales and earl of Chester (1301/7). It is difficult to speak with certainty, because there are only four extant chamberlain's accounts for this period (one of which is fragmentary) and two Macclesfield accounts which, together, cover one financial year.[88] However, the chamberlain's accounts do appear to show that the 'common form' was employed at the time, as can be seen in that for 1303–4, which is summarised in Fig. 4. This account illustrates the principal weakness of this form of accounting. The inclusion of 'arrears' in charge, and liveries in discharge, although it produces the right balance as far as the account is concerned, does not separate the 'actual' from the 'potential' account in the way the 1365 account does. Of course, there is no reason why 'common form' accounts should not have distinguished between liveries of arrears and current liveries, but it is clear from published accounts that such was not normally the case.[89] In P. D. A. Harvey's edition of the Cuxham manorial accounts for 1276 to 1359, for example, there is only one account (that for 1357–8) in which the cash liveries are distinguished into arrears and current revenue.[90] Dr. Harvey places accounts of the post-1347 Cheshire type in what he calls 'phase one' of medieval estate accounting development, and it is true that the accounting form adopted by the Black Prince's administration in the late 1340s had a venerable ancestry. This went back through the royal exchequer 'foreign accounts', beyond 1310 to the accounts of royal manors in the pipe roll in the thirteenth century (of which there are several for Macclesfield manor),[91] when the basic procedure of the reformed Cheshire accounts was employed but without the cash liveries being particularised.[92] The earliest surviving substantial application of this accounting method to Cheshire is to be found in the justiciar's accounts on the pipe rolls for August 1237 to Easter 1254; in other words, it dates from when the county first came under permanent royal control.[93] Consequently, it is likely to have originated as a modification of the royal pipe roll accounting method, adapted for use with unified estates, such as manors in the king's hands. It is possible that the earliest important English estate accounts of all, those of the lands of the bishopric of Winchester, which start in 1208, also had their origins in royal exchequer procedure: this type of accounting is normally termed the 'Winchester' method.[94] Harvey's placing of accounts such as the Cheshire examples in 'phase one' of accounting tradition is correct, therefore, but it is difficult to accept his contention that the 'phase one' method was more primitive in conception than 'phase two' (or 'common form'), which became so popular with estate managers in the later thirteenth century.

FIGURE 4

ACCOUNT OF WILLIAM MELTON, CHAMBERLAIN OF CHESTER, 1303–4[95]

1. Charge

a. Arrears	£570	8s. 5¾d.
b. Receipts of Cheshire	£1,113	6s. 3¼d.
c. Receipts of Flintshire	£428	16s. 4¼d.
d. Foreign receipts	£273	6s. 8d.
Sum total:	£2,385	17s. 9¼d.

2. Discharge

a. Expenses	£446	7s. 1½d.
b. Liveries of money	£1,514	18s. 5½d.
Sum total:	£1,961	5s. 7d.

3. Balance (1 *minus* 2)   £424 12s. 2¼d.

The 1347 reform affected both main levels of accounting in Cheshire administration. As in most large lay estates, the Black Prince's officials operated a three-tier system of accounting. The names employed to designate officials varied from estate to estate, and there were considerable variations in detail, but the scheme was usually structured as follows:

1. Receiver-general level (or keeper of the wardrobe level): for the whole estate.
2. Receiver level: for a regional group of properties.
3. Bailiff level: for one or two properties.

One important reason for having such a structure was, without doubt, that of security. In a large, scattered estate it would have been excessively dangerous for all local bailiffs to make their liveries of money to a single centre, as well as a waste of energy and time. So the usual plan was for level 3 officials to make their liveries to a local receiver, usually based in a castle containing one or more 'treasuries', that is, strong-rooms for the storage of money and documents. The importance of security of documents does not need to be emphasised for an age when financial administration so completely depended on writings both formal and informal. That very large sums could be at stake is illustrated by the fact that, in 1353, a former county sheriff was found guilty of breaking into the Chester castle treasury and stealing a recognisance which showed that he owed the prince, as earl, a sum of 1,000 marks, not a great deal less than half the normal annual revenue of Cheshire and Flintshire together.[96] From time to time during the year the various receivers would deliver cash, under armed escort, to the central office (whether it be the lord's wardrobe or the office of his receiver-general). The general principle was that no more cash than absolutely necessary should be left in the hands of either local or regional officials, and that money should be transported around the countryside in reasonably small amounts. Thus it was normal in the later fourteenth century for the chamberlain of Chester, as a 'level 2' official, to make several liveries of money throughout the year to the prince's receiver-general. In respect of his 1361–2 account, for example, there were eleven, dated, as follows:[97]

1.	14 May 1362	£566 13s. 4d.
2.	26 May	£26 7s. 2d.
3.	26 June	£33 2s. 3d.
4.	3 July	£73 0s. 0d.
5.	19 July	£17 0s. 0d.
6.	24 July	£40 0s. 0d.
7.	20 August	£120 0s. 0d.
8.	23 August	£200 0s. 0d.
9.	18 October	£764 12s. 8d.
10.	18 October	£68 11s. 4d.
11.	28 November	£33 10s. 0d.

The dates are those of the sealed acquittances made by Peter Lacy, the receiver-general, on receipt of the cash which the chamberlain, John Burnham, had to produce at the audit for discharge to be granted him on his accounts. Thus the two acquittances dated 18 October 1362 probably stand for two separate consignments of cash from Chester to Westminster which left within a very short time of each other. In most large estates three tiers of accounts appear to have been employed by the end of the fourteenth century to express the financial relationships between the three levels of financial responsibility. Compared with the superabundance of those for level 3, comparatively few for level 2 have survived, and hardly any at all for level 1. Little attention has been paid even to those higher-level accounts which do survive, since they are mainly concerned with the movements of cash. They are important, however, from the point of view of administrative history, and it is necessary to see how they relate to each other, and to the accounts of level 3.

As with other estates, what makes it difficult to describe the inter-relation of the lower and higher level accounts is the shortage of those of the top level. During the times of the three earls Edward (1301/7, 1312/27 and 1333/76) the three-level structure operated, but it is not until 1350 that the reasonably continuous series of level 3 ministers' accounts begins. The survival of chamberlains' accounts, representing level 2, is patchy, consisting of two short series (1301/6: five accounts; and 1347/62: ten accounts) and some few other examples.[98] There are only three from the time of Edward of Windsor, none of which is both complete and covers a full financial year.[99] Indeed, many of the chamberlains' accounts after the 1320s are in a poor state of physical preservaton. As for level 1 accounts, there are some fifteen from between 1301 and 1345 and none at all from the following thirty odd years. Of those fifteen, only six contain information about the receipt of revenue from Cheshire.[100] Despite the limitations of the evidence it is possible to see one important difference between the way that levels of accounting inter-related during Edward of Caernarfon's principate and the way they did in his grandson's time, after 1347.

FIGURE 5

'TRANSFER CHARGE' ACCOUNTING IN CHESHIRE, 1301/6

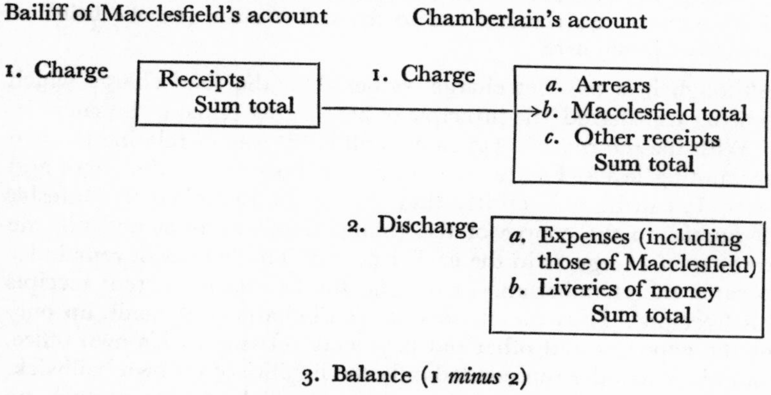

Bailiff of Macclesfield's account   Chamberlain's account

3. Balance (1 *minus* 2)

As we have already seen, the 1301/6 chamberlain's accounts, were cast in 'common form' (see Fig 4). It might be expected, of course, that the only bailiffs' accounts at this time, two for Macclesfield manor which cover the first and second half of 1304–5, are for a year when the chamberlain's account is missing. However, it is possible to see that the relationship between the two levels was as represented in Fig. 5. This system of 'transfer charge', between levels 3 and 2, appears, at first, to be a somewhat clumsy device. It was suitable, however, for an administration in which the great majority of bailiwicks were leased at farm, as was the case in Cheshire at this time. There is no discharge in the bailiff's account, so Macclesfield's entire discharge, including both *decasus* and the expenses incurred in running the manor, had to be included in the chamberlain's account. If the other manors and bailiwicks of the earldom had been 'transferred' in the same way, then the level 2 account would have become impossibly unwieldy, with a very large discharge side balanced against a charge side comprising mere sum totals. However, Macclesfield had been leased between 1301 and 1304,[101] and the administration were probably justified in feeling that its temporary need to be directly administered would not be of long duration although, in the event, it may have lasted another sixteen years.[102] As general leasing continued to be the standard policy with the royal earls until 1346 and later, the 'transfer charge' account was probably employed until that time. There is another example of it in the case of the isolated account of Frodsham manor for June–Michaelmas 1315.[103] Although this account does, in fact, have a discharge side (unlike the previously mentioned Macclesfield accounts), the 'net charge' of £50 6s. 5¾d. did not include liveries, since (in the words of the account):

William Fulburn, chamberlain of Chester, charges himself [with the £50 6s. 5¾d.] in his account for the said chamberlain for the above mentioned time of this account; and so the said William [i.e. the bailiff of Frodsham] is quit here.

Although it is the 'net charge' rather than the total charge which is being transferred, the principle of accounting remains the same.

With the reforms of 1347 came a different way of relating the two accounting levels. Figure 6 shows how it operated in the 1350s and later. It can be seen clearly that this method entailed the transfer of *liveries* to the charge of the chamberlain's account and not the transfer of *charge* as in the earlier period. The liveries of remainder became the chamberlain's *arreragia*, the liveries of current receipts his 'receipts'. Thus the chamberlain's discharge was made up only of the expenses and other out-payments relating to his own office, and his remainder represented only the liability of his own bailiwick. Consequently the sum total of *arreragia* and receipts of such an account represents largely, although not entirely, money which had actually passed into his hands and for which the subordinate officials had received acquittance as liveries. I say 'largely' because there was some revenue which the chamberlain himself was charged to collect directly and not through a subordinate accountant, although this revenue was not normally very large in amount.[104]

FIGURE 6

'TRANSFER LIVERY' ACCOUNTING IN CHESHIRE, *c.* 1347/76

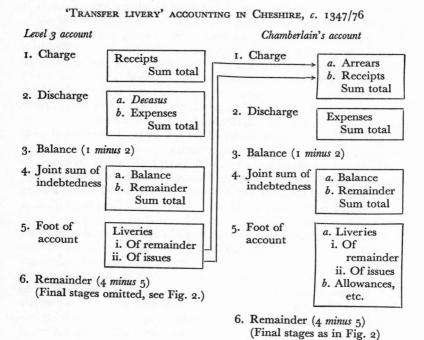

Level 3 account

1. Charge
   > Receipts
   > Sum total

2. Discharge
   > a. *Decasus*
   > b. Expenses
   > Sum total

3. Balance (1 *minus* 2)

4. Joint sum of indebtedness
   > a. Balance
   > b. Remainder
   > Sum total

5. Foot of account
   > Liveries
   > i. Of remainder
   > ii. Of issues

6. Remainder (4 *minus* 5)
   (Final stages omitted, see Fig. 2.)

Chamberlain's account

1. Charge
   > a. Arrears
   > b. Receipts
   > Sum total

2. Discharge
   > Expenses
   > Sum total

3. Balance (1 *minus* 2)

4. Joint sum of indebtedness
   > a. Balance
   > b. Remainder
   > Sum total

5. Foot of account
   > a. Liveries
   > i. Of remainder
   > ii. Of issues
   > b. Allowances, etc.

6. Remainder (4 *minus* 5)
   (Final stages as in Fig. 2)

From the point of view of medieval accounting methods in general, this change from 'transfer charge' to 'transfer livery' accounts may not be of great importance, since it was bound up with the special circumstances which pertained in Cheshire and in other royal estates in the matter of preference for leasing over direct administration.[105] However, the change does emphasise the need for adopting a 'vertical' view of financial administration as well as the commonly employed 'horizontal' one. For example, in P. D. A. Harvey's admirable edition of the *Cuxham Records*, although there is very detailed and deep discussion of accounting methods and the accounts themselves, there is only a bare reference to accounts above the level of the manorial bailiff.[106] It is unfortunate that nothing can be said here about the relationship between the Cheshire chamberlain's account and those of the central administration, since no closely corresponding examples exist. There is, admittedly, an account for John Burnham as receiver of fines in Cheshire in 1342–3 (before he became chamberlain)[107] and an account of the keeper of duke Edward's wardrobe for the same year.[108] Although the latter has entries of receipts from both the justiciar-farmer and from John Burnham, as receiver, it is all but impossible to read the sums in question, even with the aid of ultra-violet light. It is likely, though, that 'transfer livery' was used by the central accounts at all periods, since it is difficult to see how, on a large estate, any other system could work. The changes in accounting methods which took place round about 1347 do have very great importance for the history of Cheshire's financial administration, in that when 'trends' in the amount of revenue collected and spent over the whole period between 1272 and 1377 are being discussed we have to bear in mind that the chamberlain's accounts of the early fourteenth century are different in *form* from those of the third quarter and that they cannot be *directly* compared. If this mistake is made there is a great danger of confusing changes in form with changes in actuality.

There are two final remarks which need to be made to conclude this preliminary discussion of the financial records of Cheshire. The first is connected with the appointment of a controller of the county in March 1347, the second with the use of 'prests' (or *prestita*) made on the chamberlain's account for 1364–5. Roger Chester was appointed as 'controller of the chamberlain' in the royal exchequer sense of that term; in other words, his job was to act as a check on the chamberlain's financial probity and administrative efficiency rather than to act as his superior officer.[109] As such he was entrusted with the task of drawing up 'counter-rolls' which the auditors could check with the chamberlain's own records, and in order to compile these he was to be personally present when important financial transactions were being carried out.[110] This was not a wholly new concept in Cheshire administration: in 1325–6 John Ashby, the county escheator, had been described as the chamberlain's controller, but probably only in the sense that he kept a counter-roll of the receipts of Mara forest.[111] Even earlier, in 1279–80, the then chamberlain, Leo Leo's son, kept a counter-roll of the receipts of the justiciar, Guncelin Badlesmere, who was then accounting for the issues of the county.[112] It is possible that the chamberlain was always controller when the justiciar was responsible for collecting the issues of the earldom, but the survival of this single roll for 1279–80 is not a strong indication of this, since it dates from the start of an unusual period in the history of the county's finances when all the county revenues were assigned for the building work at Vale Royal abbey and they were, therefore, to pass through Leo's hands for this purpose.[113] The appointment of a permanent controller, in 1347, was a new departure, therefore, and part of the wholesale administrative reforms that were being implemented at that time. In the event, it turned out to be a short-lived measure, possibly because the chamberlain, Burnham, resented the implication that he needed a spur of this type to do his job properly, and it is likely that the appointment was rescinded a year or two after it had been made.[114]

Likewise, the making of prests to two knights and three esquires from Cheshire by the chamberlain in 1364–5 so that they could take archers to the prince in Gascony seems to have been an isolated intrusion into normal accounting methods which did not lead to any permanent change.[115] Prests, or cash advances made to an official or department for which they had to account after they had spent all (or part) of them, were much used in household accounts as a method of giving the various branches of the household an income.[116] Estate administrations, especially those of considerable size, were not really regarded as spending departments at all: their job was to collect the revenue, spend as little as possible, and hand over the greater part for the lord's use. Consequently, the voucher/acknowledgement system was used so that only expenditure which was authorised, in detail, in advance was undertaken. As we shall see, towards the latter part of the prince's life the Chester exchequer became a spending department almost despite itself, as a result of the local assignment of the payment of annuities to the prince's retainers and followers. It is perhaps in this context, therefore, that the prests of 1364–5 should be seen: as extraordinary methods employed at a time when military necessity required money to be made available without the usual safeguards, so that troops could be obtained.

IV DEBT, VALUE AND ESTIMATING REVENUE

The first job for any government finance department is to collect the revenue for which it is responsible with the greatest amount of dispatch and the smallest amount of wastage. Having achieved that, the next task is to make an assessment of the revenue in question and, by using records primarily designed to ensure efficient collection, to find out how much the 'yield' has been in the past, what it is at the present and what it is likely to be in the future. We now have to consider the extent to which the Cheshire accounts were used in this way, as instruments of financial policy rather than as records of administrative procedures. For forty out of the 104 years under discussion the county was in the king's hands and was subject to the methods devised by the royal exchequer. G. L. Harriss maintains that the exchequer regularly practised the construction of estimates of both current and future revenue from the 1320s onwards. Such estimates, he says, achieved, as they were designed to do, a degree of planning in royal finances which would have otherwise been impossible.[117] The method that was probably used was that of averaging receipts extracted from the various accounts over a series of preceding years.[118] Unfortunately, none of the published documents made as a result of such calculations survives from a time in the fourteenth century when Cheshire was in the king's hand.[119] To find such an estimate in which the county is included, we have to go back as far as 1284, when the king's exchequer made an estimate of ordinary royal revenue of £27,000-odd out of which the county contributed £700. It is suggested that £8,000 or so should be deducted from the total to allow for those royal lands which had been given away by successive kings (the *terre date* of the pipe roll), which would mean that the county produced just over 3½ per cent of royal income.[120] Sir Reginald Grey was, at that time, farming the county as justiciar for a rent of 1,000 marks (£666 13s. 4d.) a year, in addition to which he was charged to pay £32 0s. 3½d. for the lands of Gwendolen Lacy, which made £698 13s. 7½d.[121] Obviously, therefore, the Cheshire estimate was obtained by the simple expedient of rounding up Grey's total charge, with the implication that the figure for the whole country was based on the *liability* of officials to pay money rather than on what they *actually* paid. It looks as if the exchequer had made an important advance in financial forecasting between 1284 and the 1320s. The 1284 Cheshire estimate turned out to be unreliable, since the Welsh war of 1282/3 and its aftermath upset, understandably, the normal routine of financial adminstration.[122]

The lack of central records of the time of the royal earls makes it difficult to establish what methods, if any, they employed to interpret their estate accounts. Other large estates, we do know, did produce analyses of accounts of various types, particularly in the fourteenth and fifteenth centuries. These normally took the form of accounts of arrears and 'valors', by which an overall view of the estate's revenue could be obtained. The interpretative documents of the duchy of Lancaster are probably the best preserved and best known fourteenth century examples.[123] There is some indirect evidence, however, that the administrators of both Edward of Caernarfon and the Black Prince made revenue estimates. For the earlier principate the evidence is very slender indeed, comprising statements at the end of the first two chamberlain's accounts (February–Michaelmas 1301[124] and 1301–2[125] giving the vlaue (or *summa valoris*) of the two counties of Chester and Flint. The method of calculating this was not much of an advance of that of 1284 and consisted of taking the total receipts (excluding arrears) and deducting from them both foreign receipts (which were money originating outside the chamberlain's bailiwick) and expenses. Thus, in terms of the accountancy employed after 1347, the 'clear value' was equivalent to the 'net charge' (the 'balance' of Fig. 3, above). It is important to note that this figure was included as a matter of course, without the necessity for special calculation, in accounts produced by the later accounting method. Whether the valuation was an accurate forecast or not depended on how successful the chamberlain and other officials were at realising the amount of the charge. In this connection it is instructive to note that when William Melton gave up the chamberlainship in 1304 he was liable for £344 12s. 2¼d. arrears, of which he was remitted £80 by gift of the prince—a part of his charge that was never collected.

For the Black Prince's time the evidence, although still largely indirect, is much more compelling. It seems beyond doubt that his administrators did compile both arrears accounts and valors of his whole estate. After the 1347 reforms the remainder (that is the charge which had still not been paid over by the time of the audit) was distributed throughout all the accounts of the county officials. This represented potential revenue which it was important for the prince to know about in case he wanted to raise ready cash in an emergency. Consequently, in the autumn of 1352, when the accounting reforms were finally beginning to work smoothly, a new type of document appears among the Cheshire accounts called the 'great roll of debts' (*magnus rotulus debitorum*).[126] This roll had two main sections. The first was, quite simply, a catalogue of all the remainders contained in the Cheshire and Flintshire accounts, including that of the chamberlain. The other, much smaller, part contained what were, to use royal exchequer terminology, 'desperate debts' (that is, items extracted from the remainders of particular accounts because of some difficulty in collection for which the accountant could not be held responsible). This section seems to have been the successor of an older record called the 'pipe' (*pipa*), presumably named after the pipe roll of the royal exchequer, and which dated back to at least the early years of the fourteenth century.[127] It appears that the 'great roll' was compiled from the accounts when the originals had been completed and put in order, that is, after the business of the audit was over. As might be expected, the accounts were preserved in four groups, to correspond with the four white leather bags bought for their safe-keeping, as follows:

1. Chamberlain's account. (A long roll, sewn chancery fashion, kept on its own.)
2. Accounts of 'Divers Ministers of Cheshire'. This group included the accounts of sheriff, escheator and of all the other county officials except those in group 3. The abbreviated heading of this group was 'Cestria'.
3. Accounts of the ministers of Macclesfield manor and hundred, including the lordship of Longdendale. Abbreviated heading: 'Macclesfield'.
4. Accounts of 'Divers Ministers of Flintshire'. (Individual accounts in groups 2–4 were sewn together at the head 'exchequer fashion'.)

From 1353 onwards an extra group of accounts was added, which related to the lands of Sir John St. Pierre of Peckforton, a substantial Cheshire magnate's estate which was taken over by the Black Prince in 1353.[128] The estate consisted of several manors, fragments of manors, rents of rural and urban properties, and feudal rights scattered over the south-western part of the county, the responsibility for the whole of which was placed in the hands of a receiver, who made his liveries to the chamberlain. As far as his accounts went, they were an interesting compromise between levels 2 and 3 described above (pp. 29–34), in that each separate township (whether it was a whole manor, or a single rent-payer) was given a separate charge and discharge, but all the balances of 'net charge' were then brought together in a single 'foot' in which the receiver made his liveries, received allowances and so on, in the usual way.

The value to the prince's officials of a compendium of uncollected revenue such as the 'great roll' cannot be doubted. It is peculiar, though, that it is the 'great roll' for the county that has survived rather than a general enrolment for the whole of the prince's estates. In one sense, of course, it is not so strange, since the local accounts have been preserved while the central records are largely lost. On the other hand, the Cheshire–Flintshire 'great rolls', in the form that they have come down to us, are singularly futile documents. They contain no grand total of remainders and desperate debts at their foot, and so they are, in effect, only a collection of abbreviated extracts from the accounts among which they were kept, and they do not seem to have had any particular merit even as a source of ready reference. As they continued to be compiled until 1412,[129] and as it was no characteristic of the prince's government to waste its clerks' valuable time in drawing up useless documents, the implication is that a 'great roll' for all the prince's estates was compiled annually, from the local sets of extracts made at the regional audits. The very name *magnus rotulus* suggests this, since there is nothing 'great' about the surviving Cheshire 'great rolls'—they were written on parchment of the same size as the 'Divers Ministers' ' accounts to which they are attached.[130]

A general conspectus of remainders was one necessary tool which the estate administrators had to have if they wanted to provide their employer with good estimates of present and future revenue yield. It is clear that the Black Prince's auditors were able to make such estimates, since on 4 September 1355, when the prince and his army were waiting at Plymouth to take ship for the campaign which was to culminate at Poitiers, letters were sent to the chamberlains of Chester, north Wales and south Wales, informing them of how much the auditors expected would be leviable at the morrow of Michaelmas next (30 September 1355) and ordering them to ensure that the anticipated sums were collected so that the loans raised to finance the expedition could be properly serviced.[131] John Burnham, the Chester chamberlain, was given a figure of £1,383 8s. 2½d. The most recent accounts which the auditors would have had to hand were those of 1353–4, although they had probably made views of the 1354–5 accounts when the former were audited, in January 1355.[132] Consequently, it was necessary for them to indulge in a certain amount of estimation of revenue, and they appear to have been remarkably accurate.[133] Another such auditors' report, based on the accounts, may be referred to in July 1356, when a Caernarfon man was paid 18d. to convey to London the 'results' of 'the ministers accounts of the parts of Chester and the state of the prince's lands in north Wales'.[134]

Accurate estimating of revenue also depended on the making of realistic valuations of current receipts. Valuations of individual manors, through sworn 'extents', had long been made by estate managers, but it is almost never clear how such valuations were arrived at. As in other large fourteenth and fifteenth century estates, the prince's managers did make general valuations of his whole property, and, what is more, it is possible to see how the values were calculated. Three types of evidence illustrate this. The first is the existence, at the end of a number of Cheshire accounts for the 1350s and 1360s, of statements of 'value': that is, a sum of money, preceded by 'et valet'. Six of the accounts for 1354–5, for example, have these.[135] As is not uncommon with such statements of value, it is difficult to discern a consistent principle of valuation in the figures,[136] and, unlike the 'valuations' at the end of the early fourteenth century chamberlains' accounts, no indication is given of how the calculations were made. Out of the six, the 'value' is equivalent to the liveries of money in one case, in another to the charge, while in the other four instances no obvious correlation can be made. The second type of evidence is a valor made of one section of the Cheshire revenues, that emanating from the St. Pierre lands, in 1365–6.[137] This was calculated, according to its heading, 'by examining various receivers' accounts of the same lands, etc.'. Unfortunately, as the receivers' account for 1364–5 is missing, it is not possible to relate valor to accounts in any detail, but as the St. Pierre inheritance was wholly rented, and judicial receipts formed a very small proportion of the total revenue, an accurate estimate would not be too difficult to work out.

The third type of evidence consists of three copies of a valor of the Black Prince's estates which was made after his death, in June 1376.[138] Although they are undated, it is clear that the valor must have been compiled that same summer, since a copy was delivered to the royal chancery on 30 September.[139] The assignment of dower lands to the princess Joan, on the basis of the figures to be found in the valor, took place on 13 October 1376, and the chamberlain of Chester was ordered that same day to give her the Cheshire portion of them.[140] All the eleven commissioners appointed by the royal government to value the prince's lands were either present or past officials of his, and together they represented the senior and middle management of his estates towards his life's end.[141] There can be no doubt, therefore, that the method of valuation which they adopted was that which had been used on the prince's estates, at least in the previous decade or so. One of them, Richard Fillongley, had had extensive experience as an auditor for the prince in Aquitaine when he had been responsible for making an analysis of the accounts there which M. Sharp calls 'a synoptic survey of Gascon revenues for the whole period of the principality'. Consequently, it is worth quoting in full the detailed explanation which the commissioners gave of how they set about their task:

... a detailed examination was made of the account rolls of the ministers of the lord Edward, Prince of Wales, duke of Cornwall and earl of Chester, for divers years, in order to find out what lordships, lands and tenements the said prince, duke and earl held, either in demesne or in service, both in the county of Chester and north Wales and south Wales and the counties of Devon and Cornwall as elsewhere in the kingdom of England, on the day he died and how much they were worth in all their issues in accordance with the true value of the same. And because the issues and profits of the same lordships, lands and tenements are, for the most part, casual and variable in magnitude, so that the value of the same in one year hardly agrees with that in another, the figures for all these casual issues are taken for three years [that is, the forty-ninth, forty-eighth and forty-seventh years] and of them one total is made, the third part of which is reckoned to be the value for one year by [estimation], as appears below.[142]

TABLE I

MACCLESFIELD BOROUGH REVENUES, 1372/6[143]

	1372–3			1373–4			1374–5			1376		
	£	s.	d.	£	s.	d.	£	s.	d.	£	s.	d.
1. Liveries of money	32	5	7½	25	8	4¼	28	17	0			
2. Net charge	31	14	0¼	29	19	3¼	28	5	4¾	31	0	0
3. Total charge	36	5	3¾	33	8	10½	36	2	3			

As the valor was made in the summer of 1376, the commissioners naturally used the accounts for the three years most recently available (1372–3, 1373–4 and 1374–5). In normal practice the 1375/6 accounts would not be due for audit until 1377. The employment of an arithmetical mean for averaging the unpredictable issues was a commendably simple procedure and had been used, in G. L. Harriss's view, by the royal exchequer earlier in the fourteenth century. Very likely it represents yet another technique imported from the king's into his son's administration.[144] Unfortunately, there are no chamberlan's accounts at all for the years in question, while the 'Divers Ministers' series of accounts breaks off after 1373–4.[145] All that we have left to compare with the valor are the relevant Macclesfield accounts, so it is these that will have to be used in an attempt to see how the commissioners' programme was actually carried out. In Table 1, the relevant figures from the Macclesfield borough accounts are set out, alongside the valuation. The first, and most obvious, point to note is that the 'valuation' is a figure which has been rounded off in some way. Having said this, it is difficult to see immediately how the average was struck, as no reasonable combination of the nine figures approximates to £31. However, an average of *all* nine figures (ignoring fractions of pence) works out at £31 7s. 3d., and, surprising though this may seem, it looks as if that was how this particular value was arrived at. Exactly what the mathematical significance of such a figure would be is impossible to say: in only one of the three years had Macclesfield borough ever yielded as much as £31, and so the 'value' was a compromise between the actual and potential yields. This method was not used, however, in the case of the other Macclesfield bailiwicks. The reason seems to have been that in the case of the borough bailiwick there were no regular expenses and the officials' remainders were always small, so the nine figures all fall within a reasonably narrow range. In contrast, the accounts of forest and hundred exhibit large remainders, and so both their averages (in the borough sense of taking all the figures together) are considerably higher than the 1376 valuation. In these cases the commissioners appear to have used an approximation to the liveries of money as the basis for the value, perhaps recognising that the theoretical 'potential' revenue af these two bailiwicks could not reasonably be expected to become actuality.[146] Of the two remaining Macclesfield accounts, that of the parker seems to have been valued at the net charge (rounded down), while in the case of the stock keeper's account no combination of figures will produce an average low enough to equate to the figure in the valor. This account was always erratic in the sense that the liveries of money varied widely from year to year, and what the commissioners appear to have been doing is choosing a round figure (£13 6s. 8d.) about £4 or so lower than the average of the three net charges. Their reason for doing this was probably that the Macclesfield herd was being gradually sold off, as a cursory glance at the stock account would tell them, while expenses of maintenance were high, and thus they were justified in 'forecasting' a fall in revenue. They had no way, really, of knowing how large that fall would be.[147] On the whole, then, the late prince's officials appear to have used their 'method' of valuation in a flexible and discriminating way, taking into account the different problems inherent in different types of property.

With respect to the remainder of the Cheshire part of this valor, it is difficult to say anything certain because of the lack of the last year of accounts. The sums attributed to the county court (£180) and the escheator (£100) look arbitrary, and the former, in parti-

cular, appears somewhat low. Likewise with the Frodsham value of
£56 13s. 4d.: this manor's revenue had long been declining, admittedly, but in 1372–3 the bailiff's net charge had been over £76
and he made liveries of nearly £70 to the chamberlain.[148] This was,
moreover, a year when particularly bad weather had led to serious
inundations of the lower-lying ground of the manor and to the
destruction of Frodsham bridge. Such indications seem to point to
a fair degree of conservatism on the part of the commissioners, which
could perhaps be explained by the purpose for which the valor was
being drawn up. It was not that of routine estate administration but
so that the prince's lands could be divided into two parts, with the
customary third going to the dower of his widow. Consequently, the
valuations needed only to be approximate, and a degree of fiscal
conservatism was not out of place.

The Cheshire financial records survive in large numbers but unevenly through the period: there is no decade of the county's history
in the years between 1272 and 1377 when there is not a relative
abundance of some types and a relative scarcity of others. Despite
this difficulty, the Cheshire accounts and associated financial records
are witnesses to an impressively high standard of financial administration, for the times, as good as, and probably better than, that to
be found on estates of other wealthy English laymen. We might
expect that the royal government, and the associated (and closely
related) administrations of the kings' eldest sons, would be able to
employ officials of the highest calibre. Whether they were able to put
their technical expertise to good use remains to be decided in
subsequent chapters.

NOTES

[1] Dorothea Oschinsky, *Walter of Henley* (1970) and 'Notes on the editing and
interpretation of estate accounts', *Archives*, IX (1969–70), pp 84–9 and 142–52;
P. D. A. Harvey, *Cuxham Records* (1976).

[2] *Guide to the Contents of the Public Record Office*, I (1963), pp. 172–6.

[3] See R. I. Jack, *Medieval Wales* (1972), pp. 69–78.

[4] B. E. Harris, 'The Palatinate 1301–1547', *V.C.H. (Cheshire)*, II, pp. 21–2.
These rolls are now officially called 'Enrolments'.

[5] *D.K.R.*, 36, 37 and 39.

[6] For example, the roll for 1352/3 (Ches. 2/36) comprises six membranes (some
fragmentary), on which forty-six visible entries are enrolled. Among them are a
recognizance of the lessees of Frodsham manor (m. 1d) and letters of appointment
of the constable of Chester castle (m. 3d), of the collectors of the pontage of
Northwich (m. 6d: a writ of intendancy), of the above lessees of Frodsham (m. 2d),
of the lessee of Macclesfield mills (m. 2d) and of the lessee of the riding forestership
of Mara (m. 1d). The rest of the roll is largely made up of charters and recognizances:
it relates to both Cheshire and Flintshire.

[7] Ches. 2/36 m. 2: warrant for the issue of charters of pardon to the foresters of
Mara for accidental homicide.

⁸ Ches. 1/1 (parts one and two). The former file contains thirty-nine pieces, either writs or petitions endorsed with administrative orders.

⁹ The earliest rolls are calendared in R. Stewart Brown, (ed.), *Calendar of County Court, City Court and Eyre Rolls of Chester, 1259–97*, Chet. Soc., New Series, 84, 1925. They are classed as Palatinate of Chester: Plea Rolls (Ches. 29). B. E. Harris, *op. cit.*, pp. 11–18, gives the most recent and reliable discussion of Cheshire's medieval county court and its records. Genealogical material extracted from the plea rolls is calendared in *D.K.R.*, 26 (1865); 27 (1866); 28 (1867).

¹⁰ Ches. 29/12 m. 16d (1299/1300) records that the towns of Middlewich and Northwich, together with the county shrievalty, were taken at farm, with details of the leases granted. In the same roll there are also recognizances connected with the same leases (e.g. of Northwich, m. 4d) and with the farms of the serjeanty of the peace and the custody of the avowries (m. 12, 13).

¹¹ Ches. 29/17 m. 12d. (1305/6). This membrane contains Prince Edward's order to make the purveyance and also gives details of the goods purveyed. Similar entries are to be found in Ches. 29/21 m. 3d (1308) and Ches. 29/22 m. 9d (1309).

¹² Ches. 29/20 m. 19d. Orders to levy the arrears of the under-bailiffs of Macclesfield (1308), addressed to the county sheriff because the debtors had bound themselves by statute merchant recognizances.

¹³ For example, in the 1309/10 plea roll there is an inquisition into the liability of the inhabitants of Middlewich to serve in the town's offices and to pay toll in the city of Chester (Ches. 29/22 m. 4d). There were also attempts to establish the Chester exchequer as a court of revenue in the early fourteenth century, but without success (Ches. 29/22 m. 15d).

¹⁴ Harris, *op. cit.*, p. 17. These so-called 'Gaol files' form the class Ches. 24.

¹⁵ *Ibid.* These include rolls of mainprises and essoins (Ches. 23), fines and recoveries (Ches. 31), coroners' inquests (Ches. 18), warrants of attorney (Ches. 37), calendars of indictments (Ches. 20) and so on.

¹⁶ It is impossible to give even a brief summary of other useful classes of these two government departments here.

¹⁷ The roll has been edited by Hilda Johnstone as *Letters of Edward, Prince of Wales, 1304–5*, Roxburghe Club (1931).

¹⁸ S.C.8 333/E.996–1101B. 'England', in this context, excludes Cheshire (as well as Cornwall),

¹⁹ S.C.1 54/47, 52, 55, 58, 70, 73–7, 81–3, 88, 93–7, 100. Those of the letters which relate to Wales are published in J. G. Edwards (ed.), *Calendar of Ancient Correspondence concerning Wales*, Univ. of Wales Board of Celtic Studies (1935).

²⁰ The P.R.O. class numbers of the original books, in the order given, are E.36 144, 280, 279, 278. With E.36 279, (*B.P.R.*, III), has been calendared also a fragment of the register for North Wales (S.C.1 58/35). For a brief description of these registers by M. Sharp see 'The Administrative Chancery of the Black Prince before 1362', in *Essays presented to T. F. Tout* (1925), pp. 322–5; for a more detailed account see her section of *Tout*, V, pp. 400–31.

²¹ See *D.K.R.*, 20, pp. 95–143, for a list of the Ancient Miscellanea which were removed from the Carlton Ride and the Stone Tower at Westminster to the 'Record Depository' (i.e. the P.R.O.) in July 1856. A list of the 'Welsh Records', removed from 'Wales' in 1854 and 1855, is given 'as far as arranged' in *D.K.R.*, 20, pp. 160–83 and is continued in *D.K.R.*, 21, pp. 26–46.

²² S.C.6 802/17 and 803/1 are a duplicate and an original respectively. S.C.6 803/2 is a Q.R. duplicate.

²³ In 1351 the Black Prince's receiver-general was ordered to forward copies of his accounts to the royal exchequer for this purpose (*B.P.R.*, IV, p. 32).

²⁴ For the significance of 'original' and 'duplicate' see below, p. 15. Evans, in *Flintshire Accounts*, pp. xiv–xv, assumes that the 'originals' were, in fact, duplicates of the bailiffs' own accounts. There is no evidence for this until the prince's last years.

[25] *Chamb. Acc.*, p. 270.

[26] *B.P.R.*, IV, p. 201.

[27] The originals are S.C.6 771/1–23 and S.C.6 783/15, 16. A full transcript of the chamberlain's account for 7 February–Michaelmas 1301 is given as an appendix to *Ch. Pipe Rolls*, pp. 193–216.

[28] A. Jones (ed.), *Flintshire Ministers' Accounts, 1301–28*, Flintshire Historical Society, 3 (1913); D. L. Evans (ed.), *Flintshire Ministers' Accounts, 1328–53*, Flintshire Historical Society, Record Series, 2 (1928).

[29] This chamber was rebuilt in 1354–5 at the same time as the county court house, which latter then stood outside the outer bailey of the castle. (*Chamb. Acc.*, p. 230; R. A. Brown, H. M. Colvin and A. J. Taylor, *The History of the King's Works*, II (1963), pp. 608–12; R. Stewart-Brown, 'The Exchequer of Chester', *E.H.R.*, 57 (1942), pp. 291–7).

[30] *Chamb. Acc.*, p. 270.

[31] *Ibid.*, p. 272.

[32] *Ibid.*, p. 270; S.C.6 771/18 m. 2d; S.C.6 772/8 m. 2d. Canvas cash bags were used in the 1350s, leather ones in the 1360s. The letters sealed with the red wax may have been summonses to the Cheshire and Flintshire ministers to collect estreats (for which see note 41) and to attend the audit.

[33] S.C.6 772/7 m. 4d. This document, in which receipts were entered, was probably a detailed record of money actually collected and disbursed by the chamberlain and may have been the forerunner of the account later kept by the chamberlain's clerk.

[34] S.C.6 783/17–787/7; S.C.6 783/1–10; S.C.6 802/6–13.

[35] S.C.6 786/3 m. 1.

[36] S.C.6 786/8 m. 2, 2d.

[37] S.C.6 771/18 m. 2d. Admittedly this set of accounts is particularly long and detailed because of the repercussions of the prince's visit to the county in the late summer of 1353. When the auditors are known to have been at Chester at dates in three consecutive months, it must not necessarily be assumed that they were auditing Cheshire or Flintshire accounts continuously during that time, since Chester could be their base from which to go and audit the north Wales and Denbigh or even other accounts.

[38] *Cuxham Records*, pp. 42–3, 49–51.

[39] S.C.6 786/3 m. 4d.

[40] See the description of the royal exchequer's use of the abacus in Hubert Hall, *Introduction to the Study of the Pipe Rolls*, Pipe Roll Society (1884), pp. 40–2.

[41] The escheator-steward made a rental of a demesne lordship on at least one occasion (S.C.6 787/2 m. 3). A set of county court estreats for May–October 1348, addressed to the county sheriff, survives (E. 101 508/7) and part of a similar set for 1326 (S.C.6 1268/4, file two). The court rolls of the demesnes could be used to calculate the 'perquisites of the court' in the accounts, as the fines and amercements were invariably totalled for each session, with a grand total at the end of the roll. (See, for example, S.C.2 252/1.)

[42] See *Chamb. Acc.*, pp. 27–37 and pp. 46–75, or the chamberlain's particulars of receipt for 1302–3 and 1303–4. The files of inquisition post mortem with extents and other analogous documents formed the escheator's 'particulars'. Two extents and an inquisition are actually attached to the 1352–3 escheator's account (S.C.6 784/2 m. 6).

[43] S.C.6 784/4 m. 2d. This means that the yield of the 1354 pea crop should have resulted in at least twice the amount of peas sown, by volume. The accounts of the manors have corn and stock accounts, of the usual type, after the cash accounts.

[44] *Ibid.* The 'sale' yielded £4 7s. 9d.

[45] *Ibid.* See Oschinsky, *Walter of Henley*, pp. 419–37, for the recommendation of such methods to detect fraudulent officials.

[46] As Harvey maintains, in *Cuxham Records*, pp. 52–4.

⁴⁷ S.C.6 784/7 m. 9, 9d.

⁴⁸ S.C.6 784/7 m. 9d. The same inquisition found, though, that the death of one ox and two sheep had been caused by the neglect of the stockkeepers and the shepherd.

⁴⁹ P.D.A. Harvey, in his introduction to *Cuxham Records*, pp. 12–34, calls the charge of a manorial account 'items of cash received by the local agent, totalled', which is misleading.

⁵⁰ For a discussion of the *decasus* in the Macclesfield accounts see Chapter IV, pp. 89–91.

⁵¹ At the 1351 audit the lands in Sutton township (which was part of Macclesfield manor), which used to belong to Robert Alkemondelowe and which 'lay fallow, uncultivated and in common', were allowed to remain *in decasu* by inquisition taken by the auditors. (S.C.6 802/2 m. 1.)

⁵² S.C.6 1268/4 (file one). It comprises twenty items: three are writs ordering payments to be made by William Melton, the chamberlain; fifteen are sealed acknowledgements of the receipt of fees, wages and ancient alms paid by Melton; one is a sealed acknowledgement by Walter Reynolds (keeper of the prince's wardrobe) of the receipt of Melton's cash liveries; and the final document is an indenture between Melton and his successor as chamberlain, Hugh Leominster, recording the transfer of a list of the prince's debtors for which Leominster would be charged in his first account. The documents in the file are dated between 1302 and 1305.

⁵³ See Oschinsky, *Walter of Henley*, pp. 215–18.

⁵⁴ Action against slow payers is discussed in Chapter IV, pp. 101–2.

⁵⁵ There is a petition for allowance attached to the account of the receiver of the St. Pierre lands for 1363–4 (S.C.6 783/11 m. 6) and a petition for respite to the 1366–7 Macclesfield poker's account (S.C.6 803/13 m. 2A).

⁵⁶ S.C.2 786/10 m. 4.

⁵⁷ Sharp, thesis, p. 149; Curry, thesis, p. 77.

⁵⁸ Middlewich (1325/6, 1328, 1361/2, 1367) S.C.2 156/1, 2; Northwich (1328, 1355) S.C.2 156/9, 10; Shotwick (1338/43), S.C.2 156/12, 13. They were all originally part of the royal exchequer 'Ancient Miscellanea'.

⁵⁹ These are in the form of 'states of account' as employed in the exchequer memoranda rolls (*C.M.R.*., pp. xxiii–ix, xxxvii–ix.) They exist for Northwich, 22 March–30 September 1328 (S.C.2 156/9 m. 1d) and 4 October–29 November 1328 (S.C.2 156/9 m. 3); Middlewich, 29 March–10 May 1328 (S.C.2 156/1 m. 7d) and Michaelmas–29 November 1328 (S.C.2 156/1 m. 10d). These facts, plus the structure of the court rolls themselves, indicate that, at least in some cases, revenue collection was as important a reason for keeping court rolls as the necessity for having legal precedents, notwithstanding the view of P. D. A. Harvey in *Cuxham Records*, p. 80. Particularly compelling are the early Middlewich court rolls in which not only are the sums of money due from each type of court revenue (and rents) given but a digest of all the sums is presented at the end which is almost exactly the same as the charge in a later Middlewich account.

⁶⁰ Strictly speaking, the account ran from the *morrow* of Michaelmas 1363 (30 September) to Michaelmas following (29 September).

⁶¹ S.C.6 784/2 m. 10. (This is the account for 1352–3, in the foot of which Stephen Merton's rent is unpaid for that and the previous year.)

⁶² S.C.6 783/17 m. 6. This extent survives, in part, as S.C.11 894. On m. 2, under the heading *Rudheath-next-Lachemelbank*, it is stated that Ranulf Merton held 23½ acres, ½ rood 9¾ perches there, as sub-tenant of the abbot of Chester.

⁶³ S.C.6. 786/1 m. 2d.

⁶⁴ *The Estates of Ramsey Abbey* (1957), pp. 258–9.

⁶⁵ S.C.6 787/7 m. 1d.

⁶⁶ Oschinsky, *Walter of Henley*, pp. 188–9.

⁶⁷ Views of: (1) chamberlain's account, Michaelmas 1356–23 June 1357 (*Chamb. Acc.*, pp. 232–6); (2) Longdendale account, 25 March–Michaelmas 1366

(S.C.6 803/12 m. 3). (3) St. Pierre estate account, 1369–70(!) (S.C.6 783/13).

⁶⁸ This is the chamberlain's account for June–Michaelmas 1315 (*Chamb. Acc.*, p. 83). As it terminates at Michaelmas, it is more likely to be a part-year final account. There is also another account which started off as a 'view' (that of Drakelow, 1367–8) but its heading was amended to turn it into a normal whole year final account. (S.C.6 786/8 m. 2.)

⁶⁹ That is, S.C.6 771/21, which is mistakenly dated 1357–8 in *Chamb. Acc.*, pp. 237–43.

⁷⁰ S.C. 6 1241/14 m. 1.

⁷¹ See pp. 62–79 for a more detailed discussion of this period.

⁷² Chapter IV, pp. 86–9, deals with the latter aspect.

⁷³ Pynnok, who acted as auditor in the 1340s and 1350s, died before May 1356 (*B.P.R.*, IV, p. 185). Pirie had held the posts of chamberlain of Chester and of north Wales in the 1330s and 1340s, before being promoted to the office of receiver-general for a short time in 1346. (*Tout*, V, pp. 62, 436–8.)

⁷⁴ S.C.6 1241/14 m. 3.

⁷⁵ S.C.6 1241/13. This account may have been audited as late as 1344 or even 1345.

⁷⁶ *Chamb. Acc.*, p. 150. In the 1346–7 Frodsham account, which had no arrears, the liveries were first put in the 'common form' position (that is, in the discharge, before the balance) and then deleted and transferred to the foot. (S.C.6 801/13 m. 1d.)

⁷⁷ S.C.6 783/17 m. 3, 5, 8. These are the accounts of the county sheriff, escheator and the bailiff of Frodsham.

⁷⁸ *Chamb. Acc.*, pp. 111–13. The true form of this account can be seen only by examining the original (S.C.6 771/13 m. 2, 3), which shows that it had both the remainder and liveries in the '1365' position. This account may well have been audited a considerable time after July 1343 (the date of the last of the chamberlain's liveries).

⁷⁹ *Chamb. Acc.*, pp. 114–18. Again, arbitrary omissions by the editor diminish the value of the published account. The original (S.C.6 771/14) shows that both the 'arrears of the last account', written immediately after the heading, and the 'liveries of money', written in the body of the discharge, were crossed out with the notes 'because below in the foot'. The possibility cannot be ruled out, however, that this account was audited as late as 1347, when it is considered that the escheator's account for January 1333–August 1338 was not audited until 1345. (S.C.6 1241/12.)

⁸⁰ *C.P.R.*, 1346–9, p. 123; *B.P.R.*, I, pp. 41, 70.

⁸¹ See *Tout*, V, p. 325, where M. Sharp states: 'He knew the traditions and procedure of the royal exchequer, and could be trusted to propitiate that department's more conservative officials and to further the king's interests by modelling the duke's financial reforms on similar lines.'

⁸² Brown, Colvin and Taylor, *The King's Works*, II (1963), Plans: III (The Medieval Palace of Westminster).

⁸³ D. M. Broome, 'The Auditors of the Foreign Accounts of the Exchequer', *E.H.R.*, XXXVIII (1923), pp. 63–71.

⁸⁴ *Ibid.*, p. 71. One of the first three men to be appointed a foreign auditor in 1310 was William Fulburn, who had served as chamberlain of Chester 1299/1300. (*Ibid.*, p. 64; *Ch. Pipe Rolls*, pp. 183–4.) Walter Fulburn, chamberlain in 1315 and escheator, 1315–16, in Edward of Windsor's service, had become a foreign auditor by 1325 (Broome, *op. cit.*, p. 71).

⁸⁵ The original account, with many omissions, is translated in *Chamb. Acc.*, pp. 104–6 (from S.C.6 771/11 m. 3). It has, in accordance with exchequer procedure, been cancelled upon enrolment by having a line drawn through it. The enrolled account is E.372 174 rot. 44. Paynel's accounts for December 1326–13 March 1328 were audited in 1330 by Robert Nottingham (baron of the exchequer) and Hugh Glamvill (auditor), witness the 'state of account' in the Lord Treasurer's

Remembrancer's Memoranda Roll for 1330–1 (E.368 102 rot. 151d). Paynel was imprisoned in the Fleet for his final remainder on this account, 10 March 1330 (E.368 102 rot. 152).

[86] *Tout*, V, p. 335.

[87] *B.P.R.*, III, pp. 9, 15. Dr. Sharp calls the reply to this order 'evasive' (*Tout*, V, p. 342). In fact it entailed a return to the situation before the order was made. Very likely, the main difficulty was the county community's opposition to revenue cases being heard in the exchequer rather than the county court.

[88] *Chamb. Acc.*, pp. 1–77 (accounts for 1301–2, 1302–3, 1303–4 and 1305–6); S.C.6 1186/1 (Macclesfield accounts for 1304–5).

[89] Three exceptions are the account for Forncett, Norfolk, 1376–7 (F. G. Davenport, *The Economic Development of a Norfolk Manor* (1906), p. lviii); Crowland abbey estate accounts for 1258–9 (F. M. Page, *The Estates of Crowland Abbey* (1934), pp. 174–331); and R. E. G. Kirk (ed.), *Accounts of the Obedientiars of Abingdon Abbey*, Camden Soc., New Series, 51 (1892), pp. 143–4.)

[90] *Cuxham Records*, p. 580.

[91] See Appendix II(a).

[92] E.372 146 rot. 33 m. 1, 2 (Macclesfield accounts, 1296–9).

[93] *Ch. Pipe Rolls*, pp. 30–103.

[94] Oschinsky, *Walter of Henley*, p. 217. Hubert Hall, in his edition of *The Pipe Roll of the Bishopric of Winchester, 1208–9* (1903), p. xi, long ago pointed out the similarity between the method employed in the Winchester accounts and in the 'foreign accounts' of the exchequer.

[95] *Chamb. Acc.*, pp. 38–46.

[96] Ches. 29/65 m. 10d.

[97] S.C.6 772/3 m. 4d.

[98] *Chamb. Acc.*, pp. 1–77; *ibid.*, pp. 119–276.

[99] *Chamb. Acc.*, pp. 78–106. That dated in the edition 1315–16 is, in fact, for June–Michaelmas 1315 (*ibid.*, pp. 83–8). The accounts for 1326/8, although they relate, in part, to the time before Edward III was placed on the throne, were all audited subsequently by the royal exchequer. (*Ibid.*, pp. 100–6.)

[100] The six in question cover the years 1306/7, 1336–9, and 1341/4. (B. L. Harleian MS 5001; E.101 387/25; E.101 389/13; E.101 390/3.)

[101] *Chamb. Acc.*, pp. 2, 16, 38.

[102] The next recorded lease of the manor was to Hamo Massy c. 1320 (S.C.6 1090/13). There may have been other, unrecorded leases in the interim.

[103] S.C.6 801/12 m. 4.

[104] For example, the revenue from prises of wood and sea coal passing through the port of Chester and the fees payable for a grant under the seal of Chester exchequer.

[105] For which see below, p. 138

[106] *Cuxham Records*, p. 34. Moreover, Harvey's conclusions are based, as they have to be, very largely on the records and practice of the estates of ecclesiastical corporations.

[107] He was receiver of that part of the revenue from the county which was not included in the justiciar's farm. (*Chamb. Acc.*, pp. 114–18, supplemented by S.C.6 771/14.)

[108] E.101 390/3.

[109] *B.P.R.*, I, p. 65. His annual fee, of £10, was only half that of the chamberlain.

[110] His letters of appointment stated that he was to be continually resident in his bailiwick and either to write his counter-rolls with his own hand or to have them written in his presence. (*Ibid.*) In the chamberlain's account for 1347–8 the purchase of parchment for, among other things, 'the rolls and memoranda of the controller controlling the chamberlain's receipts and expenses' is recorded. (S.C.6 771/15 m. 2d.) There is no such entry in the next surviving account, that for 1349–50. (S.C.6 771/16.)

[111] *Chamb. Acc.*, p. 96.

[112] This counter-roll is published in *Ch. Pipe Rolls*, pp. 138–43. It seems to have been a copy of Badlesmere's own particulars of account with appropriate amendments, such as the deletion of the justiciar's name and the substitution of Leo's, to make it into a counter-roll (L.R. 12 42/1897).

[113] *Ch. Pipe Rolls*, pp. 136–8.

[114] B. E. Harris, 'Palatinate' p. 19. Chester was also known as Roger Shipbrook, and was parson of Grappenhall. He was summoned to appear, with others, before the king and council by Christmas 1349 to make answer concerning the things they had planned to do 'to the prejudice of both king and kingdom, and the dishonour and scandal of the whole English nation . . .' (E.368 124 m. 25). Process was continued to bring him before the King's Bench in February 1350, and it is subsequently recorded that he made a fine for 'divers contempts and trespasses committed against the king and his crown' (E.368 124 m. 24).

[115] The chamberlain's account for that year is missing, and the only reason we know about the prests is because fifty-eight of the archers, from Cheshire, Flintshire and Denbigh, did not go and so the prests for their wages were charged in the great roll of debts (which is discussed in the next section) (S.C.6 786/6 m. 8). One of the knights, Sir Thomas Dutton, also failed to set out (S.C.6 786/8 m. 12). His fellow leaders were Sir Geoffrey Warburton, William Legh of Grappenhall, William Hoton and John Roop.

[116] See E. B. Fryde, (ed.) *The Book of Prests of the King's Wardrobe for 1294–5* (1962), for the accounting methods of the royal wardrobe.

[117] G. L. Harriss, *King, Parliament and Public Finance in Medieval England to 1369* (1975), pp. 208–28.

[118] *Ibid.*, p. 217.

[119] In addition to those published by Harriss, others are to be found in Hilary Jenkinson and D. M. Broome, 'An Exchequer Statement of Receipts and Issues: 1339–40', *E.H.R.*, LVIII (1943), pp. 210–16; T. F. Tout and D. M. Broome, 'A National Balance Sheet for 1362–3', *ibid.*, XXXIX (1924), pp. 404–19.

[120] Mabel Mills, 'Exchequer Agenda and Estimate of Revenue, Easter Term 1284', *E.H.R.*, XL (1925), pp. 229–34.

[121] *Ch. Pipe Rolls*, pp. 145–6.

[122] See below, pp. 56–8.

[123] R. R. Davies, 'Baronial Accounts, Incomes and Arrears in the Later Middle Ages', *Ec.H.R.*, Second Series, XXI (1968), pp. 214–18.

[124] *Ch. Pipe Rolls*, p. 213.

[125] *Chamb. Acc.*, p. 13.

[126] S.C.6 783/19. This, the first of the 'great rolls', is separate from the other accounts; subsequent rolls were bound up together with the 'Divers Ministers' ' series. The Flintshire portions of this roll are printed in Evans, *Flintshire Accounts*, pp. 91–4, and that for 1352–3 *ibid.*, pp. 117–19.

[127] *Chamb. Acc.*, p. 55; it appears that this 'pipe' continued to be compiled after 1352 as well (S.C.6 784/7 m. 3d).

[128] S.C.6 783/1.

[129] Curry, thesis, p. 90. In 1367–8 a set of the 'feet' (*pedes*) of the 'Divers Ministers' and Macclesfield ministers' accounts was compiled on two rolls (S.C.6 786/8 m. 14–17d; S.C.6 803/14). What the purpose of these rolls was, and whether they were produced regularly, is impossible to determine.

[130] Again, the prince's officials may well have been consciously echoing royal exchequer terminology, since the official name of the pipe roll is 'magnus rotulus scaccarij'. This does not imply any coincidence of accounting methods in this case, but the pipe roll's 'great' size and comprehensive coverage may well have been suggestive parallels.

[131] *B.P.R.*, III, pp. 214–15.

[132] S.C.6 784/3 m. 1.

[133] The actual wording of the 4 September order does not make it clear whether the phase 'levyable at the morrow of Michaelmas, next' means the revenue relating to Michaelmas term 1355 (and thus falling in the financial year 1354–5, as it was the Michaelmas term at the *end* of the year that applied) or the revenue due for the first part of the year 1355–6. There is no chamberlain's account for 1355–6, but that for 1354–5 has an unusual feature in that the liveries made to the receiver-general were divided into two groups: those made 'before Michaelmas' (i.e. 1355) and those made after. This shows, then, that what the auditors had in mind was that revenue from 1354–5 which still remained uncollected at the close of the account. Burnham made nine liveries to Peter Lacy 'after Michaelmas' which totalled £998 13s. 7d. (S.C.6 771/19 m. 3d), being £384 14s. 7d. short of the sum required. However, out of Burnham's remainder of £692 12s. 2¾d. at the end of the account, £341 16s. 8d. was respited to him because he claimed to have paid it to various knights and esquires, as well as 300 Cheshire archers (and 100 of Flintshire) who were going to Plymouth for the expedition, as well as the cloth for their uniforms (S.C.6 771/19 m. 4d). If this sum is added to the liveries it produces a total of £1,340 10s. 3d. for war expenditure, which is remarkably close to the auditors' estimate.

[134] *B.P.R.*, IV, p. 201.

[135] S.C.6 784/5.

[136] E.g. in R. I. Jack (ed.), *The Grey of Ruthin Valor, 1467–8* (1965), hardly any connection at all between the accounts and the 'values' can be made. The important, and elaborate, series of valors (and related analyses) for the duchy of Lancaster from 1362 onwards appears to have been based on the same principle as the early fourteenth century Cheshire 'values' (that is, 'net charge'): R. Somerville, *The Duchy of Lancaster*, I (1953), pp. 107–9. Another important set was that of the dukes of Buckingham for their Welsh marcher lordships in the fifteenth century (T. B. Pugh (ed.), *The Marcher Lordships of South Wales, 1415–1536*, Univ. of Wales Board of Celtic Studies (1963), p. 154. Again, these valors are 'net charge' based and, as a result, as Carole Rawcliffe notes, they are 'essentially optimistic'. It is surprising, therefore, that she goes on to say that they 'reveal a significant tendency towards profit-and-loss accountancy', in *The Staffords, Earls of Stafford and Dukes of Buckingham, 1394–1521* (1978), pp. 50–1.

[137] S.C.6 783/12 m. 2.

[138] Two copies are original, C.47 9/57 (a roll, complete) and S.C.12 22/97 (a book, fragmentary), while S.C.12 4/27 is a fifteenth century copy. The first version is given, in summary form, in Appendix III.

[139] C.47 9/57.

[140] *C.P.R.*, 1374–7, p. 374; *C.C.R.*, 1374–7, p. 407.

[141] M. Sharp calls the valor a 'valuation made . . . by his old servants after his [the prince's] death' (*Tout*, V, p. 363).

[142] C.47 9/57. The other two copies have the following brief heading: 'Valor terrarum, reddituum et omnium aliorum proficuorum que fuerunt Edwardi principis Wallie in diversis dominiis suis subscriptis [factus per] examinacionem compotorum ministrorum suorum de annis xlix, xlviij et xlvij°'. The similarity of this short heading to that of the St. Pierre valor of 1365–6 is striking.

[143] For references, see Appendix II (a).

[144] G. L. Harriss, *King, Parliament*, p. 217.

[145] S.C.6 787/7 is the last before the break.

[146] For the reasons for this, see Chapter IV.

[147] S.C.6 804/6 m. 3. See Chapter IV, pp. 95–7.

[148] S.C.6 787/5 m. 3.

CHAPTER III

FINANCE AND THE ADMINISTRATIVE STRUCTURE OF THE COUNTY

With the acquisition of the earldom of Chester by the crown after 1237 there began a new phase of the county's history in which its peculiar status and institutions were crystallised in the service of the government.[1] In 1254 Henry III granted the county to his son, the lord Edward, and established a pattern which was to last until after the end of the Middle Ages.[2] Henceforth Cheshire was either in the king's hands or in the hands of the heir-apparent to the English crown, and the county's administrative history is one of oscillation. In 1301 Edward I made his son, Edward of Caernarfon, earl of Chester and, likewise, when the latter had succeeded to the throne as Edward II he created his own son earl, in 1312. During Edward III's reign, what proved to be the 'model' for the king's eldest son's endowment with land was established. Edward of Woodstock, known to later generations as the 'Black Prince', was made earl of Chester in 1333, duke of Cornwall in 1337, and Prince of Wales in 1343.[3] Thus, throughout the whole period between 1272 and 1377, Cheshire formed only a part of a complex of landed possessions. Whether it was the crown estate, or the king's son's appanage, this complex required and had a central administrative structure. Consequently, we need to examine administration, in terms of structure and of actual decision-making, at two main levels: at the centre, and in Cheshire itself.

Henry III took over the system of county government in Cheshire which he already found in existence. It was divided into two main departments, headed by officials who certainly existed before 1237, but about whom little is known in detail. The justiciar, as well as having general oversight of the county's affairs, was responsible for military matters (including custody of the earl's castles) and the maintenance of public order, and acted as president of the higher courts of justice in the county. The chamberlain had special responsibility for finance, under the justiciar's supervision, and kept the seal of the earldom of which he was virtually 'chancellor'. Although this basic structure survived until the end of our period, important modifications were introduced. Henry III, for example, appointed an escheator for the county and farmed (that is, leased) county revenues to the justiciar. Both these innovations were strongly resented by the community of the shire.[4] The purpose of this section is to see how this local government office worked, how it related to the 'centre', and how decisions relating to matters of finance were arrived at.

I CHESHIRE LOCAL GOVERNMENT, 1272/1377

The general nature of Cheshire's government in the thirteenth and fourteenth centuries, together with accurate lists of the names of the officials who served it, was established in an exemplary fashion by Dr. Margaret Sharp over half a century ago in her doctoral thesis, which, unhappily for students of Cheshire history, has remained largely unpublished.[5] Local government was, at the time under review, the responsibility of a small group of five 'chief officers' at Chester castle who were themselves in charge of a staff of clerks and laymen (the latter being bailiffs, serjeants, reeves and beadles). A few of these subordinates worked at the castle, but most were distributed throughout the county. Of the five chiefs, three were laymen: the justiciar, the lieutenant-justiciar and the county sheriff; two were clerks, the chamberlain and, originally at any rate, the escheator. The office of justiciar was, in theory, extremely onerous and time-consuming. During the whole period his bailiwick included territories other than Cheshire itself, and from 1284 onwards he had the custody of another county, that of Flint.[6] This explains the institution of a lieutenant (*locum tenens justiciarii*) who could act as the justiciar's *alter ego*. Before the 1350s it is all but impossible to find evidence for the lieutenant's function because of the convention, which was in operation throughout the Middle Ages, that even when the lieutenant was standing in for him it was the justiciar's name which went on the record.[7] It is likely, however, that the lieutenant did, at times, preside over the county court and eyres of the hundreds and, indeed, carry out the full range of official duties in the justiciar's absence. After all, Sir Richard Mascy, who was lieutenant of Sir Reginald Grey during his second ministry of 1281/99, succeeded to the justiciarship himself at the end of Grey's term.[8] In 1353 the justiciarship became what it remained for the rest of the Middle Ages, a sinecure, leaving the lieutenant with the substance of the office.[9] This change eased the transition of the justiciar of Chester from the position of omnicompetent administrator to that of a judge.[10] At the same time the chamberlain rose from his apparent subordination to the justiciar to being undisputed head of the exchequer of Chester, the finance department of the earldom, and of the county's financial administration.

In the early part of our period, before 1346, when the justiciar normally had the main responsibility for the county's revenue, both chamberlainship and exchequer were sunk in obscurity. It is only from the 1350s onwards that a clear notion of the chamberlain's activities can be obtained. They have been set out in detail in the discussion of the mechanism of the audit at this period.[11] It is likely that, in the thirteenth century, the exchequer had been no more than the chamberlain's office for collecting and disbursing county revenue. Possibly, it was also the place where an informal audit was carried out when the justiciar farmed the county, since the actual audit took place in the royal exchequer at Westminister. It is important to emphasise that the Chester exchequer, by itself, never developed into a county audit, since under the royal earls, although the audit was actually done in Chester, it was the responsibility of specially commissioned auditors sent from the centre. The main source of financial control was, therefore, external to the county.

There were attempts, it is true, to carve out a more important administrative role for the local exchequer. In the early fourteenth century, for example, there had been an unsuccessful bid to make it into a court of revenue along the lines of the royal 'exchequer of pleas'. This failed because the community of the county refused to allow lawsuits concerning the earl's revenue to be tried anywhere except in the county court.[12] A much more ambitious plan was hatched in March 1351, when the Black Prince's officials ordered the chamberlain

to hold at the prince's exchequer at Chester all manner of pleas that belong to the court of the exchequer, and to order and manage the said exchequer, as far as he can, by the same course and laws as are used in the king's exchequer in England.[13]

This order, without doubt, would have been wholly unacceptable to the county community and, moreover, would have imposed an unnecessary degree of elaboration on the local institution. It is not surprising that it was repealed shortly after being issued.[14]

Under the justiciar (before 1353), the lieutenant and the chamberlain, the county sheriff and escheator were the officials mainly responsible for executing financial policy. They had much in common with their English counterparts.[15] The sheriff in Cheshire was, it is true, a subordinate official, but it was he who was primarily responsible for the executive side of public order maintenance in the county. He enforced the orders of the county court, collected its fines and amercements and summoned its juries, as well as generally maintaining the peace at the justiciar's direction.[16] It was the escheator's task to 'seize' (that is, take control of) lands which, usually because they were held of the earldom by knight-service, temporarily fell into the earl or king's possession. After seizure, he valued the property in question by the sworn extent and then managed it until it was decided how it should be disposed of.[17] On two occasions in the later fourteenth century the county headquarters staff, already reduced to four by the disappearance of the active justiciarship, was further reduced to three as a result of the sheriff and escheator being the same person.[18] These were obviously only interim arrangements, but they illustrate that the old distinction between the lay officer (wielding the sword) and the clerical officer (wielding the pen) had become meaningless.

The sheriff was the most important of the county's revenue collectors. Until *c.* 1346 it was usual for him to farm his office (the *vicecomitatus*) at a rent which had been £140 a year at the beginning of our period. By 1320 this farm had risen by £60, and in 1326 it was £240 a year.[19] Apparently the farm did not encompass all the revenues which the sheriff had to collect, since the county court and other judicial perquisites were excluded.[20] Exactly what revenues were included in the farm is not clear. Possibly they comprised not only the miscellaneous rents collected by later sheriffs, and other payments such as those for 'sheriff's aid', 'sheriff's stuth' and so on but also more informal emoluments exacted by this official. Instructive in this regard is a complaint made by William Praers, who was sheriff during the first part of 1332. In a petition to King Edward III and the royal council he stated that the execution of a writ in a plea of land had been taken from him and given to the coroners by the doomsmen of the Cheshire county court on the grounds that he had been 'favouring and aiding' one of the parties. His view was that because he had not actually been accused of 'procuring and maintaining' on his client's behalf the doom should be countermanded, otherwise he would not be able to pay the high rent which was due for his office. The council's reply was clearly favourable to his contention.[21] His successor, later in 1332, was David Egerton, who suffered a far severer depletion in the revenues which he collected in return for paying his farm. He had been appointed sheriff by the justiciar, Sir William Clinton, for three years at an annual farm of £240. In that same year another judgement in the county court resulted in the abolition of customary payments exacted by the sheriff from the freeholders of the county, payments which were held to be the result of 'undue oppressions and extortions'.[22] It was estimated that the disappearance of this custom resulted in a loss to the sheriff of £68 10s. 0d. a year, but Egerton had to petition parliament before his farm was reduced.[23]

The first surviving account of the sheriff as 'approver' rather than as farmer is for 1349–50. In this, the sheriff is paid an annual fee of £20, and it is interesting to note that, in the auditors' view, the abandonment of the farm had entailed a financial loss to the earl.[24] A further important change affecting the sheriff's account occurred in 1354–5, with the forfeiture of the serjeanties of the peace of Sir James Audley and his four fellow serjeants on account of the 'extortions and outrages' which they had perpetrated. As a result, all the beadle-bailiffs of the hundreds of the county (except Maccles-field) were to farm the serjeanty within their own hundred, and pay the farm to the sheriff.[25] Both these changes resulted in a consider-able tightening-up of central control over the sheriff of Cheshire and over the subordinate peace-keeping officials, and a loss of control on the part of the magnates of the county.

The escheator was not, primarily, a collector of revenue. Lands rarely remained in his hands for any length of time, since it was usual to dispose of them by way of patronage, at least until the 1350s, and later. His receipts varied widely from year to year, and so it was never possible for the office to be farmed or for it to be included within the justiciar's farm. Moreover, it was important for control to be maintained by the centre over the disposal of 'escheats' even when the collection of all other sources of revenue was decen-tralised. Consequently, in the thirteenth and early fourteenth cen-turies, the writs of *diem clausit extremum*, which ordered the holding of inquisitions post mortem, issued from the royal chancery and were addressed to the justiciar.[26] Also, the escheator had to account separately at this time for his issues before special auditors appointed by the royal exchequer.[27] Despite such precautions it was not always possible to stop an escheator succumbing to the temptation to conceal the earl's rights in return for cash or favours proffered by members of the local community. For example, in 1344 Peter Arderne, who had been escheator from 1333 to 1338, was accused of having falsified an inquisition post mortem in favour of some local landowners who had rewarded him, appropriately enough, by selling him the ward-ship of the heir in question. Arderne's behaviour when summoned before the prince's council to explain himself was so odd that his guilt seems to be unquestionable.[28] From the 1350s onwards the escheator himself was the recipient of writs of *diem clausit extremum* now issued from the Chester exchequer and held the resultant inquisitions. In 1352 he was made ex-officio steward of the demesne manors and towns of the earldom (except for Chester city and Macclesfield), a natural extension of responsibility for an official who was normally concerned with the valuation and management of landed property. The following year he was given the task of administering Flintshire as well as Cheshire escheats.[29]

Of the many subordinate county officials little needs to be said here. When the detailed 'Divers Ministers'' accounts begin after 1346 a somewhat motley crew are revealed as paying over the earl's revenues to the chamberlain. They range from the constable and the

hereditary gardener of Chester castle, through the variously titled
keepers of the demesne manors and towns, to the sheriff and
escheator. Mention should be made here of three salaried officials,
the master plumber, carpenter and mason who had oversight of the
prince's works not only in Cheshire and Flintshire but also in north
Wales as well. They did not render account themselves but featured
in the accounts of others.[30] The master carpenter had a particularly
important part to play in raising revenue as the supervisor of the
very large sales of timber from Mara forest and Peckforton park
which took place in the Black Prince's later years. Actual expenditure on works themselves was, in the last couple of decades of the
period, very small indeed.[31] Similar financial roles were played by
the 'law officers' of the earldom, the serjeant of pleas and the
attorney, whose job it was to safeguard the earl's legal and financial
rights in judicial proceedings.[32] At a time, in the second half of the
fourteenth century, when judicial revenue formed an increasingly
important part of the county yield, the financial importance of these
officials does not need to be emphasised. Likewise the establishment
in 1353 of a new post of 'bailiff-errant', that is, a revenue collector
with general responsibility to assist other officials, especially with
the collection of judicial receipts, is an indication of an important
revenue-raising campaign which will be discussed in detail below.[33]

II ROYAL ADMINISTRATION OF THE COUNTY
(1272/1301; 1307/12; 1327/33)

'Farming out' was the royal exchequer's preferred method of administering royal estates in the Middle Ages. It is tempting to equate
such a policy with conservatism, laziness and general inefficiency.
It is difficult to justify such a view in the case of Cheshire. In the
1270s the farm of the county (or rather of the justiciar's bailiwick)
had been £533 6s. 8d. a year.[34] It was raised, in stages, to 1,000
marks (£666 13s. 4d.) in 1281, £1,000 in 1311, £1,200 in 1336 and,
finally, to 2,000 marks (£1,333 6s. 8d.) in 1342. On the face of it,
the thirteenth century farm rents compare poorly with the £1,000
a year, or more, charged on the chamberlain's accounts between
1301 and 1307, and even the higher farms of later on look puny
beside sums of up to £3,000 charged in the later part of the Black
Prince's life. Does this mean that the royal exchequer was content
with a poor return from Cheshire? One thing which is clear is that
simple comparison of total figures is the most misleading way of all
of attempting to trace financial trends. It is necessary, first, to
establish what the government was using Cheshire for during the
periods of royal administration and, secondly, to compare the
detailed figures for revenue then with those for the years of the
apparently more successful royal earls.

To start with Edward I's reign, his financial policy in Cheshire was determined by two considerations: the Welsh war and the building of Vale Royal abbey. In the two decisive campaigns of 1277 and 1282/3, Chester was the springboard for the king's attack on the heartland of Welsh resistance in Gwynedd. In accordance with contemporary practice, both the county's revenues and its reserves of able manpower were largely spent on the prosecution of the war. The voluminous records of the royal chancery, supplemented by the survivals of more informal letters between the king and his officials (and among themselves) which are now in the P.R.O. class 'Ancient Correspondence of the Chancery and Exchequer' illustrate this very clearly.[35] Luckily, the Cheshire sections of the royal exchequer's pipe roll have been published in a good edition and so it is possible to discern both the working out of administrative policy and its financial consequences.[36] When the 1277 war broke out, Sir Guncelin Badlesmere was justiciar of Chester. He had replaced Sir Reginald Grey three years earlier when the latter had fallen victim to Edward I's general administrative purge which had taken place on the king's return from the Crusade. Badlesmere was appointed, unusually, as 'approver' of the county revenues, that is, he had to account for them item by item.[37] This practice was resorted to by the royal exchequer when it wanted to find out the level at which a farm should be set in the future. Badlesmere was charged approximately £700 on his 1276–7 account, nearly all of which was spent on the war, which was brought to a swift conclusion by the Welsh surrender in the autumn of 1277. In July of that year the king and queen came to Chester, and on 13 August they laid the foundation stone of Vale Royal abbey. This grandiose building project was to be the main regular call on the county's revenue up to 1301.[38]

In the three years between 1277 and 1280 the chamberlain, Leo Leo's son, paid over more than £1,500 to the building works. All the county revenue, up to 1,000 marks a year, had been assigned for this purpose in 1277, and control of its collection had been taken away from Badlesmere. In 1281 Reginald Grey was reappointed as justiciar, to farm the office for an eight-year term at 1,000 marks a year. This figure was obviously based on the yields in Badlesmere's and Leo's accounts. Grey's second ministry was to last nearly eighteen years, and in his appointment it was stated that his farm was to continue to go to the Vale Royal works.[39] He very soon had to cope with the Welsh revolt which broke out in the spring of 1282 and with the war that followed it and lasted just over a year.[40] In July 1283 the exchequer recognised that Grey could not be held to account for his farm, since he had spent all the revenue he had collected on soldiers' wages, munitions and the like, and as a result he was allowed to account in the royal wardrobe as 'approver'.[41] Grey played an important part in the war as commander of that section of the royal army which pushed from Chester to Hope and then to Ruthin. For his part in the conflict he was generously rewarded by the king with the gift of the cantref of Dyffryn Clwyd, which later became the marcher barony of Ruthin.[42] During the justiciar's involvement in the campaign William Perton, a royal clerk, took over financial responsibility for the county from his bases in Chester, Flint and Rhuddlan.[43]

Reconquered Englefield, together with other Welsh lands, was transformed into the new county of Flint by the statute of Rhuddlan of 1284. The new shire was to be administered by the justiciar and chamberlain of Chester, but with its own separate judicial system, sheriff and escheator.[44] From that time onwards Grey, who had resumed his role of farmer, was responsible for running two counties. Of course, the greater part of the new county had already been included in the justiciar's bailiwick before 1282. Nevertheless, it is surprising that his farm was reduced to 785½ marks in 1284 (£523 13s. 4d.) and to 727 marks 8s. 0d. (£485 1s. 4d.) in 1291. The loss of the cantref of Rhos to the new lordship of Denbigh was given as the reason for the first reduction; no reason was given for the second. The farm was by the latter year lower than it had been in 1270. One explanation for this 'leniency' must be Grey's central role in the pacification of north Wales, and his involvement in two more Welsh campaigns after 1283. In 1287 he led a Cheshire force to west Wales to help the earl of Cornwall in putting down Rhys ap Maredudd's rebellion. A much more serious uprising occurred in 1294/5 which resulted in his being responsible once again for raising, feeding and leading an army against the Welsh.[45] His own comments on the financial repercussions of that rising were made in 1298, when his account for those years was audited.

At this time [i.e. 1294–5] he could not levy the issues and farms of the said counties [of Chester and Flint] because of the war. In the county of Flint there was no peace, nor did the tenants of the county heed the king's ministers from Michelmas to August.[46]

During Edward I's reign Cheshire's financial administration became what it was never designed to be, a revenue spending department. The king's wars of aggression against Wales and Scotland were made possible only by charging the lands nearest the conflicts with the brunt of the expenses for feeding and maintaining the royal forces. Even when there was no trouble in Wales (or, later, Scotland) Grey was still bound to pay large sums of money to Vale Royal. He gave the works there over £1,760 between 1284 and 1291, and £451 between 1291 and 1298. By 1299 more than £500 assigned to the project had still not been paid, a sign of both slackening royal support and of Edward I's financial difficulties towards the end of his reign. During the whole period between 1272 and 1299 comparatively little money reached the royal exchequer from Cheshire. This did not stop the exchequer, however, from keeping its customary firm grip on the minutiae of financial obligation. Audits, however, when the justiciar was farmer of the revenues, came only at intervals of years, when his leases came to the end of their terms, and little more than a 'clearing-up operation' was then possible. Even the separate financial control over the escheator looks less convincing when it is realised that the exchequer-appointed auditors of the escheator's account in 1290 were Richard Mascy (Grey's lieutenant-justiciar) and Peter Bromington (the chamberlain).[47] The surviving records show that the king's government was greatly concerned with mobilising and spending Cheshire's resources but gave less consideration to the county's governmental well-being.[48] That was left to men such as Reginald Grey, and it is important to remember that Grey founded the fortunes of his house on his tenure of the justiciarship of Chester. His good service to the government at a time of military crisis enabled him to reach the ranks of the parliamentary baronage. In 1297, when the king was abroad in Flanders, Grey acted as chief military adviser to his then sole surviving son, lord Edward.[49] A little later on, when the same lord Edward had been made Prince of Wales, Grey took on the position of 'elder statesman' in his household affairs.[50] His retirement from the justiciarship in 1299, nearly thirty years after he had first assumed it, was bound to be the end of an era of decentralisation. At first it seemed that the royal exchequer itself was determined to exploit more positively the county's revenues by appointing Sir Richard Mascy as justiciar but not farmer, leaving the chamberlain, William Fulburn, with the responsibility for collecting and accounting for them. However, before this plan could be implemented it was decided to endow the king's son with the earldom of Chester and the principality of Wales. As a result, Mascy's tenure of the office was changed to that of farmer at the rent of 1,000 marks a year.[51]

In 1307 Prince Edward himself became king as Edward II, thus beginning another period of royal control of Cheshire, but which turned out to be as different from the previous one as it possibly could have been. In 1312 the king made his son Edward, earl of Chester, with his own household and administration, but the transfer was only nominal, since the new earl was a baby. In as much as the king had control of the government of England he retained control of Cheshire until the effective end of his reign in 1326. What Edward II's rule of Cheshire had in common with that of his father was that financial policy was largely overshadowed by royal necessity. It is impossible in the compass of this work to do justice to the history of Cheshire in the years between 1307 and 1327. Control of the county closely followed the political convolutions of the reign which resulted from the various conflicts between the king, his supporters and their baronial opponents.[52]

That the justiciarship became something of 'a political football' during this time can easily be demonstrated. Sir Robert Holland, of Upholland in south Lancashire, was justiciar three times. He was the right-hand man and chief supporter in the North-west of the king's cousin, earl Thomas of Lancaster, who, soon after 1307, became the leader of the king's baronial opponents. Holland's first ministry began in 1307, when king and earl were still on good terms, and ended on 14 October 1309, when Lancaster had come out firmly in opposition to royal policy.[53] A year later the political scene had turned upside down in that Edward had been forced to accept a measure of baronial control of his counsels which resulted in the 'Ordinances' of 1311. Holland was reappointed justiciar at the end of 1311, therefore, but lost the office a year later during the prelude to the treaty which was agreed between Edward and earl Thomas after the murder of the king's 'favourite', Piers Gaveston.[54] Holland's third term, which began in late 1318 or early 1319, was the result of yet another reconciliation between the king and the earl, before what proved to be the final rupture of relations. At a later stage the justiciar was present at one of earl Thomas's unofficial gatherings in Yorkshire in the summer of 1321 through which support was rallied against the king, and Holland was obviously at this time wholly on the earl's side.[55] The Lancashire knight's loyalty, however, did not stretch to actually fighting on earl Thomas's behalf, and he abandoned his patron's cause twelve days before the battle of Boroughbridge, which was fought on 2 March 1322, when Lancaster was defeated and executed. Despite this timely treachery, Holland lost both his office and his lands.[56]

Holland was not the only justiciar at the time who won and lost the post through the shifts of political events. His successor in 1311, Sir Payn Tiptoft, had originally been an opponent of Edward II but became reconciled to his cause,[57] and when ordered to surrender the office to Holland at the end of that year refused to do so. As a result the latter was ordered to take over the county, by force if necessary.[58] With Holland's second dismissal in 1312, he was replaced by Sir Hugh Audley the elder, who, with his son, was a knight of the king's household.[59] After 1322 the Despensers, father and son, rose to power in the king's favour, and it was no doubt through their influence that Sir Richard Amory, the steward of the king's household, was appointed justiciar in 1325.[60] Amory's credentials were good: the king had made him governor of his son's household and estates in 1318,[61] and as such he had held an inquiry into misgovernment of the earl's officials which had resulted in the removal of Sir Hugh Audley as justiciar.[62] His brother, Sir Roger Amory, was a member, with the younger Audley, of a new party

of 'king's friends' that was taking shape at the time. Audley's replacement in Cheshire was Sir John Sapy, a royal official whose exclusion
from office had been one of the stipulations of the Ordainers in
1311.[63] The rise to power of the Despensers brought about the last
conflict of all in Edward II's reign, which resulted in the king's
deposition and murder. In the autumn of 1326 his queen, Isabella
of France, landed in England with an invasion force commanded
by her lover, Sir Roger Mortimer of Wigmore. One of those who
threw in his hand with the rebels was the seneschal of Gascony, Sir
Oliver Ingham. Ingham had already been involved in Cheshire
affairs, having been sent with a military force to the county at the
time of Boroughbridge to organise resistance in the North-west to
the threatened Scottish invasion.[64] He had then served as justiciar
for three years. Even before the breach between king and queen
Ingham had received patronage at Isabella's hands, so it is not surprising that he was put on the regency council through which the
queen and Mortimer governed in the name of the young Edward
III.[65] In February 1328 he was rewarded by being reappointed
justiciar, but this time for life. He stayed in office until October 1330,
when Edward III overthrew his guardians and assumed power
himself.[66]

It has long been known that the political turbulence of these years
had serious social effects on the North-west. Indeed, J. R. Maddicott
has stated that the political problem, exacerbated by the famine of
1315 and the Scottish invasions of 1316 and 1322, led to a 'breakdown of authority' in northern England.[67] In Lancashire the groups
which supported and opposed the power of Robert Holland clashed
in miniature civil war in 1315, leaving the county in a disordered
state for many years afterwards.[68] Cheshire suffered from similar
symptoms during Edward II's reign. They appeared as early as
1308, when one of the master-serjeants of the peace and the baron
of Shipbrook were accused of both attempting to murder a royal
bailiff and being involved in a seditious gathering which had allegedly
assembled at Barrow. The jury summoned to investigate these allegations at the county court responded with an attack on one of the
royal officials in the county for corruption.[69] The following year
the bailiff of Northwich town was attacked in the street and a riot
resulted.[70] By 1310 the government was so concerned about the
general state of lawlessness in Cheshire that the joint master-serjeants
of the peace were ordered in strong terms to remedy the deteriorating
situation.[71]

In 1318, when outright civil war first began to threaten in England,
Cheshire's problems flared up disastrously. On 5 September a 'great
multitude of armed men' from the county laid siege to the city of
Chester on the day of the county court and arrowshots were exchanged. When the besiegers failed to break through the walls they

set fire to the suburbs and set up road blocks so that no one could get in or out of the city. This paramilitary attack was serious enough for the king's government to call in the justiciar of Wales, Sir Roger Mortimer, who, with the treasurer of England, the earl of Surrey, Sir John Grey and the sheriffs of three neighbouring counties, was commissioned to repress the disorder.[72] The cause of this attack is not known. It is clear, though, that the 'keepers' (that is, serjeants) of the peace were involved in it, and also the followers of earl Thomas of Lancaster.[73] Not surprisingly, financial administration was affected by difficulties such as these. As Appendix I shows, many accounts for this reign are missing, and it is not certain whether this is because they never existed in the first place. No accounts have so far been found on the pipe roll for any of the farmers of the county during the reign: Robert Holland had all the £1,000 due from his second term (1311/12) remitted, and, when a general report was made in 1337 on revenue still outstanding in Cheshire, over £4,250 was said to be owing from the justiciars and chamberlains for the years between 1307 and 1327.[74]. This was, it must be admitted, an exaggeration, yet it was claimed then that Sir Oliver Ingham had rendered no accounts at all for the five years when he was farmer, and this statement, coupled with the fact that in 1337, after his rehabilitation by the new regime, Ingham was pardoned his Cheshire arrears, would explain why all his accounts are missing.[75] It is very likely that considerable sums of money due in these years were eventually written off as impossible of collection.

With the accession of Edward III in 1327 there came about what was virtually an administrative re-run of the previous reign, but with different political problems. In 1333 the king created his son, Edward of Woodstock (the Black Prince), earl of Chester, but actually retained control of the running of both his household and his estates until 1346, when the prince was deemed capable of independent initiative. Thus in 1336 the king appointed Sir Henry Ferrers, a member of the royal household who had previously served as warden of the Channel Isles, justiciar of Chester in his son's name. He was to farm the county at a rent of £1,333 6s. 8d., and if, indeed, it was he who served as chamberlain of the royal household between 1337 and 1340 he must, of necessity, have delegated most if not all of his day-to-day authority in Cheshire to others.[76] This impression is confirmed by a survey of the demesnes and castles of the earldom which was made, in 1337, by two royal clerks acting in concert with 'members of the council of Sir Henry Ferrers, then justiciar of Chester'.[77] In March 1341 he was deprived of the farm for a year, as part of the revenge of Edward III against those officials whom he suspected of corruptly preventing him from receiving sufficient money to finance the French war.[78] After receiving the office back again, Ferrers died in 1343 without having rendered any accounts.

His debts passed to his brother, and executor, Sir Thomas Ferrers, who took over the justiciarship as well. When the account was finally rendered it made clear that Sir Henry had been making large cash liveries to the earl's wardrobe of £1,000 a year between 1331 and 1334 and £4,250 in all up to 1341. This success was continued during his last eighteen months, when a further £2,000 was paid over.[79] This shows that the farming out of the county revenues (remembering that the farm did not include the escheats) could raise large sums of money for the central administration. Sir Thomas Ferrers probably managed to continue in the same way, as he is known to have paid more than £1,200 to the keeper of the prince's wardrobe between Michaelmas 1343 and July 1344.[80] He surrendered his farm in 1346, not because of financial difficulties but because in that year the prince took over full control of his lands, and farming the justiciarship was not compatible with his officials' new ideas for a thorough investigation into every possible way of raising increased revenue. In fact, he stayed on as justiciar, although not as farmer, until his death in 1353.[81]

The handling of Cheshire finances by the royal exchequer, either directly or under its influence, between 1272 and 1346 does not reveal the king's government to have been financially conservative or incompetent. Naturally, though, financial administration of the county had to be subservient to royal policy. During Edward I's reign this entailed most revenue being spent locally, while in the early years of Edward III preparations for the Hundred Years' War resulted in the collection of most revenue by the centre. Again, in Edward II's reign, when royal policy virtually fell apart, revenue collection could not help but be affected. Administrative and financial control of the county was decentralised to a large extent, which magnified the power and importance of the justiciars such as Reginald Grey and, perhaps to a dangerous extent, left the matters of detailed policy in their hands.

III ADMINISTRATION UNDER THE ROYAL EARLS
(1301/7; 1312/27; 1333/76)

This discussion will be limited very largely to the administrations of the first and third of the earls Edward, since few materials relating to the second, Edward of Windsor, survive. Edward of Caernarfon's household and governmental offices were organised in ways like those of any other landed magnate in contemporary England.[82] Nevertheless, the system was devised and run by clerks detached for the purpose from government service.[83] Thus the prince drew on the abilities of men of talent and importance who regarded themselves, and turned out to be, the future government of England. Walter Reynolds, keeper of the wardrobe (which was the prince's central financial office), later became treasurer of England, chancellor of England, and archbishop of Canterbury. His colleague, William Melton, served as chamberlain of Chester from 1301 to 1304, was promoted to the royal wardrobe after 1307 and mirrored Reynolds's rise to the highest offices. At the end of his career he was consecrated archbishop of York. He was also one of the few prominent Englishmen to emerge with credit from Edward II's reign. The prince's wardrobe performed secretarial as well as financial functions, since its controller kept the prince's privy seal. Edward also had a great seal and a chancellor who played an important part in estate administration as the head of the prince's council, a body which was composed of his chief officials. As far as is known, the purely domestic officers like the steward and chamberlain were not concerned with administering the prince's estates. The council issued orders for the government of his lands, and it controlled the actions of local officials both through the medium of letters and by the annual visits of auditors of accounts to the estates themselves. It is in the function assigned to these auditors that the main difference between the administrative methods of kings and earls is to be found.

When the 1301–2 chamberlain's account was audited in the summer of 1303 the auditors were William Blyborough (the prince's chancellor) and two others who were, presumably, full-timers, appointed by 'the prince and his council'.[84] All the main county officials were 'new men', appointed by the prince when he had taken up the government of the earldom on his visit to Chester in April 1301. Mascy then lost his post of justiciar-farmer, and was replaced by Sir William Trussell. William Melton was appointed chamberlain, with the responsibility of accounting for all the issues of the earldom under Trussell's supervision.[85] The accounts of Walter Reynolds, as keeper of the wardrobe between 1301 and 1304, show that the large cash liveries made by Melton during these years were, by themselves, almost sufficient to cover the normal domestic expenses of the household.[86] This explains the necessity for more detailed and central control of county finances: in the exchequer valuation of 1284 Cheshire's contribution to the normal royal revenue (excluding extraordinary taxation) had been only some 3½ per cent of the whole.[87] The short-lived principate of Edward of Caernarfon produced a model for running the heir-apparent's estates which was used, and further developed, during the Black Prince's time.

Tout argued that the earlier Prince Edward's household remained under his father's strict control even after 1301. The king, it is true, did appoint a commission of inquiry into the government of Cheshire in 1304, apparently without reference to the prince, although the commissioners were largely Prince Edward's officials.[88] Even closer control was exercised by Edward II over his son's administrative arrangements, although the infant earl was provided with his own household and a central administration similar to that of 1301/7. Edward of Windsor had a wardrobe, to which the chamberlain of Chester made liveries, and its keeper in 1320, Nicholas Hugate, had been a clerk in Edward of Caernarfon's office.[89] The young earl also had a council, since the wardrobe keeper and other members of that body were in Cheshire on official business in 1315.[90] In 1327 it was recorded that the earl's auditor came from London to Chester castle, where he audited, in conjunction with the county escheator, the chamberlain's account.[91] On the other hand, in July 1320 it had been the chamberlain who travelled to London, where he was present at the audit of the account of his predecessor, William Burstow (chamberlain 1315/20), which was rendered before the barons of the king's exchequer.[92] The young earl also had officials of high calibre. Richard Bury, who had begun his career in the royal exchequer as clerk to the treasurer, Walter Langton, served as chamberlain of Chester between 1320 and 1324. He then returned to the royal service in the wardrobe and assisted with Edward III's seizure of power in 1330. Later he was made bishop of Durham and then treasurer and chancellor of England.[93] Under Edward of Windsor the royal clerks who filled the office of chamberlain accounted for the county's issues, as far as is known, with the possible exception of the years between 1322 and 1325, when Sir Oliver Ingham may have farmed the county.[94] As no full-year chamberlain's account survives from this period, it is not possible to say anything with certainty about the total revenue collected and how it was spent.

When Edward of Woodstock was created earl of Chester in 1333 he was a small child, and so, for the next ten years or so, his administrative arrangements were similar to those of the other two earls.[95] His wardrobe in those early years doubled as a household and estate finance office. Like his predecessors, he had both a council and a privy seal, together with the usual domestic officials. He also had an estates steward, plus a 'master' who superintended his education and his general affairs. Edward received his estates in stages: he acquired the duchy of Cornwall in 1337 and the principality of Wales in 1343. The structure of his administrative establishment had to change to meet new requirements, and in the latter year a central exchequer was set up, at Westminster, as the department of receipt for the revenue from his whole appanage. This meant that revenue collection was to be separated from revenue spending, which latter remained the task of the wardrobe and other household departments. It was the council which had to act as a bridge between the two departments and work out a coherent financial policy. Behind these changes was the figure of Peter Gildesburgh, the keeper of the prince's wardrobe since 1341, who had come to that office from a subordinate position in the royal exchequer. He was made head of the prince's exchequer in 1344 with the new title of receiver-general,

and was replaced by John Hale at the wardrobe.[96] In March 1347
his dominance in the prince's financial administration was demonstrated beyond doubt when he was promoted to the newly created
post of 'keeper of the prince's exchequer, chief auditor, and controller of the receiver-general', for which he took 5s. 0d. a day
wages.[97] Although this grandiose title did not survive Gildesburgh
himself, in essentials the office was continued after the Black Death
in the persons of two laymen, Sir John Wingfield and Sir John
Delves, who were successively 'business managers' to the prince.[98]
This new office replaced the older one of estates steward. It seems
to have had no real parallel on other large English estates at the
time, and is an indication of the large measures of both centralisation
and professionalisation in the prince's administration.

From 1344 until the prince's death in 1376 Cheshire revenue was
paid to his Westminster exchequer, of which the receiver-general
from 1346 to 1371 was Peter Lacy.[99] The only exception to this rule
was the short period between December 1352 and July 1355 when
it was ordained that the revenues of Cheshire, Flintshire and Cornwall should go, as of old, to the wardrobe. The reason given for this
was that

the prince [desires] very earnestly that payments for the expenses of his
household be made henceforth more promptly than heretofore, and that his
household be directed and governed more regularly and with greater honour
and profit to himself and less harm to his people.[100]

It seems that this remedy, of assigning substantial revenues to the
wardrobe, was decided upon because the alternative was the extensive use of the prince's right to prises, that is, the forced purchase
of supplies, on credit, from the tenants of his estates. This could
'harm' them in that they might receive considerably less than the
market price for their goods and might also have to wait a long
time for payment. The royal household had exactly the same difficulty at this time, and responded in the same way, by assigning
revenues to the wardrobe.[101] These years were particularly significant
for the prince in that they were the time when the plans were being
made for his great campaign which led to the victory of Poitiers,
with the resulting expansion of his wardrobe from a simple household finance bureau to a war treasury.

With the death of Sir Thomas Ferrers in 1353 a change took place
in the office of justiciar of Chester. He was replaced, eventually,
by the prince's retainer, Sir Bartholomew Burghersh the younger,
who treated the post as a sinecure, leaving the substance of responsibility to John Delves, who had been appointed lieutenant-justiciar
about three weeks previously.[102] Delves, who came from a minor
Staffordshire landed family, had been lieutenant-justiciar of north
Wales since 1348, and he retained this office together with the

Chester one.[103] His career is a compelling example of the rewards open to a trusted administrator in the Black Prince's service, even to someone from a relatively humble background. Although not yet even an esquire, in 1359 he was given the general responsibility for the government of the principality, the earldom and the lordship of Denbigh. In the early 1360s he reached the highest point in the prince's administrative hierarchy as his 'business manager' in succession to Sir John Wingfield. As he assumed these heavy responsibilities in the central administration he needed assistance to carry out his local responsibilities, which, significantly, he did not shed. Thus John Pole was made joint lieutenant-justiciar of Chester some time before 1362, and Delves himself only gave up the lieutenancy round about 1364.[104]

From 1346 to 1370 the office of chamberlain of Chester was held by one man, Master John Burnham the younger. At both the centre and in the localities the Black Prince's regime was characterised by the long service of his officials, contrasting markedly with Edward II's reign, when there had been six justiciars and ten chamberlains.[105] Burnham was probably the nephew of his elder namesake, who had an even more distinguished career in the financial service of the king and prince.[106] The younger man first appeared as 'receiver of Cheshire' in 1342–3, in respect of the revenue, largely judicial, which was not included in Henry Ferrers's farm. In 1351 his fee of £20 a year was increased by £6 13s. 4d. in recognition of his extra responsibilities in receiving the revenue of Macclesfield lordship.[107] The following year the county escheator was ordered to make his liveries to the chamberlain rather than to the prince's central exchequer, as had previously been the case.[108] It is no exaggeration to call this self-effacing 'petit clerk' of the prince the lynchpin of the financial administration of Cheshire during the prince's maturity.[109] His job was to be an efficient collector of revenue in accordance with a financial policy which was almost wholly imposed on him from above. In this limited task there can be no doubt that John Burnham the younger was a complete success.

No further changes of importance took place in the actual administrative structure of which Cheshire was a part. Except for the actual accounting forms adopted after 1346, nothing can be pointed to in the methods that were used under the three royal earls which was essentially different from those employed on any other large lay estate of the time. Yet the men who devised and operated the structure came from the royal finance departments of exchequer and wardrobe. Even during the later decades of the Black Prince's life, when it was possible to train recruits within his own governmental set-up, links with the king's government remained strong. Royal justices were retained to give both legal and general advice on the prince's council, and Peter Lacy, his receiver-general from 1346 to

1371, was also keeper of the king's privy seal during his last four years in that office.[110] On the basis of such connections, and with our knowledge of the centralisation of detailed concern with financial administration which was typical of the Black Prince's time, it is impossible to agree wholly with B. P. Wolffe's assertion that the royal exchequer maintained only a limited, 'residual interest' in the exploitation of the royal patrimony in the thirteenth and fourteenth centuries during 'the brief periods needed to replace one life grant by another'.[111]

Over the period as a whole between 1272 and 1377 the most significant administrative shift affecting Cheshire was towards a fully professional, salaried staff. In the thirteenth century the justiciar had been a landed knight, a 'magnate' within the limited horizons of county society, whereas the sheriff usually belonged to a prominent local family. Both officers commonly farmed their bailiwicks (the sheriff normally, until 1349) and thus were not subject to the scrutiny of detailed financial control. If 'feudalism' entails the decentralisation of governmental authority on the basis of the ownership of land, then this was a truly feudal system, but without the element of hereditary succession. In the beginning only the two clerical officers, the chamberlain and the escheator, were 'professionals' : by 1354 all the chief county officials were paid salaries and held office at the prince's pleasure. Similarly, the demesnes within the county had normally been disposed of by being granted for life to those whom the kings or earls wished to reward until the mid-fourteenth century, when the revenue which could be raised from them became the significant factor.[112] In the second half of the fourteenth century Cheshire was governed from London in a way it had never experienced before, and one of the consequences was that rewards for loyal service had to be dispensed in ways different from those sanctioned by tradition: by the grant of life annuities rather than of manors, and by the disposal of the fixed capital of the earldom (for example, its growing timber) rather than touching its revenue. It was an obvious lesson from Edward II's reign that weak and divided government had a bad effect on financial administration: the Black Prince's officials may have hoped, by strong centralised control, to produce both good government and a healthy financial position. The difficulty was not so much that the two objectives were incompatible but that the needs which the administrators existed to fulfil were determined by forces almost wholly outside their control.

It has been suggested that the change discussed above was accompanied by a progressive increase in the amount of money that was exacted from Cheshire over the whole period. Is it true, as Appendix I suggests, that, under the royal administration of Edward I, less revenue was collected from the earldom, compared with the time of Edward of Caernarfon? Richard Mascy, as justiciar-farmer, had to pay an annual rent to the king of £666 13s. 4d. while William Melton, as chamberlain accounting for the issues of the county in 1301–2, was charged to collect £1,904 4s. 10¼d. for Cheshire and Flintshire. Whether this apparent disparity represented a real financial difference can be determined only by deducting from Melton's charge those items which Mascy either did not receive or which he had to pay out of his own pocket whereas Melton was allowed them on the discharge side of his account. (Table 2.) The difference between Melton's adjusted charge of £740 4s. 3d., and Mascy's farm is only just over £70. The 'excess' is accounted for not by an element of 'profit' collectable by the farmer, since he had much greater responsibilities for finance and administration than the chamberlain, who did not farm the county, and £70 is only a bare recognition of that fact. There is no justification, therefore, for J. R. Maddicott's contention that the farmers of the justiciarship were able to make a 'good profit' out of the office.[113] On the contrary, Sir Payn Tiptoft's farm of £1,000 a year was based on a distinct overvaluation of the issues of the justiciarship, the terms of his tenure being similar to those of Richard Mascy twelve years earlier.[114]

TABLE 2

COMPARISON OF THE ACCOUNT OF SIR RICHARD MASCY (1299–1300)[115] WITH THAT OF WILLIAM MELTON (1301–2)[116]

Mascy's farm	Melton's total charge (Cheshire and Flintshire		
£666 13s. 4d.	£	s.	d.
	1,904	4	10¼
1. Mascy did *not* receive revenue from:			
a. Arrears	294	7	6¼
b. Wardships	50	9	0¼
c. Some demesnes[117]	388	0	0
d. Englefield (lead mine and escheats)[118]	31	18	7
2. Mascy had to pay:			
a. Ancient alms	51	6	6
b. Fees (including his own)	145	10	6
c. Expenses on repairs, etc.	202	8	6
Total (1 and 2)	1,164	0	7½

Similar comparisons have been made between the revenue from Cheshire in the early 1300s and half a century later, when the disparity can be made to appear quite staggering. In the words of H. J. Hewitt, whereas county revenue had been nearly £1,900 in 1302–3 'it was driven up to £3,928 in 1353–4 . . . and to about £3,450 in 1359–60'.[119] Table 3 provides an item-by-item comparison of the accounts for 1302–3 and 1359–60. Those manors and towns which were 'in hand' in one period, and not in the other, have to be discounted, so that like is being compared with like. It will be noted that one item of income that the Black Prince was not able to exploit was wool customs revenue. The royal direction of the wool trade which came about as the result of the Hundred Years' War meant that Chester ceased to be a port from which wool could be exported. It is easy to see that nearly all the significant difference between the two accounts is provided by item 17, the financial results of the

TABLE 3

COMPARISON OF THE CHESTER CHAMBERLAIN'S ACCOUNT FOR 1302–3[120] AND 1359–60[121]

		1302–3				1359–60		
		£	s.	d.		£	s.	d.
1.	Chester fee farm	100	0	0		100	0	0
2.	Dee Mills	200	0	0		199	11	3
3.	Forest of Mara	{ 20	3	4		21	0	4
		{ 6	2	0		35	11	10
4.	Macclesfield and Overton	232	0	0	(Macclesfield and Longdendale) 192	17	5
5.	Northwich	76	0	0		–		
6.	Middlewich	90	0	0		58	18	0
7.	Shrievalty	140	0	0				
8.	Avowries	48	0	0	}	335	13	4
9.	County court, etc.	250	13	9				
10.	Wardships	72	9	7¾		67	6	8
11.	Prise of wine	10	0	0		–		
12.	Wool custom	19	1	8½		–		
	Total	1,264	10	5¼		1,010	18	10
13.	Shotwick	–				24	10	0
14.	Frodsham	–				76	2	2½
15.	Rudheath	–				6	10	0
16.	Overmarsh	–				13	15	2¾
17.	Forest eyre fines	–				698	9	7¾
18.	Old atterminations (fines, etc.)	–				160	5	4¾
19.	New atterminations (fines, etc.)	–				48	7	4
20.	Atterminations of fines (breach of the peace)	–				13	6	8
21.	Fee of the seal	–				4	1	8
22.	Temporalities of the bishopric of Coventry and Lichfield	–				20	13	11¾
23.	Issues of St. Pierre lands	–				320	17	2

A. *Total* (1 *to* 12) £1,264 10s. 5¼d. B. *Total* (13 *to* 23) 1,386 19 3½

C. *Total* (1 *to* 23) 2,397 18 1½

1357 forest eyre. Likewise, in 1353–4, when charged receipts were even higher again, the reason was the levy of extraordinary judicial revenue: the common fine of 1353, and the individual fines imposed in the trailbaston sessions of that year.[122] The question that remains to be answered, therefore, is: how and why was such extraordinary revenue raised in the Black Prince's time, and did it really result in the county being 'milked dry' by his administration? This will be looked at in some detail in Chapter V.

IV DECISION-MAKING AND FINANCIAL POLICY

Most of the decisions relating to Cheshire finances in the Middle Ages were matters of office routine, sanctioned by custom and practice. Such decisions rarely, if ever, appear in records, since there was usually no need for them to be recorded, unless the routine itself was being modified in a serious way. At all times, however, there were decisions which had to be referred to a higher authority: in Edward I's time, for example, we have seen that appointments of escheators were reserved to the royal government. As 'higher authority' was external to Cheshire, such important decisions would usually be incorporated in letters addressed to the justiciar or the chamberlain. It was in the interests of these administrators at the 'lower level' to preserve any evidence there might be that they were acting only as a result of orders received, so that they could be absolved of any consequences that the order in question might have. Thus the chamberlains of Chester in the fourteenth century kept files of incoming letters, and by the 1350s they were copying some orders on to the recognisance rolls as warrants for the actions they had taken. Little 'warrant evidence' survives from before 1351 and a very large amount subsequently. However, it does appear that in the three periods of royal government most of the decisions with regard to matters such as the appointment of county officials and granting of leases of demesnes were made locally. In 1277, for example, Guncelin Badlesmere was authorised to lease the royal demesnes in Cheshire for terms of up to five years.[123] In 1333 it was made clear that David Egerton had been granted a lease of the office of sheriff by the justiciar, Sir William Clinton.[124] It was probably Clinton who wrote to the government in 1330, or early 1331, pointing out that no appointments should be made to county offices except by the advice of himself and the chamberlain, 'who have the greater knowledge of where the king's advantages may be lost in the said county . . .'.[125] What the royal government reserved for decisions at the centre was very largely matters of patronage: namely, grants and certain leases of demesnes, as well as control of the escheator's office.

Under all three royal earls decision-making was more centralised than this. Edward of Caernarfon's auditors, as council delegates, had power to remove unsatisfactory officials from office and could appoint new ones in their places.[126] During this time, and that of Edward of Windsor, the machinery was certainly capable of making and implementing detailed decisions about financial policy in Cheshire. However, it was the justiciar who appointed a keeper of the avowries in 1305–6 and possibly the county sheriffs at the same period.[127] There is simply not enough evidence at this time to decide on the precise balance between central and local decision-making. With the survival of the four volumes of the so-called *Black Prince's Register* between 1346 and 1365 we are presented, however, with an embarrassment of riches in this regard. Volumes II (Cornwall and Devon), III (Cheshire and Flintshire) and IV ('England') of these privy seal letter books which cover the years 1351 to 1365 inclusive are particularly useful, since many of the letters copied in them have 'notes of warrant' which indicate who authorised their issue. All together these three books contain about six thousand letters, of which something over two thousand have warrants. If the two lost register books, for north and south Wales, are taken into account an average of nearly 700 letters a year may well have been issued by the central administration: probably nearer a thousand in the earlier years, when the record-keeping was more careful.[128]

The first and crudest way of classifying the notes of warrant is by adding up all those attributable to one of three sources: the prince himself, his council or any of his officials (or 'ministers'), as in Table 4. The second way of classifying the warrants, almost equally crude, is to see how many of each class were issued from month to month. This information is set out in the form of a graph in Fig. 7. Fig. 7 shows that virtually all the 'conciliar' warrants are confined to three or four 'peaks' each year and hence must relate to the meetings of the prince's great council, which is known to have met annually at Easter, midsummer, Michaelmas and Hilary. Similarly, letters (or orders) issued 'by petition endorsed' without further qualification

TABLE 4

WARRANTS IN THE BLACK PRINCE'S REGISTER, VOLUMES II–IV, 1351/65[129]

1. *Princely.* Letters issued 'by command of the prince', either by himself, or on the advice of the council or of someone else; also letters issued on the authority of the seal used by the prince when abroad, 'by warrant of Gascony' or some such phrase. *Total*: 760
2. *Conciliar.* Letters issued 'by advice of the council', either in the salutation clause or the note of warrant; letters issued 'by petition endorsed' or by warrant of four, or more, officials acting together. *Total*: 568
3. *Ministerial.* Letters issued 'by ordinance . . .', 'by command . . .' or 'by advice . . .' of between one and three of the prince's officials. *Total*: 1,112

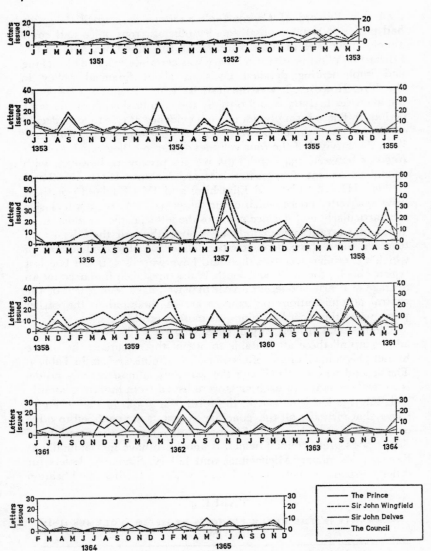

Warrants in the *Black Prince's Register* volumes II-IV 1351/65

also appear in the same clusters of warrants and so they have been included in the 'conciliar' class in Table 4.

It must be remembered that these warrants were not the actual records of decisions made at the centre, only the *consequences* of those decisions. Many of them can be interpreted in more than one way. Thus an order to the escheator dated 4 August 1353 is warranted thus:

par avis monsire William de Shareshull monsire Roger Hillary monsire Richard de Willughbi monsire Johan de Wengfeld Henri Grene Robert de Thorp et autres.[130]

What does 'advice' mean in this context? It could mean that the keeper of the prince's privy seal was told by the group (or by one person representing them) that the letters were to be issued. Or the advice could have been proffered to the prince himself, who would then order that the letters be issued. The former alternative is, in my view, more likely, since the second one is covered by the warrant to the letter next on that same folio:

par command' le seignur meismes et avis de son conseil.

Bearing in mind that warrants were a form of protection both for those who drafted the official letters and those who executed orders contained in them, it seems right to assume that the two formulae given above, both representing decisions by the prince's council, mean different things, and that in the first the prince was not involved in the decision. Moreover, it is likely that when letters were issued 'by command of . . .' or 'on the advice of . . .' or 'on the information of someone' the person or persons to whom the phrases applied had a decisive part to play in making that particular decision. What is worrying is that the three different phrases employed must have represented different levels of 'decisiveness', but exactly what the differences were cannot be recovered. In his study of the notes of warrant on the royal chancery rolls of Henry IV's reign A. L. Brown put forward the suggestion that we can, more or less, accept what they say at their face value.[131] We can assume, without too much risk, a similar general correspondence between warrants and reality in the *Black Prince's Register*.

The classification given in Table 4 is therefore rather surprising. 'Ministerial' warrants outnumber the 'princely' variety by over 300, and the 'conciliar' type comes a very poor third.[132] Moreover, Fig. 7 shows that between 1351 and 1361 the prince's business manager, Sir John Wingfield, was responsible for the issue of the largest number of letters in the prince's name, either on his own authority or in conjunction with other officials. The only exception was between October 1356 and August 1357, which can easily be accounted for by the fact that Wingfield spent those months in Gascony, where he distinguished himself by his military service and probably lent a hand with the organisation of the expedition.[133] It is no exaggeration to say that Wingfield was the principal maker of policy for the prince's estate administration at this time, and indeed until his death in 1361. He first appeared in the prince's service shortly after the Black Death, when he had already reached a position of such importance that the record clerks were uncertain by what title he should be called: 'steward of (all the prince's) lands', 'chief councillor' and 'governor of the prince's business' were all tried on occasion. Normally 'Sir John Wingfield' was sufficient designation. In one way, as has already been remarked, he succeeded the clerk, Peter Gildesburgh, in the control that he assumed of the prince's affairs, but Gildesburgh had had a lay colleague, the steward of lands, Sir Richard Stafford, whereas Wingfield ruled alone.[134] Until 1361 the routine of central administration was Wingfield's responsibility, acting either alone or in conjunction with two or three fellow councillors. He came to Cheshire in February 1351 and took part in the audit of the accounts for 1349–50 and again during the prince's visit of 1353.[135] In the autumn of that latter year a decision about the payment of rent by the abbot of Chester in Rudheath had to be postponed because Wingfield was out of London.[136] Most compelling of all, it was he who, in 1359, gave John Delves the responsibility for general supervision of the government of the principality of Wales, Cheshire and Flintshire, and thus designated him as his successor.[137]

Delves first became prominent at the London end of the prince's administration when Wingfield was absent on the Aquitainian expedition during 1356/7. After his predecessor's death he filled Wingfield's place, but only to a limited extent. The notes of warrant make it clear that he shared his decision-making powers with other councillors much more than Wingfield had ever done. It is unfortunate that the registers themselves start to tail off quite markedly from about 1363 onwards, but Fig. 7 shows that, as far as the sheer number of warrants were concerned, Delves was far from having reached by 1365 his predecessor's pre-eminence as a decision-maker. A typical warrant of this later period is one relating to a letter of 8 February 1364 concerning a payment for services in the lordship of Denbigh which was issued 'by advice of Stafford, Delves, Lacy and Spridlington', the last two being the receiver-general and chief auditor.[138] Indeed, if Delves's appointment (or, rather, the order to pay his wages) as 'governor of the prince's business' in 1363 had not survived, we should not have guessed that Wingfield had ever had a successor.[139] John Delves rose from his very modest landed background through training in the common law. We know nothing specifically about this, but it must have been thorough, because, between February 1364 and Easter 1365, he was seconded to king's service as a puisne judge of the court of Common Pleas at West-minster.[140] He may with justice be regarded as an early member of one of the new breed of lawyer-administrators which was to be so important in the subsequent history of English landed estates, sup-planting the clerks (like Gildesburgh) and the soldier-administrators (like Wingfield and Reginald Grey) who had predominated hitherto.

Because of lack of evidence it is impossible to determine whether Delves's administrative authority increased between 1363 and his death in 1369, or whether he himself had a successor. Sir Hugh Segrave was acting as steward of lands by 1372, which may indicate a regression to the older type of 'supervisor' of which Sir Richard Stafford had been the previous example. On the other hand, Wing-field had also been designated in this way while wielding a power which made that title an inadequate description of his functions. At any rate, Segrave succeeded to the expectations of high royal office which Gildesburgh, Wingfield and Delves probably all enter-tained in their turn, becoming steward of Richard II's household and then treasurer of England.[141]

The prince's council, as a body, was far less important adminis-tratively than the individual councillors referred to above. In fact, it seems to be a mistake to think of it as a corporate body exercising a regular administrative role. What might be termed the 'ordinary' council was between 1346 and 1365 a small group, composed largely of administrators and lawyers. It was not a household organ: the officials of the prince's wardrobe, chamber and privy seal depart-ments played a relatively small part in it. When the prince was abroad (on the campaigns, which culminated at Crécy and Poitiers and, from 1363 to 1371, as prince of Aquitaine) he left behind, to look after his estates, an 'English council' with which he communi-cated by letter. Of the laymen on the council, Sir Richard Stafford was the most consistent member throughout the whole period. Of the clerks, William Spridlington, the chief auditor, was usually a member, and of the lawyers Sir William Shareshull, chief justice of the King's Bench, stands out in particular. Although Shareshull played an important part in general administrative policy, particu-larly relating to finance, the part-time royal justices and other lawyers dealt largely with specific matters which raised legal diffi-culties, often in response to a petition from one of the prince's subjects or tenants. They were, in effect, a legal committee of councillors who disposed of those matters which would obviously fall in their province. For example, in November 1355 Shareshull and eight other lawyers, plus the receiver-general, ordered that an investigation should be undertaken in the Flint sessions into allegations of fraudu-lent and extortionate actions against Basingwerk abbey.[142]

To the prince's secretariat, however, the term 'council' normally meant the 'great council'. This was an institution which met, in theory, four times a year so that the prince's *dominium* might be made publicly available. It was, therefore, the main body for dealing with petitions to the prince.[143] It also acted as an administrative court of appeal in which the actions of the prince's officials could be corrected. For example, in July 1357 Chester abbey petitioned the council, saying that the lieutenant and chamberlain were preventing them from exercising certain lawful rights which they claimed.[144] What the great council did not do was act as a court of appeal in the strictly judicial sense. Petitions came from inhabitants of Cheshire, among others, complaining about some defect of justice in the county court. The remedy the great council could provide was an order to the lieutenant-justiciar, or someone, to hurry up and do his job properly. In fact, the great council had to be very firm in limiting the number of petitions it could deal with, and in 1351 an ordinance was made that only exceptional matters could be entertained, and that everything else should be dealt with locally.[145] Exactly who was summoned as a member of the great council is not wholly clear: its core would obviously consist of those councillors who were active in between the 'great' sessions—the administrators and the lawyers. In addition, it is likely that the prince's military retainers would attend, and a proportion of his household staff. The great council did have an administrative function: matters of the highest importance were its province. In December 1352 it was an ordinance made 'by advice of the prince's great council' which assigned the revenues of Cheshire, Flintshire and Cornwall to the wardrobe. This was a matter which concerned the spending as much as the collecting of the prince's revenue, and so the fuller body was more appropriate. Even so, Sir John Wingfield is recorded as having had an important part to play in the actual *framing* of the ordinance.[146] Somewhat earlier, it was stated that the method of audit employed in respect of the Chester chamberlain's account for 1349–50 had been laid down 'by ordinance of the great council'.[147] Administrative decisions, even of the highest importance, could be and were made elsewhere: the great council was both a body and an occasion, the *prime* purpose of which was not to administer, but to be open to the complaints and requests of the prince's people. In the earldom of Chester and the principality of Wales, where, in the Prince's time, the inhabitants did not normally have recourse to the king in parliament by way of petition, the great council carried out part, at least, of a parliamentary function.[148]

What of the role of the prince himself in the government of his estates? All administration in Cheshire, of course—financial, judicial or of any other kind—was carried out in his name, and charters, letters and writs issued under his privy seal or under the seal of the earldom were drafted as if their contents were his own personal concern. The notes of warrant, however, tell a different story. They demonstrate that between 1351 and 1365 the prince left the government of his lands and matters concerned with the collection of his revenue very largely to his professional administrators. Until 1361 this meant Sir John Wingfield. The field that was reserved for the prince's own personal involvement was that of 'grace', or 'patronage'. In such matters nothing was too small to escape his attention. In the surviving petition file for 1375/6 there is a request from one of the unfree tenants of the manor of Princes Risborough, who had taken a bachelor's degree at Oxford and needed the prince's 'letters of freedom' before proceeding to take Holy Orders. Administratively and financially this was of little consequence indeed. Nevertheless, the council had it endorsed 'speak to the prince about it', not because of its importance but because it fell within his recognised province of concern.[149] Likewise, in the flood of grants which followed the Poitiers expedition, the prince was responsible for ordering not just the payments of large life annuities to his military retainers but, for example, a grant of 'two oaks in the park of Peckforton' to Thomas Done 'for good service in Gascony' so that he could repair his house.[150] This is not to say that the prince had no concern at all with detailed financial administration. He had appointed the top officials in the first place, they held office during his pleasure, and, no doubt, matters of great financial importance relating to his estates were referred to him for consultation. The questions of spending rather than collecting of revenue, the financing of the overseas expeditions, and raising loans for general expenditure, were different matters. They did concern the household and the prince's own person in very important ways, and his personal involvement in them was patent.

To illustrate the 'division of labour' that operated in the 1350s, Table 5 sets out all the seventeen warrants to be found on the twenty-seven letters copied into the Cheshire/Flintshire register for June 1353. From the prince's point of view, therefore, the task of his estate administrators was to govern his lands sufficiently well, and without referring decisions to him unnecessarily, so that the large amount of revenue he required could be paid over regularly. Moreover he needed a 'patronage pool' of lands, offices and privileges of one sort or another which he could draw on to reward retainers and other dependants. As far as Cheshire administration was concerned, such a centralised system left far less initiative in the hands of local officials than had once been the case. What this meant as far as the granting of leases of the prince's demesnes and appointments to offices was concerned, in the context of the interplay between patronage and financial administration, will be discussed later on.[151] It is already clear, though, that under the Black Prince the weight of decision-making was shifted much more towards the centre than had been the case even during Edward of Caernarfon's principate.

TABLE 5
WARRANTS OF JUNE 1353 (CHESTER REGISTER).
NUMBERS IN BRACKETS ARE DATES IN JUNE

A. *Conciliar*
1. (3) Order concerning an inquisition on a wardship.*
2. (10) Order to escheator to restore seized lands.*
3. (10) Order to escheator to enquire into a seizure for unlicensed alienation.*
4. (12) Order to justiciar and chamberlain to 'do right' in accordance with a petition (not extant).*
5. (13) Order to chamberlain to pay wages to steward of Hopedale which he claims are being withheld.
6. (3) Order to escheator to cease distraining abbot of Chester for fealty, which he has performed.*
7. (3) Order to same to deliver to same his manor of Saighton.* (Presumably result of 6.)
8. (8) Order to justiciar and chamberlain not to distrain Chester abbey for lacking stocks on their manors, as indictments to that effect have been made maliciously.*
9. (15) Order to justiciar and chamberlain to hear an 'appeal' in a case of novel disseisin.*

B. *Ministerial* (all on the authority of Sir John Wingfield)
10. (3) Order to justiciar, chamberlain and escheator to deal leniently with widow of Hugh Hamson for his arrears as bailiff of Northwich.
11. (7) Notification to justiciar, chamberlain and escheator that prince and council have decided to take Chester abbey into his protection, and giving details in connection with this. The matter is to be resolved when the prince or his great council come to Chester.
12. (8) Order to forester of Wirral to deliver to Chester abbey oaks in Saughall wood which the prince has granted it.
13. (8) Order to chamberlain to cease levying £500 from citizens of Chester, as the matter is to be discussed further.
14. (15) Order to escheator to deliver manor of Bollin, etc., to Richard Fitton, as he has paid fine for unlicensed alienation.
15. (30) Order to chamberlain to arrange for purveyors of prince's household to buy supplies for his coming to Cheshire.

C. *Princely*
16. (18) Order to chamberlain to issue charter to Thos. Dutton granting him free warren in his Cheshire manors.
17.   Order to chamberlain about a grant of licence to Alan Cheyne, the prince's yeoman.

* Letters issued in response to a petition.
Source: *B.P.R.*, III, pp. 104–11.

However, the balance of power depended not upon abstract constitutional arrangements but on the relationships of particular officials to each other and to the prince himself at any particular time. There was a degree of flexibility which permitted change and development. Nothing illustrates this better than the policy for administering escheats in Cheshire in the 1350s. As had already been seen, it had always been usual to keep a stronger central control over the running of the escheator's department than over other parts of the county's administration. In 1352, when it was decided that the escheator should make his liveries to the chamberlain instead of to the Westminster exchequer, it was with the reservation that all decisions relating to his office were still to be made centrally.[152] Yet less than two years later Wingfield decided that Delves, acting in conjunction with Burnham, should be empowered to sell all wardships and marriages worth ten marks (£6 13s. 4d.) or less on his own authority.[153] Then, in September 1359, Delves, Burnham and the escheator were given power to sell all wardships and marriages in Cheshire (and Flintshire) 'by agreement among themselves, as quickly and profitably as possible'.[154] We are thus faced with the paradox that at a time when administration was centralised to a degree which had no precedent, devolution of control over the middle-range county patronage (which escheats represented) yet existed to an extent that would once have been unacceptable. One reason for this was the position of Delves himself, who from the mid-1350s onwards was rising even higher in the prince's central counsels. This was why he was given progressive command of local patronage, not because he held the local office of lieutenant. An additional factor was the prince's need for ready cash in large quantities, which meant that 'profitability' had, perforce, to loom very large in his calculations. This was the direct result of his commitment to the French war in general, from 1346 onwards, and to Gascony in particular up to 1371, which was productive of a tension between good financial administration and good government that even the most professional, fair-minded and efficient administrator would have found difficult to resolve.[155]

NOTES

[1] R. Stewart-Brown, 'The End of the Norman Earldom of Chester', *E.H.R.* XXXV (1920), pp. 26–54.

[2] Robin Studd, 'The Lord Edward's Lordship of Chester', *T.H.S.L.C.*, 128 (1979), pp. 9–10.

[3] See B. E. Harris, 'The Palatinate 1301–1547', *V.C.H.* (*Cheshire*), II, pp. 9–11.

[4] *Close Rolls*, VI, 1247–51 (1922), pp. 185–6.

[5] Margaret Sharp, 'Contributions to the History of the Earldom and County of Chester, 1237–1399 . . .,' Univ. of Manchester Ph.D. thesis, 1925. This is cited henceforth as 'Sharp, thesis'. I am grateful to Professor J. S. Roskell for first drawing my attention to this magisterial work.

[6] Harris, 'Palatinate', pp. 9–35.

[7] *Ibid.*, pp. 12–13.

[8] *C.P.R.*, 1281–2, p. 308; *Ch. Pipe Rolls*, pp. 180, 183. In 1298 he took an inquisition, as lieutenant, at Middlewich. (S.C.6 1268/4.)

[9] See pp. 65–6.

[10] Harris, 'Palatinate', p. 12.

[11] See above, pp. 15–35.

[12] Ches. 29/22 m. 15d.

[13] B.P.R., III, p. 9.

[14] Ibid., p. 15.

[15] Harris, 'Palatinate', pp. 26–9 (sheriff) and 25–6 (escheator).

[16] Sharp, thesis, pp. 171–207.

[17] For this onerous and unpopular job the wages were, at first, surprisingly low. They had been 12d. a day in 1312–13 (Harris, 'Palatinate', p. 25) but fell to 2d. a day in 1350, when the then escheator, Hugh Hopwas, had to be given an extra ten marks a year not to give up the post. (Chamb. Acc., p. 205.) His successor, Thomas Young, was at first paid only 2d. a day, which was raised to ten marks a year in 1355 and £10 a year in 1357. (B.P.R., III, p. 268.) £10 a year was the annual fee paid to royal escheators up to 1350 (Willard and Morris, The English Government at Work, II, p. 159).

[18] From 1359 to 1361 and 1367 to 1370. Thomas Young, escheator 1352/61, was made sheriff for his last two years (P.R.O., List of Sheriffs, p. 174); John Scolehall, escheator 1365/84, was sheriff 1367/70 (ibid., p. 174). For the list of escheators see Sharp, thesis, appendix, p. 25.

[19] Ch. Pipe Rolls, p. 117; Chamb. Acc., p. 20; E.372 174 rott. 44, 47.

[20] Chamb. Acc., p. 2.

[21] S.C.8 16/765; Rot. Parl., II, p. 400A.

[22] C.F.R., 1327–37, p. 327; C.C.R., 1330–3, p. 509; D.K.R., 29, p. 25.

[23] C.C.R., 1333–7, p. 183.

[24] Chamb. Acc., pp. 132–8.

[25] S.C.6 784/5 m. 3d. In 1353–4 the puture which had customarily been exacted by serjeants of the peace in the county, both those of the earl and of his barons, was abolished by the justiciar. (S.C.6 783/1 m. 1d.) It looks as if the Black Prince's officials intended the emasculation if not the complete abolition of this office. With his take-over of the St. Pierre estates in 1353 the prince had acquired a portion of the master-serjeanty of Cheshire.

[26] Ches. 29/18 m. 5.

[27] Several of these early escheators' accounts survive: S.C.6 1241/7 (1283–9), 1241/8 (1283–9), 1241/9 (1326), 1241/10 (1328), 1241/11 (c. 1328–c. 1329), 1241/12 (1333/8), 1241/13 (1342–3), 1241/14 (1345–6).

[28] S.C.6 1241/12.

[29] B.P.R., III, pp. 78, 136.

[30] S.C.6 772/3, 4. They were paid their wages by the chamberlain for the time when they were actually working within his bailiwick. Ad hoc appointments to carry out the same functions had been made earlier in the period. (Chamb. Acc., pp. 7, 103; C.C.R., 1330–3, p. 186). All the Black Prince's officials did was to put the 'control' of works on to a systematic and permanent basis.

[31] See below, pp. 136–41.

[32] Again, this work was systematised under the Black Prince. See B.P.R., III, pp. 180, 292.

[33] B.P.R., III, p. 209. See below, pp. 120–22.

[34] For this and subsequent figures see Appendix I.

[35] Formal and semi-formal orders together with grants and appointments by the royal government in Cheshire are to be found on the chancery rolls (Close, Fine, Patent, Welsh, Charter). Appointments of county officials are shared between the Patent and Fine Rolls, while the latter contain most of the orders relating to the escheator's department; of the class S.C.1, those items relating to Welsh history (and thus many to Cheshire's also) are included in C.A.C.W.

[36] Ch. Pipe Rolls.

[37] C.P.R., 1272–81, pp. 6, 116.

[38] F. M. Powicke, King Henry III and the Lord Edward, II, pp. 722–3.

[39] C.F.R., 1272–1307, p. 155; C.P.R., 1272–81, pp. 464–5.

FINANCE AND ADMINISTRATION

[40] F. M. Powicke, *The Thirteenth Century* (1962), pp. 419–30.

[41] *C.C.R.*, 1279–88, p. 216.

[42] Powicke, *Thirteenth Century*, pp. 424–5; *C.Ch.R.*, II, p. 262.

[43] Edwards, in *C.A.C.W.*, gives a number of letters (pp. 161, 163–4, 201–5) showing that Perton was involved in collecting revenue, providing military equipment, purveying stores for the army and recruiting craftsmen and labourers in both Cheshire and Englefield. In September 1282 he and John Maidstone were called 'receivers at Chester' (S.C.1 22/19), and Perton's connection with the royal wardrobe is shown in several letters written to him by William Louth, its keeper (e.g. S.C.1 30/148, 30/151). Later on Perton was described as having been 'receiver of Cheshire' (*C.C.R.*, 1307–13, p. 383). He also acted as one of the receivers of the fifteenth of 1283 (J. F. Willard, 'An Exchequer Reform under Edward I' in L. J. Paetow (ed.), *The Crusades and other Historical Essays presented to Dana C. Munro* . . . (1928), pp. 225–44.

[44] T. F. Tout, 'Flintshire: its History and its Records', *Collected Papers*, III, pp. 29–32.

[45] *Ch. Pipe Rolls*, pp. 159–74. Note the mistake in the commentary on this account (see below, p. 152). Virtually all Grey's £2,303 18s. 3½d. in this account, which covered the years 1291–8, was spent on matters connected with military policy. See also S.C.6 1268/3; *C.A.C.W.*, p. 80.

[46] S.C.6 1268/3. Grey maintained that judicial revenue had been lost in Cheshire because of the virtual suspension of the law courts which was customary in the county in wartime. This matter had also arisen in 1277, when Badlesmere felt that such a custom was unjustifiable (S.C.1 22/94).

[47] *C.P.R.*, 1281–92, p. 391. Likewise, Badlesmere and Perton were auditors of the accounts of the collectors of the fifteenth in Cheshire in 1281 (*C.P.R.*, 1272–81, p. 434); Grey and the abbot of Vale Royal audited the farmer of the Dee mills' account in 1284 (*C.P.R.*, 1281–92, p. 137).

[48] Of course, if the records of the privy seal had survived they might have told a different story.

[49] H. Johnstone, *Edward of Carnarvon* (1946), pp. 73–4.

[50] H. Johnstone (ed.), *Letters of Edward, Prince of Wales, 1304–5*, Roxburghe Club (1931), p. 13.

[51] *Ch. Pipe Rolls*, pp. 182–5. Mascy's appointment as justiciar-farmer, on a five year lease, although dated 22 October 1299 (that is, three weeks later than his first appointment), was notified to the people of Cheshire only on 7 June 1300. It is likely that the change from approver to farmer was made not long before this date, and on 1 April 1300 John Havering had been appointed justiciar of Wales in preparation for Edward of Caernarfon's take-over. (M. Rhys, *Ministers Accounts for West Wales, 1277–1306*, I, (1936), p. 67.)

[52] What follows is largely based on J. R. Maddicott, *Thomas of Lancaster* (1970) and 'Thomas of Lancaster and Sir Robert Holland: a study in noble patronage', *E.H.R.*, LXXXVI (1971), pp. 449–72. See also J. R. S. Phillips, *Aymer de Valence, Earl of Pembroke, 1307–24* (1972).

[53] Maddicott, *Thomas*, pp. 104–10.

[54] Sharp, thesis, appendix, p. 5; Phillips, *Aymer*, p. 50. The excuse for Holland's dismissal was probably the grant of the earldom to the king's son.

[55] Maddicott, *Thomas*, pp. 269–74.

[56] *C.C.R.*, 1327–30, p. 192; C.260 37/33.

[57] T.F. Tout, *The Place of the Reign of Edward II in English History* (1936), p. 335; Maddicott, *Thomas*, pp. 73, 100; J. C. Davies, *The Baronial Opposition to Edward II* (1918), pp. 366–7.

[58] *C.F.R.*, 1307–19, p. 122; *C.P.R.*, 1307–13, p. 427; *C.C.R.*, 1307–13, p. 396.

[59] Maddicott, *Thomas*, pp. 193, 271, 305. Both Audleys deserted to Thomas of Lancaster and the elder was imprisoned after Boroughbridge, dying in 1325 (C.

Moor, *The Knights of Edward I* (1930), p. 27). He was a cousin of the Audleys of Newhall, who were considerable landowners in south Cheshire.

[60] Sharp, thesis, appendix, p. 6; Conway Davies, *Baronial Opposition*, pp. 209–10; Tout, *Place of Edward II*, p. 337.

[61] *C.C.W.*, p. 485.

[62] *C.P.R.*, 1317–21, p. 21.

[63] Tout, *Place of Edward II*, p. 114.

[64] *C.P.R.*, 1321–4, pp. 72, 174.

[65] Ingham was made riding forester of Mara, at the queen's request, in 1320 (*Chamb. Acc.*, p. 91); McKisack, *The Fourteenth Century*, p. 102.

[66] Ingham was arrested and his lands were seized (*C.F.R.*, 1327–37, p. 194). He was replaced as justiciar by Sir William Clinton, who had assisted the king in his *coup d'état* (*C.F.R.*, 1327–37, p. 193). Clinton had been granted the honour of Halton for services to Queen Isabella, after the overthrow of the Despensers in 1326 (E.372 174 rot. 44).

[67] Maddicott, *Thomas*, p. 161.

[68] G. H. Tupling, *South Lancashire in the Reign of Edward II*, Chet. Soc., Third Series, I (1949), pp. v–lxi.

[69] Ches. 29/20 m. 28, 28d.

[70] Ches. 29/22 m. 9.

[71] Ches. 29/23 m. 5d. They were informed that 'the king has made prohibition many times in full county court against those who presume to make secret and unlawful conventicles to the terror of the people of the county, the injury of our dignity and the sword of Chester. Moreover ... very many malefactors and disturbers of our peace frequently make such unlawful conventicles and practise daily homicides, depredations, arson and other very great crimes and are at large in your bailiwick.'

[72] *C.C.R.*, 1318–23, p. 12.

[73] *C.P.R.*, 1317–21, p. 200; *C.C.R.*, 1318–23, p. 23.

[74] *C.P.R.*, 1338–40, p. 31.

[75] John Paynel's arrears as chamberlain were not as high as was stated in the 1337 report (see above, note 74); *C.P.R.*, 1334–8, p. 467.

[76] S.C.6 1268/3. See J. H. Le Patourel, *The Medieval Administration of the Channel Islands, 1199–1399* (1937), p. 126; *Tout*, VI, p. 46.

[77] S.C.12 22/96. This phrase, in itself, suggests that Ferrers was largely an absentee justiciar.

[78] William Beauchamp and Hugh Berwick were ordered to seize Cheshire and Flintshire, and Berwick subsequently held a commission of oyer and terminer, nominally of the duke of Cornwall (i.e. the Black Prince), to try unspecified criminal offences in Cheshire (*C.F.R.*, 1337–47, p. 214; *Chamb. Acc.*, pp. 114–15; *cf.* opinion of M. Sharp in *Tout*, III, p. 122).

[79] S.C.6 1268/3.

[80] E.101 390/3.

[81] *B.P.R.*, I, p. 47. See below, p. 65.

[82] See H. Johnstone, *Edward of Carnarvon, 1284–1307* (1946), 'The Wardrobe and Household of the Sons of Edward I', *B.I.H.R.*, II (1925), pp. 37–45, and (ed.), *Letters of Edward, Prince of Wales, 1304–5*, Roxburghe Club (1931); also *Tout*, II, pp. 165–87, on which the following is based.

[83] Johnstone, *Letters*, pp. xviii–xxv.

[84] *Chamb. Acc.*, p. 13; Johnstone, *Letters*, pp. 36–7.

[85] *Ibid.*, p. 61; *Chamb. Acc.*, pp. 13–14. See also W. H. Waters, *The Edwardian Settlement of North Wales* (1935), pp. 31–44.

[86] *Tout*, II, p. 174. It is clear that Prince's Edward's military and political responsibilities later led to increasingly heavy expenditure, which resulted in his receiving subventions from the royal exchequer (J. F. Willard, 'Ordinances for the Guidance of a Deputy Treasurer, 22 October 1305', *E.H.R.*, XLVIII (1933),

pp. 84–9). These were not enough to prevent the prince's wardrobe being over £4,000 in deficit by 1307 (Michael Prestwich, 'Exchequer and Wardrobe in the later Years of Edward I', *B.I.H.R.*, XLVI (1973), p. 4).

[87] M. H. Mills, 'Exchequer Agenda and Estimate of Revenue, Easter Term, 1284', *E.H.R.*, XL (1925), pp. 229–34.

[88] *Tout*, II, pp. 174–8; *C.P.R.*, 1301–7, p. 238.

[89] *Tout*, VI, p. 31. He was promoted to cofferer of the king's wardrobe in 1314.

[90] S.C.6 801/12 m. 2.

[91] *Chamb. Acc.*, p. 96. The audit took seven weeks. It is very unexpected to find the escheator as co-auditor, and he was probably acting in his capacity as surveyor of works in the earldom and in that sense 'controller' of the chamberlain.

[92] *Ibid.*, p. 94.

[93] N. Denholm-Young, 'Richard de Bury (1287–1345)', *T.R.H.S.*, Fourth Series, XX (1937), pp. 135–68.

[94] See Appendix I.

[95] See M. Sharp's article on 'The Central Administrative System of Edward, the Black Prince' in *Tout*, V, pp. 289–400, and 'The Administrative Chancery of the Black Prince before 1362', in *Essays in Medieval History presented to T. F. Tout*, ed. A. G. Little and F. M. Powicke (1925), pp. 321–3.

[96] *Tout*, V, pp. 434, 438.

[97] *B.P.R.*, I, p. 61.

[98] Gildesburgh himself had been described as 'governor of the prince's lands' and 'keeper of the prince's lands' in 1349 (*Tout*, V, pp. 390–1, 440).

[99] *Tout*, V, pp. 438–9.

[100] *B.P.R.*, II, p. 41.

[101] G. L. Harriss, *King, Parliament and Public Finance in Medieval England to 1369* (1975), pp. 376–83; E. B. Fryde, 'Parliament and the French War, 1336–40', in *Essays in Medieval History presented to Bertie Wilkinson*, ed. T. A. Sandquist and M. R. Powicke (1969), pp. 258–9.

[102] *B.P.R.*, III, pp. 125, 128.

[103] *Tout*, VI, p. 60.

[104] For Delves's career see Booth, thesis, pp. 313–14.

[105] Sharp, thesis, appendix, pp. 5–6, 12–13.

[106] For the early career of the elder Burnham see A. B. Emden, *A Biographical Register of the University of Cambridge to 1500* (1963), p. 109.

[107] *B.P.R.*, III, p. 11.

[108] S.C.6 784/2 m. 5.

[109] He was self-effacing in two ways: first, nothing really bad is known of him, which is quite and achievement for a medieval estate administrator. Secondly, in two letters from him to the prince's council in 1345 he expresses himself in terms which were unusually cringing and subservient even for that benighted age. (S.C.1 54/83; S.C.1 54/93.)

[110] *Tout*, III, p. 267; *Tout*, V, p. 439. When the king was compelled to dismiss his clerical ministers and replace them with laymen in the parliament of 1371, Lacy lost both posts.

[111] *The Royal Demesne in English History* (1971), p. 54.

[112] Life grants began to creep in again after 1356, but they never became as widespread as before 1349.

[113] 'Thomas of Lancaster and Sir Robert Holland: a study in noble patronage', *E.H.R.*, LXXXVI (1971), pp. 465–6. Likewise Sir Guncelin Badlesmere, when accounting for the issues of his office between 1274 and 1277, was charged to collect between £695 and £800 a year, from which he was allowed to deduct ancient alms, fees and running expenses. See Appendix I.

[114] *C.F.R.*, 1307–19, p. 5.

[115] *Ch. Pipe Rolls*, pp. 180, 183.

[116] *Chamb. Acc.*, pp. 1–14.

117 I.e. Macclesfield and Overton (£220), Northwich (£76) and Middlewich (£92).

118 Value in 1302–3 account (*Chamb. Acc.*, p. 22).

119 *Cheshire under the three Edwards* (1967) pp. 8–9.

120 *Chamb. Acc.*, pp. 15–27 (checked with S.C.6 771/2).

121 *Chamb. Acc.*, pp. 258–76 (checked with S.C.6 771/23).

122 *Chamb. Acc.*, pp. 206–19. Hewitt's comparison also failed to allow for the fact that arrears were treated differently in the accounting systems employed in the two periods. For this see above, pp. 20–24.

123 *C.P.R.*, 1272–81, p. 190.

124 See above, p. 53 and E. 159/81 m. 15.

125 S.C.1 37/81. At the beginning of Edward III's reign the chamberlain, sheriff and escheator were all appointed by letters patent of the royal chancery (*C.F.R.*, 1327–37, pp. 85–6, 88–9, 193, 207, 253).

126 *Chamb. Acc.*, pp. 24, 41; *Ch. Pipe Rolls*, p. 214.

127 *Chamb. Acc.*, p. 76; Ches. 29/17 m. 21d.

128 By 1364 the registering of the prince's letters had fallen a couple of years in arrears (*B.P.R.*, IV, p. 526).

129 This classification is modelled on that devised for similar warrants which appear on the royal chancery rolls by H. Maxwell-Lyte in *Historical Notes on the Use of the Great Seal in England* (1926) pp. 141–222. See also B. Wilkinson, 'The Authorisation of Chancery Writs under Edward III', *Bulletin of the John Rylands Library*, 8 (1924), pp. 107–39.

130 E.36 279 f. 6ov (*B.P.R.*, III, p. 112).

131 'The Authorization of Letters under the Great Seal', *B.I.H.R.*, XXXVII (1964), pp. 125–56. The notes discussed by Brown are briefer and apparently more straightforward than those in the *Black Prince's Register*. He assumes that *per ipsum regem* means that the king himself made the decision, *per consilium* that the council (without the king) made it and that *per regem et consilium* refers to co-operation between the two.

132 This contrasts with Brown's findings in relation to Henry IV's administration, where ministerial warrants tended to be of small importance.

133 He had also fought at Crécy (*Tout*, V, p. 387). At Poitiers, Wingfield took prisoner the Sire d'Aubigny, whose ransom he sold to the king for 2,500 marks (M. H. Keen, *England in the Later Middle Ages* (1972) p. 146). See also Duchy of Cornwall Office, Henxteworth's Jornale, 1355–6, for his involvement in the campaign. He was also abroad, for a shorter time, between November 1359 and March 1360.

134 Stafford acted as 'steward and surveyor of all the prince's lands in Wales, Cheshire, Cornwall and elsewhere in England' in 1347 (*B.P.R.*, I, p. 48). His commission states that he is to 'loyally make survey of the said lands, of the prince's under-stewards and other ministers, and report to the prince or his council on the state of his lands and the bearing of his ministers, to the end that any defaults may be redressed by the said council'. Stafford appears not to have acted as steward after November 1347, but he remained an active and prominent member of the council until the prince's death.

135 S.C.6 801/14 m. 1; S.C.6 784/4 m. 1; *B.P.R.*, III, p. 112.

136 *Ibid.*, p. 129.

137 *Ibid.*, p. 368. This order is warranted 'by advice and ordinance of Sir J(ohn) W(ingfield)'. The same phrase is employed in the warrant for the appointment of Thomas Young as escheator four days later (*ibid.*, p. 369).

138 *Ibid.*, p. 464.

139 *B.P.R.*, IV, pp. 500–1. Delves received 6s. 8d. a day, while Wingfield had taken 10s. 0d. (*ibid.*, p. 163). For a memorandum of the prince's council to Delves, as governor, see P. J. Morgan, 'Cheshire and the Defence of the Principality of Aquitaine', *T.H.S.L.C.*, 128 (1979), p. 140.

140 *B.P.R.*, III, p. 199; *C.P.R.*, 1361–4, p. 461; G. O. Sayles (ed.), *Select Cases in the Court of King's Bench*, Selden Soc., 82 (1965), p. lxxi.

141 Steward, 1378/81; treasurer, 1381/6. He also served as one of the keepers of the great seal in 1382. (*Tout*, VI, pp. 16, 23, 44.)

142 *B.P.R.*, III, p. 218. The citizens of Chester's request for a new charter in 1354 could not be answered immediately because the legal members of the council were not in London (*ibid.*, p. 152).

143 See above, pp. 71–3. The survival of the *Record of Caernarvon* shows that, at least as far as north Wales was concerned, the earlier Prince Edward's council also heard petitions. See Waters, *Edwardian Settlement*, p. 44.

144 *B.P.R.*, III, p. 266.

145 *Ibid.*, p. 6.

146 *B.P.R.*, III, pp. 84–5; *B.P.R.*, II, p. 41. Lesser administrative matters could, of course, be dealt with at a great council simply because the prince's administrative councillors were then present.

147 S.C.6 771/16 m. 2.

148 P. H. W. Booth, 'Taxation and Public Order: Cheshire in 1353', *Northern History*, XII (1976), p. 22.

149 S.C.8 333/E.1042.

150 *B.P.R.*, III, p. 249. The prince's administration did, it is true, sometimes have to act as a brake on the prince's exercise of patronage by, for example, pointing out the financial consequences of particular gifts. When the prince was abroad on the Crécy–Calais campaign he decided to commit the keeping of the lordship of Bromfield and Yale, which had come into his hands by the death of the earl of Surrey, to the custody of five named people. Letters were sent to Peter Gildesburgh to that effect, but Gildesburgh, instead of executing them, consulted the 'English council' that was responsible for the government of the estates in the prince's absence. Together they decided that the commission was financially damaging to his interests and wrote back saying that they were not willing to put the commission into effect unless changes were made. (July 1347: *B.P.R.*, I, pp. 96–7.) Similarly, in 1357 letters were sent to the lieutenant and chamberlain 'by command of Sir John Wingfield' saying that the prince had granted pasture rights in Cheshire to 'certain persons' who were with him in Gascony but because the grants had turned out to be more expensive than the prince had realised they would have to be cancelled and the recipients compensated in cash. (*B.P.R.*, III, pp. 244–5.)

151 See below, pp. 138–41.

152 *B.P.R.*, III, p. 100.

153 *Ibid.*, pp. 190, 193. In 1315 a wardship in Frodsham manor worth only £5 had been sold by Hugh Leominster, keeper of the earl's wardrobe. (S.C.6 801/12 m.2.)

154 *B.P.R.*, III, p. 368.

155 A. L. Brown's discussion of the role in government of the king's council in what might be termed 'normal times' between the late fourteenth century and the early Tudor period suggests a number of parallels with the Black Prince's central administration ('The King's Councillors in Fifteenth-century England', *T.R.H.S.*, Fifth Series, 19 (1969), pp. 95–118). See also R. Virgoe, 'The Composition of the King's Council, 1437–61', *B.I.H.R.*, XLIII (1970), pp. 134–60, and J. L. Kirby, 'Councils and Councillors of Henry IV, 1399–1413', *T.R.H.S.*, Fifth Series, 14 (1964), pp. 35–65. Allowing for differences of scale, it can probably be asserted that, from the point of view of government and administration, the Black Prince's rule of his English and Welsh estates provided him with experience that would have been directly relevant to his task as king of England.

CHAPTER IV

PROFIT AND LOSS:
THE LORDSHIP OF MACCLESFIELD

I THE MANOR AND THE LIBERTY

In the thirteenth and fourteenth centuries the successive lords of Cheshire received only a small proportion of their revenue in the county from the profits of agriculture. Indeed, the possibility of managing the county demesnes directly hardly ever seems to have been seriously considered, except for the twelve years or so after the Black Death. Macclesfield manor, which is by far the best documented of the earldom's estates, stands as the only exception to this rule, and cattle farming on a reasonably large scale was carried on here for over twenty years in the second half of the fourteenth century. It is worth looking at the history of the manor in some detail to try and find out why this should have been so, how successfully the enterprise was managed, and how its management fitted in with the financial administration of the lordship as a whole.

Macclesfield had belonged to the earls of Chester from at least the time of Domesday Book.[1] However, for the greater part of the period between 1270 and 1347 the manor had been all but severed from the county to be given in dower to two queens of England: first to Eleanor, Edward I's consort, who held it from 1270 to 1290, and then to Isabella, wife of Edward II, who possessed the manor, with significant breaks, between 1309 and 1347.[2] This long separation meant that by the mid-fourteenth century official opinion was in some doubt as to whether Macclesfield manor, and its annexed hundred, had ever been part of Cheshire at all.[3] The two royal ladies had been granted such extensive privileges during their tenure of the manor that the officials of Cheshire had been all but excluded from any possibility of interfering in what had become known as 'the liberty of Macclesfield hundred'.[4] Thus Macclesfield's governmental institutions became self contained: for example, the hundred had its own master-serjeant of the peace, and under-serjeants, who were not subject to the authority of the master-serjeant of Cheshire.[5]

There is no doubt that the existence of such a privileged area on its eastern extremity caused problems for the county's government, since there are very strong hints that the manor experienced a high level of misgovernment under the two queens. For example, Edward III was petitioned by 'the poor men, his lieges, of the forest of Macclesfield' in 1335 to the effect that the queen mother's bailiff, Thomas Hampton, had 'destroyed and wasted' the lordship by illegally hunting deer, destroying the woods, by making sure that the justiciar's eyre could not investigate the damage done to the park and in the forest, and so on.[6] At various times inquiries were undertaken into allegations of oppression, extortion and negligence perpetrated by the officials there, as well as into damage done by the inhabitants and others.[7] It is not wholly surprising, then, that the Black Prince persuaded his grandmother in 1347 to release Macclesfield to him in exchange for two manors (in Wiltshire and Dorset) and some other revenue besides.[8] The decayed and demoralised state of the lordship is well illustrated by the extensive repairs which had to be carried out on the manorial buildings[9] and by the special court of justice which the prince set up to deal with all 'damages, trespasses, wastes and destructions . . . and . . . all felonies, misprisions, extortions and other grievances' committed over the previous few decades.[10]

It is more or less from this time onwards that the virtually complete series of Macclesfield official records survives, with a full succession of both manorial estate accounts *and* court rolls between 1349 and 1376, something which occurs for no other Cheshire lordship at that time, and which enables an unusually detailed investigation of the manor's administration to be undertaken.[11] Moreover, Macclesfield is again unusual in that nineteen manorial accounts survive from the two centuries before the Black Death. They relate to three main periods: 1182–5,[12] 1237/48[13] and 1296–9,[14] and, in addition, there are a few scattered examples between 1299 and 1347.[15] Thus an overall view of the manor's financial history for the best part of two centuries (1182/1376) can be obtained, by setting out the summary figures extracted from the accounts (see Appendix II).[16]

Medieval estate managers were usually great believers in the virtues of leaving well alone as far as administrative structures were concerned, and were only rarely willing to make radical changes. Consequently, it is not surprising that the prince's administration of Macclesfield after 1347 was continuous, in an institutional sense, with the manor's previous history. It had been usual, whether it were in the hands of king, queen or earl, for the manor to be committed to the management of an individual, either as 'farmer' or as 'keeper'. In the former case, of course, the manager would pay the lord a fixed rent instead of accounting for individual items of revenue. At some periods it had been normal to give the keeper/farmer of Macclesfield additional responsibility for the manor of Overton-on-Dee and its dependent territory, the southernmost part of what became known as Flintshire.[17] Such custodians were powerful men locally, and two of them, Thomas and Jordan Macclesfield, formed something of a local dynasty in the late thirteenth and early fourteenth centuries.[18] Little is known about the elder man, but Jordan, who was apparently a younger son of his, studied at Oxford, and after his ordination acquired the benefice of Mottram-in-Long-dendale in Macclesfield hundred in 1300. While he was away gaining his master's degree the then bailiff of Macclesfield and Overton attempted to deprive his older brother, Roger, of some family lands in Worthenbury (in Overton lordship). Edward II ordered their restoration in 1316.[19] After his local governmental service to both Queen Isabella and Edward II and their son as keeper of Macclesfield and farmer in the 1320s and 1330s, Master Jordan apparently survived the Black Death and was listed in the 1352 rental as one of the manor's most substantial tenants. He held land in the borough as well as in the demesne townships of Hurdsfield, Pott Shrigley and Upton.[20] There is no doubt that the position of power exercised by such figures served to reinforce the sense of separateness from the rest of Cheshire which the community there already possessed to a considerable degree.

So the prince's council was faced, in 1347, with the problem of re-integrating this semi-independent lordship into the county administrative structure without dismantling any of its administrative or judicial 'liberties' (however recently acquired). It took almost four years, and the intervention of the pestilence, to produce a satisfactory solution. Continuity of personnel was provided by drafting into the prince's service one of Queen Isabella's local officials, Robert Legh of Adlington, who was given the keeping of the manor at the prince's reception of seisin and who, although he did not retain this position for very long, continued to play an important role in local (and county) administration for several decades.[21] He was replaced in December 1347 by a Welsh official who was clearly appointed on a temporary basis while the council made up its mind what to do.[22] The opportunity came in that same winter of 1347/8, when a high-powered group of the prince's central officials, including his chief finance officer, Peter Gildesburgh, and his principal councillor, Sir Richard Stafford, visited Cheshire. On 9 December a general inquiry was ordered into the whole of county government, to be held in nine days' time, and the councillors were 'to attend to other great matters that concern the prince and the state of his lands and lordships there and at Macclesfield'. Just over a week after that, the judicial sessions of inquiry into misgovernment and disorder in the manor in Queen Isabella's time, already mentioned, were announced.[23]

In the event, the decision the council arrived at was that Macclesfield should be only partially re-integrated into the county structure. This was achieved by appointing Sir Thomas Ferrers, justiciar of Chester, to the unusual post of steward *and* bailiff of the manor and hundred, with effect from 16 March 1348. This plan meant that Ferrers was to be locally responsible for the government of the lordship (as the former keepers/farmers had been), and that he would account for its revenue direct to the prince's central exchequer at Westminster, thus by-passing the county's own financial bureau, which was headed by the chamberlain.[24] Whether this was meant to be a permanent solution is difficult to say, because it was overtaken in just over a year by the Black Death and all the administrative dislocation that ensued. It did have an inherent weakness in that the link between Macclesfield and the county was a purely personal one, through Thomas Ferrers, who happened to hold two separate offices. At any event, whatever the reason, the 'solution' of 1347/8 turned out to be short-lived.

II THE BLACK DEATH

Ferrers's second surviving account, for 1348–9, is of peculiar interest because it is one of only two Cheshire accounts covering the period of the arrival of the Black Death in the county. The pestilence had taken a firm hold by the early summer of 1349, the last sessions of the manorial courts having taken place on 21 June, after which they ceased because of the epidemic.[25] Some idea of the horrific mortality can be grasped by the fact that forty-six holdings of tenants of the manor were *in decasu* in the 1348–9 account (that is, no rent could be levied from them), of which only six had been so classified in the March–Michaelmas account of 1348.[26] Moreover, the stock side of the 1348–9 account lists sixty-six heriots due from dead tenants, only eighteen of whom bear the same surnames as the tenants of the lands *in decasu*.[27] Thus at least eighty-eight tenants of Macclesfield manor died in that one year. An actual death rate is difficult to calculate, first because no detailed manorial extent or rental for the manor survives from before 1349. Moreover, the putting of a holding *in decasu* occurred only when no one was willing, after the tenant's death, to take it up. Further, it is not clear what proportion of the tenants here were liable to pay heriot; it may only have been a minority.[28] Consequently, the tenant death toll of eighty-eight could be an underestimate. What does survive is the new, detailed rental of the manor which was made in 1351 or 1352.[29] This document lists 172 tenancies (excluding the borough of Macclesfield itself). If it is permissible to hazard an opinion here, had a similar number of tenancies existed at the beginning of 1348-9, which is not unlikely, a tenant death rate of some 50 per cent is not out of the question. Unfortunately, as has been seen, Cheshire lacks nearly all the fourteenth century demographic data which are available for other parts of England (unsatisfactory as those may be), and such guesses are all that can be made.

It is clear that, despite the horrors of such a pestilence, the Black Prince's administration adopted a tough-minded policy with regard to revenue collection. For example, officials were ordered to levy the value of the rent from thirty-nine of the tenancies *in decasu* by the expedient of seizing corn and other goods which were found on the holdings.[30] Moreover, it was alleged a few years later that Adam Mottram, the hereditary gaoler and rent collector of the manor, had taken the opportunity of some illegal 'private enterprise' at that time. Of one accusation he was found guilty: of stealing a colt, the heriot of Christiana Pigott. Of the second he was acquitted (of stealing 100 of the prince's oxen), and also of the third, which stated that

... in the time of the pestilence and afterwards he destroyed the poor tenants of the lord earl, as well as children under age, and their lands and tenements to the grave damage of the lord earl and the diminution of his rent.

It went on to accuse Mottram of having done this by keeping the goods impounded for non-payment of rent after the amount of the rent had been realised from them.[31] The juxtaposition of the supposed destruction of the tenants with the effect on the rent payable to the prince is an interesting comment on the priorities of the prince's administration at this time (and later), markedly financial in nature as they were.

The administrative dislocation caused by the Black Death was, in the short term, severe. The 1348-9 Macclesfield account was not audited until 1351, a year late, for example.[32] However, general recovery took place remarkably quickly. As has been seen, a new rental of Macclesfield had been made by 1352, probably the first completely new one for over forty years. By 1355 all but six of the 1348-9 holdings *in decasu* had been let to new tenants. This had not been achieved without a great deal of effort, and indeed a readiness to compromise immediate revenues in return for long-term interests, on the part of the administration. In May 1354 the prince's council ordered the Cheshire officials to re-let holdings in the manor without demanding rent arrears, or the customary relief of two years' rent, if that was the only way it could be done.[33] It is possible, through the accounts and court rolls, to trace the steps by which the holdings were let. This inducement was used on at least one occasion: in the 1354/5 halmote roll it is recorded that two tenants were admitted, in Stanley and Sutton, each of whom had their reliefs pardoned 'because the land is poor and has been in the lord's hands for a long time'.[34] Such a rapid administrative recovery has parallels elsewhere in England.[35] It suggests the existence of a considerable surplus in the pre-1349 population, which accounts for the number of survivors who were able to take on the empty holdings. It must be noted, however, that unlet holdings were not exactly unknown in the first half of the fourteenth century. In Jordan Macclesfield's manorial account for 1329–30 twenty-six had been in decasu (including six burgages)—in all nearly 19 per cent of the total charged rents.[36] Without further evidence it is impossible to say whether this situation was caused by some economic factor, such as the progressive soil exhaustion posited for the early fourteenth century by M. M. Postan.[37] It is as likely to have been due to the political and administrative upheavals of the time, remembering that Edward III seized power from his mother, Queen Isabella, in 1330 and as a result took over all her landed possessions, including Macclesfield, as well.[38]

The Black Death undoubtedly helped to cause the second major change in the administration of Macclesfield since 1347. By March 1351 Thomas Ferrers had accumulated over £200 arrears on his steward's account, well over the normal annual revenue.[39] This was obviously unacceptable and could only in part be excused on account of the pestilence and the prior problem of reducing the manor to a state of good governance. Sir Thomas was caught in the web of personal responsibility which threatened all medieval financial administrators. Those arrears, as well as other debts to the prince, were still not paid off when he died in 1353, and as a result all his goods in England were seized.[40] It was to be seventeen years before his estate was finally acquitted of the burden.[41] The new arrangements for Macclesfield were, once again, part of a general overhaul of the county's finances, this time recorded in the Black Prince's Register in meticulous detail. Ferrers's three-year-old office of 'steward and bailiff' was abolished. Those officials of the manor, hundred and borough, who had previously collected the revenue of Macclesfield in Ferrers's name, were to render account separately to the prince's auditors. In addition, they were to make their liveries of money to the chamberlain at Chester castle and be under his, and the justiciar's, joint financial control, as was the case with all the other Cheshire demesnes.[42] Robert Legh retained the responsibility for holding the manorial courts, but in this capacity he had little financial or administrative responsibility.[43] The new dispensation had the merit of being economical: Ferrers had received a fee of £20 a year as steward, whereas the chamberlain was given only £6 13s. 4d. annually for the responsibilities added in 1351 in connection with 'receiving the issues of Macclesfield'.[44] Also, it subjected the manor to the chamberlain's financial control at the local level and spread the ultimate acounting responsibility between three bailiwicks (later five), a lesson which was undoubtedly learned from Ferrers's accumulation of debt. The original three accounting units of 1351 were:

1. Hereditary bailiff of the hundred, also called the 'poker'.
2. Hereditary gaoler of Macclesfield and collector of revenue within the manor and forest.
3. The borough: the revenue of which was collected by two elected officials, the reeve (responsible for the burgage rents) and the catchpoll (the rest).

The two later ones were:

4. Keeper of the stock and stud at Macclesfield, who began to account separately from 1353–4.[45]
5. Keeper of the stud and park: separated from the previous baili-wick in 1358–9.[46]

It must be realised that although all these accounts were bound together for convenience, and the liveries which the various accountants made to the chamberlain were grouped together in his account under the heading of 'Macclesfield', they were structurally quite separate. From 1357 until 1374 yet another set of accounts joined the Macclesfield bundle, those for the lordship of Longden-dale, which comprised two manors, Tintwistle and Mottram-in-Longdendale, which, together with their dependent territory, formed the north-eastern 'panhandle' of Cheshire. They were, in fact, an escheat and were separately administered from the rest of Maccles-field, but their accounts were filed in this way because of con-venience.[47]

Before examining the actual administration of the manor it is necessary to say something about its structure. To simplify, Maccles-field consisted of a hundred annexed to a manor. Of the sixty-one townships within the (geographical) hundred, only fifteen constituted the manor proper, and they were situated on the land to the south and east of the borough on the slopes of the Pennines.[48] Over the tenants and lands of the manor the lord had forest jurisdiction: consequently, the manor tended to be called simply 'the forest', thus leading the manor court to be called by the strange name of 'halmote of the forest'. One of the fifteen townships of the manor-forest was specially privileged: the borough of Macclesfield. Of the remaining fourteen, five were in the hands of lords who held them as tenants of the manor, while the other nine were demesne townships whose tenants held immediately of the lord of the manor.[49] The borough, (the remainder of) the manor and (the remainder of) the hundred formed separate, independent areas of jurisdiction and administra-tion. What provided the central co-ordinating mechanism of these circles of jurisdiction was the presidency of the courts of the manor, borough and hundred (held by Robert Legh, using different titles at different times) and the eyre of the justiciar, which was held once a year and exercised jurisdiction over the whole geographical hundred.[50]

As far as revenue collection went, the division of labour was as follows:

1. *Hundred bailiff (poker):* collected the perquisites of the hundred court, rents from those manors held of the lord of Macclesfield by socage (and outside the manor-forest), the fines of those residents of the hundred arising from cases in the county court and the eyre, and a customary render called renegald, apparently due from the lords of all townships in the hundred.
2. *Gaoler: forest collector:* collected the assize rents of the tenants of the demesne townships, the farms of the manorial mills (of Macclesfield, and in Rainow, Whaley and Shrigley), rents of the demesne pastures, perquisites of the halmote, fines of manor residents levied in the county court and the eyre, and various other payments such as for coal mines and forges in the forest.
3. *Borough:* the reeve collected the burgage rents, the catchpoll other rents, market and fair tolls, the perquisites of the portmote and county court/eyre fines relating to borough residents.

Despite the firm and highly centralised approach to the rule of his estates that the Black Prince's council adopted from the late 1340s onwards, Macclesfield's privileges were left intact. There was probably little else it could have done. What now has to be asked is: how successfully did it run the new structure?

III THE CATTLE FARM

It might be thought that the management of a cattle farm would be the best test of the success, or otherwise, of the activities of the prince's ministers. Within the forest there were six areas of demesne pasture: the park of Macclesfield, Handley, Harrop, Midgeley vaccary, the Coombs and Shutlingsloe crofts.[51] Once there had been demesne arable as well, but that had long been rented in plots to the burgesses.[52] 'Four vaccaries' had been mentioned in 1240, and the sale of seventy-nine head of manorial cattle that year shows that it was not unknown for the lord to keep stock there.[53] Between 1240 and 1348 the evidence in the accounts suggests that the demesne pastures were normally either leased or agisted, as was the case in 1348–9.[54] A stud had been in existence in Macclesfield park in 1296–7, comprising seven mares but having only a borrowed stallion.[55] By 1332 the stud had grown to eight mares, together with twenty-one young horses and two stallions.[56] The stud had been dispersed by Michaelmas 1348.[57]

One of the effects of the Black Death was a short-term slump in the demand for land, which resulted in all six pastures returning to the prince's hands.[58] By 1350–1, the next surviving account after the epidemic, Midgley, Handley and Harrop were leased once again, although the grass of the park could find no takers.[59] It looks, therefore, as if the administration's intention was to return to the old method of management, that of leasing the pastures for high rents. However, the Black Prince's visit of 1353 to Cheshire (and Macclesfield) supervened and resulted in a change of policy in this area. It was decided to re-establish the stud in the park and start a cattle farm on the pastures. A new parker, Alexander Crosse of Prestwich, was appointed in January 1354 and he was given charge of all the prince's livestock throughout Cheshire.[60] His first task was to build up a herd at Macclesfield, which he did by removing there nearly all the cattle held on the other demesne manors of Drakelow, Frodsham and Shotwick. Dr. Hewitt mistakenly interpreted this process as demonstrating a 'working connection' between the four manors for the purpose of stock breeding and fattening.[61] For the stud, four in-foal mares were bought, three of them from the abbot of Vale Royal.[62] In theory, the prince's council was in favour of some money being spent to buy cattle, and up to £20 a year was authorised for this purpose in May 1354. However, it was a time of great financial stringency, and this permission conflicted with the council's general ordinance that the revenue of Cheshire and Cornwall had to be reserved for the expenses of the prince's household, and no expenditure was to be undertaken, except for wages and so on, without a specific order from London.[63] In the event, the central administration was reluctant to give permission at a time when the very expensive preparations were being made for the prince's great expedition to Aquitaine. To get round this, it was suggested by the prince's business manager, Sir John Wingfield, at the beginning of 1355 that the Cheshire officials might, in consultation with the auditors, look about for some unexpected 'windfalls' of money which they could use to buy stock.[64] In the end little money was spent in this way, and nearly all of the Macclesfield herd of cattle had either been born there, or had come from the other Cheshire manors, or from Ashford in the Peak.

Between 1354 and 1363 the herd rose to its peak size of over 700 head. Crosse's successor, John Alcock, who had taken over from him in 1355,[65] was largely responsible for this achievement. In September 1358, as part of the tidal wave of patronage which resulted from the Black Prince's victory at Poitiers, the custody of the stud, manor house and park was taken away from Alcock and given to William Chorley 'for good service in Gascony'.[66] From a purely administrative viewpoint this change had little to recommend it, especially since the stud was removed to Denbigh in 1360,[67] leaving the park keeper, who had been appointed for life, with virtually nothing to do at a salary of 3*d*. a day. From 1363 the number of cattle fell steadily. In some years the death rate in the herd was very high, especially among the younger animals, and, moreover, tithe of calves had to be paid to the abbot of Chester in his guise of rector of Prestbury. Consequently the volume of sales had to be controlled carefully if the herd was to be maintained, and at this time large numbers of animals were sold, more than a hundred head in each of six of the financial years between 1363 and 1376, and on average nearly ninety a year. By the end of the period, then, the herd was almost exactly half the size it had been at its peak.

It is possible to calculate from the stock keeper's accounts how much money was spent on this enterprise, and how much revenue the sale of cattle yielded.[68] These figures, it might be thought at first glance, should allow some sort of calculation to be made of 'profitability', and thus of the efficiency of the prince's officials. In fact, despite assertions to the contrary, it is not possible to apply modern notions of profit-and-loss accountancy to medieval accountants, largely because of the lack of stock valuations.[69] Of course medieval officials were just as concerned to measure their performance against agreed standards as their modern counterparts. It is just that the standards they used are irreconcilably different from those of the present day. Medieval auditors, primed with their manuals of husbandry and estate management, were mainly concerned to detect fraud and negligence, their main principle being the notions of reasonable returns of crops and stock which they carried in their heads.[70] In livestock management they were concerned that sale prices, death rates and live birth rates should not fall below acceptable norms. This introduces an added complication in that it cannot be assumed that the prices for livestock sold which are given in the accounts were necessarily always market prices, since it was always open to the auditors, if they felt the price actually realised to have been too low, to charge a higher one in the account. Admittedly, the officials in their turn would not normally have tolerated this sort of action without some kind of protest, and so we should expect a note on the account if such a surcharge were being made.[71]

What we can do is to examine the overall costs and yield of an enterprise such as the Macclesfield cattle farm and see how the two figures compare. First, though, we have to face up to one serious difficulty: good though the Macclesfield series of accounts is, there are three gaps (1355–6, 1357–8 and 1370–1). We have to assume, therefore, that the missing figures would make no substantial difference to the relative proportions of costs to revenue in the whole period. This is a bold assumption, since, in a cattle farm, the costs incurred might frequently relate to revenue realised in two or three, or more, years' time. Until 1372–3 the lactage of the herd was leased, but in this year no one was willing to pay for it, and so the stock keeper was compelled to buy cheese-making equipment so that the milk would not be wasted.[72] Over the twenty financial years £784 8s. od. was realised. Little was spent on running repairs or on investment in new stock. Labour was the most expensive charge of all, the stock keeper himself, the three stockmen, and the two dairymaids being paid in corn liveries as well as in money. This wage bill, with fluctuations, tended to rise over the whole period and reached its highest level in 1375. In addition there were two types of 'hidden cost' which are not expressed in the accounts in monetary terms at all. The first consists of those customary hedge repairing and hay carting services which were owed by the tenants of the manor. Although they are not valued, as described in the accounts they do not appear to have been particularly onerous and so would probably not have added much to the expenses if it had been possible to value them. The other is much more of a difficulty, being the cost of the 418 head of cattle transferred from other places to Macclesfield. They were not noted as purchases in the accounts, and it is impossible, therefore, to attribute prices to them, bearing in mind both annual fluctuations and the different prices attracted by different qualities of animal of the same age.

And so we are left with an apparent surplus of revenue over expenditure of £425, an average of some £21 a year. If the cost of the transferred cattle could be calculated, this would have to be reduced to £15 or £10 a year. What can be done is to compare these last two figures with the amounts that the pastures yielded when they were leased :[73]

1348   £23 13s. 4d.   (March–Michaelmas)
1348–9   £34 10s. 2d.   (Handley, Harrop, Midgley and the park)
1350–1   £20 11s. 2d.   (same)

Neither the Coombs nor Shutlingsloe crofts are mentioned in the above accounts, although they may have been silently included under other headings. The former was an important source of hay, as well as being a hunting area, and so may have yielded no pasture revenue at all. The latter could have been the place where the heriot beasts, paid at the time of the Black Death, were kept. With the formation of the prince's herd from 1353–4 onwards, five of the six pastures were used for maintaining it and the stud. Handley pasture continued to be leased at a rate of £10 a year, and with the disappearance of the stud in 1360 the park was let for a similar sum.[74] Taking the lower figure of yield for the cattle enterprise, and adding the £20 a year of the two leases, it looks as if this stock management venture was just about breaking even in comparison with the obvious alternative use for the pastures—that is, of leasing them all out. At the very best, on the figures that we have, direct management produced a very modest surplus, hardly enough to balance the extra amount of administrative attention that such a system required. With wage costs tending to rise during the period as a whole—reaching over £15 in 1375/6, compared with nearly £8 in 1356–7[75]—it is not surprising that the stock underwent reduction in the 1360s and 1370s. What is surprising, perhaps, is the administration's decision to launch the venture at all once it had become clear that the demand for land was beginning to pick up again by the mid-1350s. After all, most of the Cheshire demesnes were let without too much difficulty by the end of that decade. One explanation is that the herd was regarded not so much as an income-generating enterprise but as a method of saving, and one which had the added attraction that it could be used for provisioning the prince's household and armies (although, in fact, it never was). It was no accident that both cattle and stud were asembled at a time of intensive war preparations, and that this 'savings account' was drawn upon at a time of great financial need, in the 1360s, when the prince was almost wholly concerned with the government of Aquitaine.

IV THE REST OF THE LORDSHIP

The revenue from the remainder of Macclesfield lordship, comprising as it did mainly rents, court perquisites of various types, and leases of mills, entailed a different administrative approach. As far as the rents of tenants went, since they were fixed by custom the task was, first, to re-let vacant holdings as soon as possible (which was done) and then make sure that the rents were duly collected. The new rental of 1351/2 is a sign of the administration's eagerness to do this job well. It was not until the account for 1371–2 that any reduction in the demand for tenant land became apparent. In that year the steward of the manor confiscated eight villein holdings for not being cultivated.[76] This raised the *decasus* to 14.7 per cent of the total rent charge. Some of the confiscated holdings had not yielded rent for up to twelve years, which indicates that a problem of surplus land had begun to surface in the early 1360s. Macclesfield did suffer from the second outbreak of pestilence in 1361, but its effects were only slight in that there was no disruption at all of the routine of administration.[77] Until the 1360s the overall trend of rents remained upwards, with new land being taken into cultivation as late as 1358–9[78]

Other manorial revenues did not fare as well. Some sources of income disappeared almost completely, such as the two iron forges in Macclesfield forest, which had been charged to yield over £17 in 1348–9.[79] By 1350–1 only one was operative, being leased for £6 13s. 4d.,[80] and by 1353–4 there was none at all 'for lack of farmers'.[81] In subsequent years the position seems to have become little short of hopeless.[82] It was a similar story with the forest coal mines.[83] One of the important causes of decline in both these industries was a shortage of skilled workers, and indeed, in the account for 1371–2, it is stated that there were no forges in the forest that year 'pro defectu servientium'.[84] Another demesne monopoly was that of corn milling. The seven manorial mills were charged to yield over £35 in 1329–30, but only £20 in 1353–4. Appendix II(a) shows that a slight recovery then resulted over the next twenty years, to about £24–£25 a year, although Rainow and Shrigley mills did worse than this figure implies.[85] A positive attempt was made to increase the yield of the fixed capital of the water mills by building two new fulling mills. One was constructed on the Macclesfield millpond round about 1356, the other at Yeardsley–Whaley shortly before 1367–8.[86] The investment was a depressing failure: the Yeardsley mill functioned for only one year, after which no one could be found to farm it. That at Macclesfield was out of action for three years (1372–5) because of damage to the millpond, while the farm it attracted before this amounted to only £1 6s. 8d. a year.

If contemporary witness is to be believed, the part of Macclesfield lordship which declined most in the years after the Black Death was the borough itself. In 1359 the mayor and community petitioned the prince, complaining that they were being hindered from taking their customary estovers in the woods, and asked him 'to have regard to their great poverty'.[87] John Wingfield, the prince's business manager, and John Delves, the lieutenant-justiciar, apparently accepted this self-description as accurate, although neither could have been accused of being 'soft' towards the prince's tenants.[88] In fact, it is difficult to find any signs of such decline in the accounts. Macclesfield borough was administered by its elected officials, the reeve and catchpoll, in accordance with its 1261 charter.[89] Although the total amount of annual revenue collected by them was small in comparison with that of the forest bailiwick, it was a remarkably reliable source of income, amounting to a little over £30 a year, which appears to have been collected without any difficulty between 1350 and 1376.[90] The livery profile (Appendix II(b)) demonstrates this convincingly. This is very difficult to reconcile with any plea of extreme impoverishment, which ought to have been reflected in some way in financial administration. It is true that the tolls and stallage of the market and fairs were low in 1356–7 and 1358–9, possibly the result of a temporary recession in the borough's trade in the later 1350s, and which might, therefore, lend some credence to the 1359 petition.[91] The only item of burghal revenue which proved difficult to collect was the rent of the town's common oven, but this was not the result of either economic difficulties or mal-

administration but of a lengthy legal wrangle between the burgesses
and the prince's officials as to how it should be collected.[92]

Over the whole period the borough rents showed a slight tendency
to rise, which suggests that the town's population was not falling.
Indeed, there were attempts in 1357 and 1359 to make the burgesses
pay considerably more for their tenancies. In the earlier year, following a 'tip-off' from one of the informers who assisted the prince's
government in this way, it was decided that the Rowode, which the
townsmen regarded as their own field, was, in fact, assarted forest
land and that, therefore, a relief equal to double the annual rent
should have been paid every time a plot in it had changed hands
over the last couple of centuries or so. Robert Legh was ordered,
as acting steward, to collect all such outstanding reliefs. The shock
among the burgage plots must have been tremendous, since it
meant not only that large sums of money would have to be paid
but also that future alienations of land would attract reliefs and
have to be registered in the court rolls.[93] The second attempt, of
1359, led to the assertion, already mentioned above, of the town's
'impoverishment'. It arose out of 'the false suggestion of Robert
Foxwyst and through the ill-will of certain persons' who, the burgesses complained, had caused them to be indicted for cutting wood
in the forest.[94] Neither of these assaults on the borough's financial
liberties appears to have come to anything, but they are good illus-
trations of the methods that the prince's government was prepared
to use in the intensive exploitation of his rights, some of which were
quite shadowy, in the interests of raising revenue.

Other types of borough revenue fluctuated in size much more. As
has already been suggested, tolls and associated payments were probably firmly anchored to the fortunes of trade and industry. Judicial
perquisites were, then, the only source amenable to being 'milked'
by the administration. In 1362–3 and 1363–4, when the town's total
charged revenue amounted to more than £40, this was partly due
to the increased yield of tolls and partly to higher judicial revenue,
especially from the annual eyre. This emphasises how misleading it
can be to look at totals and try to find simple explanations for why
they fluctuate. It is possible that the high yields in the two years
referred to could have been the result of two totally unconnected
causes, with the tolls being the result of increased trade, whereas the
fines in the eyre could have been fixed at higher levels because of
an administrative campaign to help set up the Black Prince as ruler
of Aquitaine.

Turning to the other two bailiwicks, that of the hundred bailiff
was dominated by judicial revenue and consequently subject to the
revenue-raising pressures already mentioned. Thus when such revenue
was particularly high the poker had the greatest responsibility for
collecting it. For example, in 1374–5 the total charged judicial

receipts for the whole lordship was over £115.[95] Of that, more than
£90 appears in the poker's account, distributed as follows:

1. Perquisites of the hundred courts (and associated revenues)
   £8 11s. 10d.
2. Issues of the justiciar's eyre at Macclesfield   £30 12s. 8d.
3. Fines and amercements (of Macclesfield hundred residents) in
   the Chester county court   £51 14s. 11d.[96]

Of these sums no less than £67 11s. 9d. was respited as being not
immediately leviable. The park keeper needs no more discussion
here, as his was a bailiwick which was created wholly for the purpose of patronage, and it had little or no financial importance.

It is necessary to conclude by mentioning two new sources of
revenue (in addition to the lordship of Longdendale referred to
above) which were a feature of post-1349 Macclesfield administration, one of which was part of a very carefully worked out policy,
the other being a sheer bonus. So far Macclesfield forest has been
considered simply as an appurtenance of the manor, and so, in a
sense, it was.[97] Trespasses of vert and venison, and escapes of beasts,
were presented before the justiciar's eyre, yielding small sums of
money each year.[98] There was, however, little intensive exploitation
of ordinary forest rights or of the demesne woods within the forest
(such as Lyme). Small numbers of stakes and crops of trees were
sold, licences to burn charcoal were granted, but no great sales of
timber took place as was the case with Mara forest and the prince's
woods of Peckforton and Bickley.[99] It is true that a rather more
systematic attempt to catch 'escaped' beasts (that is, those that were
pasturing without permission) was made towards the end of the
period by paying the foresters a gratuity based on the number they
caught. For example, in 1372–3 Robert Legh (as riding forester)
received £2 3s. 2d. for capturing 1,036 'escapes' (horses and oxen)
and the escape money paid to the prince was charged at over £9.[100]
It was, however, through the introduction of forest eyres into
Cheshire from 1347 onwards that the prince's administration hoped
to raise really substantial sums, and Macclesfield was naturally included in this campaign, which is discussed in the following chapter,
dealing with taxation and other types of extraordinary revenue.[101]
The 'bonus' revenue accrued from fines imposed for contraventions
of the 1349 and 1351 labour legislation. From 1349 onwards the
fines of workers for either taking higher wages than they had done
before the pestilence, or for leaving their employment, were recorded
in the court rolls of the lordship, particularly in those of the eyre,[102]
although they were also imposed by specially commissioned justices
of labourers (of whom Robert Legh was always one).[103] This increase
in revenue, which fluctuated in size, arose simply because English
legislation was applicable to Cheshire.

V EFFICIENCY OF REVENUE COLLECTION

Of the five accounting bailiwicks which existed from 1358, only one (that of the stock keeper) was managed by an official who held his place at the prince's pleasure. Two bailiwicks were hereditary, the borough officers were elected (admittedly under the acting steward's supervision), while the parker was a life appointment. Consequently, it was even more difficult than usual for the administration to ensure that the policies on which it had decided were carried out. The main sanction it employed was the one which has already been discussed in connection with Thomas Ferrers: the accountants were held personally responsible for the revenue in their bailiwick. This even applied if, as was not uncommon, the hereditary bailiffs performed their offices through deputies. For example, when Adam Mottram's account, as what was now beginning to be called 'bailiff of the forest', for 1356–7 was audited on 2 May 1358, his deputy, Robert Cliff, should have appeared. Mottram had, after all, been with the prince in Gascony at the time in question and could not have administered the bailiwick in person. Robert Cliff, however, absented himself from the audit for the very good reason that, out of the total net charge of some £110, over £45 was still uncollected.[104] On 5 May Mottram was arrested as the prince's debtor, whereupon he complained that Cliff should be held responsible for the arrears, as he had had 'complete administration' of the office during Adam's absence in the prince's company. Next day a writ was issued ordering the deputy steward to arrest Cliff and send him to Chester castle (where Adam was already presumably imprisoned) to answer the allegation. Mottram lost his case and the doctrine of strict responsibility triumphed: on 3 June he was given leave to pay, by instalments, the £45 arrears, 'as he is said to have lost that sum by default of Robert de Clif'.[105] At the 1356 audit, when he had still been in Gascony, Adam had also come up against this unbending attitude. The 1354–5 accounts were being heard (that is, for the period before the Poitiers campaign started) and Mottram's account left a 'clear' remainder (after respites) of £36-odd. It was then stated in his account that he had set off for Gascony in obedience to the lord, who had given him letters of protection for his goods: 'therefore, let execution (for the debt) be made from his lands'.[106]

There were three other instances of defaulting Macclesfield officials being imprisoned at this time. In March 1355 John Somerford won his claim to share the forest bailiwick with Adam Mottram (the office was inherited through their respective wives), and from then on they held the bailiwick in alternate years until 1365, when Mottram bought out Somerford's moiety.[107] At the 1365 audit the arrears on the 1363–4 accounts of Somerford and the hundred bailiff were found to be over 35 per cent of their total net charges.[108] Both were imprisoned, but no further action was taken in either case. William Poker died and was succeeded in office by his two daughters' husbands, while Somerford sold his part of the office, although he retained the obligation to pay off his own arrears. Arrears remained with the person responsible even after he had left office, and at his death they were payable by his estate, first through his executors and then through his heirs, until they were either paid off or excused. In 1368 Mottram himself was imprisoned for a second time, again because of a deputy who, this time, was paying over arrears too slowly. Imprisonment in such cases was a formality, a prelude to settlement of the debt being agreed between the accountant and the auditors, normally taking the form of payment by instalments. Adam, the best documented of all the Cheshire 'middle managers' of the second half of the fourteenth century, was unfortunate enough to experience yet another type of sanction, at the audit of his 1364–5 account, when he was ordered to pay his remainder of £22-odd to the chamberlain in two instalments on pain of having to pay double if he failed to do so.[109] Imprisoned, impoverished or otherwise discontented bailiffs were not necessarily very good at their job, and so the administration had to maintain a very fine balance between the enforcement of the prince's rights and so alienating the accountants as to detract from his financial advantage. Negotiation of instalments of arrears and other debts, on a basis which was acceptable to both parties, was the main way of doing this, and references to such instalments, more often than not payable at the time of the county court, are scattered liberally throughout all the Cheshire accounts.

In order to achieve efficient financial administration, rewards had to be given as well as punishments, and such were particularly important in the case of hereditary officials, who normally received no salary. Adam Mottram, again, is the best example of the opportunities that were open to those who had their eye on the main chance. He first appears as 'hereditary gaoler of Macclesfield and collector of the revenue within the forest' in autumn 1347.[110] The only revenue accruing from the office appears to have been the fees he was paid as gaoler, and in 1355, when John Somerford put in his claim to half the bailiwick, Adam described it as being 'very poor'.[111] Despite the obvious self-interest of this statement, he does seem to have been, as far as wealth went, a very insignificant member of county society. In the 1351/2 rental all he is recorded as possessing is six acres plus an 'offenome' (or enclosure) in the fields of Macclesfield borough.[112] He needed to adopt, therefore, an entrepreneurial attitude if he wanted to improve his family fortunes. The right sort of connections were essential to this, and his first one of importance was with William Soty, a man who was in the service of Sir Bar-

tholomew Burghersh the younger, the prince's military associate
and (sinecure) justiciar of Chester from 1353 to 1369. At Burghersh's
request the prince had granted Bollington and its mill to Soty, for
life, in 1354.[113] By September 1358 Mottram was acting as Soty's
attorney and as his steward for Bollington. Shortly afterwards he
and William Downes, of Shrigley, took a joint lease of the township
from Soty. Neither of them was popular with the tenants there, who
accused them of fraud in trying to establish that they, the tenants,
held by knight-service. An inquisition was ordered to look into the
matter, and, it was alleged, when the two lessees saw that the jury
could not be packed 'with men of their covin', they disrupted the
proceedings so that no decision could be arrived at.[114] Downes, unlike
his partner, was a substantial local landowner with some 150
(Cheshire) acres of land in Macclesfield, Shrigley and Rainow, which
put him in the top rank of manorial tenants.[115]

The other string to Adam Mottram's bow, which was no doubt
calculated to help him move into the Downes stratum of society,
was the leases he took on of manorial enterprises: Shrigley mill
(1347–9),[116] Macclesfield town mills (1352–9)[117] and the town's
common oven (1352).[118] What men like Adam hoped to gain from
such leases (including that of Bollington) has been examined elsewhere,[119] but there is no doubt that they assisted his rise to fame
and fortune. As an accounting bailiff of the Black Prince he was
well placed to acquire the leases, not so much because of any considerations of patronage as because the administration required
lessees who were (relatively) reliable, and being already committed
to the system was a reasonable guarantee of performance. To thrive
in the circumstances of the second half of the fourteenth century
also required a certain spicing of ruthlessness which Adam seems
to have possessed. The allegations of his activities at the time of the
Black Death have already been mentioned.[120] Another of the offences
of which he was accused in the 1353 trailbaston sessions (of which
he was found guilty this time) was allowing Sir John Hyde to take
and mutilate his servant, John Scott, who was imprisoned in Adam's
custody in Macclesfield gaol, and then sending him to the gaoler's
house to recover.[121] This points to another powerful connection. At
that time Hyde was actively (and corruptly) recruiting soldiers in
east Cheshire for the prince's Gascon expedition, a campaign in
which, we have already seen, Mottram himself fought and at the
end of which he received that cheapest form of 'terminal gratuity'
with which the prince paid off his troops, namely a general free
pardon.[122] Social climbers, and perhaps especially those whose
original *point d'appui* was an hereditary gaolership, must have found
it difficult not to make enemies. Places at the higher level to which
they aspired were, after all, few and there was usually much
competition for them. Thus Adam Mottram had to be prepared to

defend himself and his interests, if necessary by the use of violent direct action or by indirect action waged through the law courts. His main opponent in the 1350s was Robert Foxwist, one of the foresters of Macclesfield and thus his colleague and associate in the prince's service. In February 1352 Mottram won a lawsuit with the other for two carucates of land in Sutton.[123] In the April following, Foxwist had to be taken into the prince's special protection because, it was said:

... divers men in the prince's lordship of Macclesfield and elsewhere in the county of Chester, hardened ill-wishers of Robert de Foxwist, ... are threatening him in life and limb ... so that he dare not remain upon the keeping of his bailiwick.

The letter went on to order Sir John Legh and Robert Legh (the acting steward) to take steps to preserve Foxwist's life, as it was well known to the prince who was behind these threats, adding that

... if any harm or damage of body should happen to Robert he [i.e. the prince] knows very well to whom to impute it, and will never take any fine or ransom from the guilty party, of whatever rank he be, but will have judgement appropriate to the deed.

Finally, a proclamation to the above effect was to be issued in the county court itself.[124] It is clear that Mottram must have been one of these unnamed ill-wishers, for when he had won the lawsuit earlier that year Foxwist had been awarded £5 worth of crops growing on the land in question and, in order to recover them from Adam's possession, had had to obtain an order for restitution which was specifically addressed 'to persons who are not his enemies'.[125] Then, two years later, in February 1354, an accusation was brought against Mottram of assaulting Richard Janny, who turns out to have been Foxwist's deputy forester.[126]

Exactly why the prince's officials should have been so concerned to preserve Foxwist from harm was never explicitly stated. It is very likely, though, that it was because his activities as a forester were, in some way, specially profitable. Much of the intensive exploitation of the prince's juridical/financial rights, for which forest law proved to be such a very fertile soil, depended on the secret activities of officials, landowners and others who were acting either as informers or as *agents provocateurs*. When Foxwist was taken into the prince's protection in 1352 it was stated that

... he has great matters to prosecute against divers persons in the court of Chester, and many matters in hand for the prince's profit.

It looks, then, as if this particular forester was intimately involved in the administration's plans to raise very large sums of money from the Cheshire forests by means of both rigorous interpretation of the forest law and by introducing English forest practices and customs

into Cheshire. This was supposed to have culminated in a forest
eyre in 1353, but had to be postponed until 1357. It is possible that
eyre, and when that was cancelled the information he had gathered
Foxwist's secret business was connected with the projected 1353
was stored up and used in 1357. This would explain why the burgesses
of Macclesfield complained in 1359, as has been seen, that indictments for forest offences were being made against them 'by the false
suggestion of Robert de Foxwist', although by 1359 Foxwist had
actually disappeared from the Cheshire scene.[127]

In the event, the prince's protection proved insufficient. In 1353
Foxwist had been fined £40 and bound over to keep the peace on
penalty of forfeiting another £40, for what offences we are not
told.[128] Hugh Tytherington and Robert Shrigley were his two pledges
for payment.[129] Not long afterwards, probably in the winter of
1353/4, he was denounced to Chester castle for having alienated
some of his lands without licence (he held High Lee as appurtenant
to his forestership), as a result of which he suffered the seizure of all
his landed property. In February 1354 he complained that this had
been done 'at the instigation of his enemies' although he had previously paid a fine for the alienation in question.[130] He may already
have decided that the only solution to his problem was flight, his
enemies now having the upper hand. His two pledges, however,
got wind of his plans and immediately tried to stop him, since if
he fled the county they would have been left with the responsibility
for paying his fine. They contacted Delves and told him that Foxwist
was beginning to move his cattle out of Cheshire, and asked that
his lands be handed over to them as security for the payment of the
1353 fine. That could not be done, of course, since the lands were
already in the hands of the county escheator because of the unlicensed alienation. So William Asthull (presumably an under-serjeant
of the peace) was sent to arrest him, and was murdered by Foxwist,
who immediately fled justice without further ado.[131] As a result, he
was outlawed as a fugitive felon and his lands and office were confiscated.[132] On his second visit to Cheshire, in 1358, the Black Prince
granted his former servant's lands and forestership to John Cresse-
well.[133] It is unlikely that the downfall of Robert Foxwist was of a
wholly innocent man, but it is instructive that it appears to have
happened after he had completed secret work on behalf of the prince,
work which was to be used 'for the prince's profit' as long as five
years after his flight from the county.

Mottram was also involved in other, somewhat less spectacular,
disputes. In 1354 he petitioned the prince in connection with land
in the manor which was in dispute between himself and Thomas
Fitton of Gawsworth (yet another forester).[134] Three years later he
was found guilty of an affray with Robert Legh the younger which
took place in Macclesfield town, in which William Downes was also

involved.[135] Bearing in mind that this Legh was probably the son of the deputy steward of the manor, there is very likely a connection between the incident and another one which occurred two years later, in June 1359, when Adam was beaten up in the halmote of the manor, which was in full session before the deputy steward. Robert Legh the younger was one of his attackers.[136] Despite the difficulties of being a minor civil servant in fourteenth century Cheshire, Adam Mottram obviously had the qualities of a survivor, since in 1376 he was still in office, the longest serving of all the prince's officials. However, the inheritance which he passed on to his son, John, did not stay intact for very long. The Mottram bailiwick and lands had to be mortgaged to John Savage in the early fifteenth century because of mounting debts, and they were, in the end, permanently lost.[137]

Life was difficult for all officials of the lordship of Macclesfield, for one reason or another, in the second half of the fourteenth century. The question now remains to be asked: how successful were they at collecting the earl's revenue, and paying it over to the chamberlain of Chester? The construction of 'livery profiles' from the accounts is one good way to attempt to answer this question. (See Appendix II(b).) The borough liveries show that most of the revenue in any one financial year was normally collected by the end of the *next*: that is, a standard two-year collection period was allowed, which also entailed a standard carry-over of arrears. This makes sense when it is realised that if distraint failed to compel tenants to pay their rents, then action had to be taken against them by writ of *cessavit per biennium*, which implied that the rent had not been paid for at least two years. The two-year collection cycle also applied to the hundred bailiwick in normal years: admittedly, it becomes difficult from the 1360s onwards to construct clear livery tables because a missing year's accounts can distort the record of payments in several of the years both before and after it, and also many of the later accounts are decayed at the outer edges of the roll, which is where the liveries appear. There are, however, signs of increasing problems of collection in the later years of the hundred bailiwick, possibly because of the characteristic reliance on increased judicial revenue, much of which was extremely difficult to collect.

The forest bailiwick and stock keepers' accounts present very different livery patterns. As has already been seen, the forest bailiffs found it difficult to keep their arrears within acceptable limits. Thus by the 'third year of payment' after 1361–2 (that is, 1364–5) over £38 out of a net charge of nearly £130 was still outstanding. Likewise, in respect of the accounts for 1364–5, 1365–6, 1367–8 and 1368–9, sums were still not accounted for by the third year after the original charge. By 1374–5, therefore, Mottram's remainder (that is, his total accumulated indebtedness to date) stood at £52, or some

57 per cent of his total net charge for that year. His difficulties must not be exaggerated, however, since in ten of the eighteen financial years between 1358 and 1376 he collected the vast bulk of the money with which he was charged within two years. Nevertheless, difficulties he did have, and these were eventually inherited by, and were the ruin of, his son. To what extent were they the result of his mismanagement, as distinct from unrealistic expectations on the part of the government? It is very difficult to say, but both considerations appear equally weighty. Manorial rents were beginning to be something of a problem in the 1360s and 1370s, as has been seen, and the reliance of the administration on judicial receipts to make up shortfalls or even to expand the revenue at a time of falling population was bound to cause difficulties for the local administrator. However, Adam Mottram's career, with its somewhat unsavoury aspects, makes it difficult to maintain that all his problems of revenue collection were the result of over-rigid expectations on the part of his superiors.

Of all the livery profiles, that of the stock keeper is the most erratic. On his account for 1358–9, for example, he had a remainder of £6 which was not paid over until 1362–3, while, on the other hand, *all* his current net charge for 1363–4, over £57, was delivered within the year of that account. What caused these differences was not slack administration but the structure of his bailiwick and its account. Unlike the other accountants, he had no receipts from rents or court perquisites but only that from the sale of stock. On the other hand, he had to pay out heavy expenses each year. Large numbers of stock were sold only when a good price could be obtained for them, or there was pressure from the central administration to raise funds quickly. Consequently, his receipts were erratic, his expenses heavy and constant, and it was necessary for him to have a 'float'—a sum of money to be carried over as remainder to meet the next year's expenses. This is shown in the 1358–9 account, in which, after the final balance was struck, giving him a remainder of £6 or so, a marginal note was added saying that this money was carried over to be used for various expenses payable from Michaelmas 1359.[138] It was the 1363–4 account which was exceptional, in that all the current net charge and remainder was paid over in that year, a fact that was no doubt due to the financial results of the prince taking up residence in Aquitaine in the summer of 1363.[139] Luckily, the following year, 1364–5, was one when a considerable number of cattle were sold, and so it was not necessary for the stock keeper to call on the chamberlain for a cash advance (to be charged in his account as 'receipts'), as would have otherwise been the case.

All in all, then, the administration of the revenues of Macclesfield lordship during the quarter-century or so after the Black Death was characterised by a great measure of success. Apart from the growth due to additions such as Longdendale and forest eyre receipts, the revenues overall held their value and were normally collected within a reasonable time. The prince's rights of lordship were maintained rigorously and extended wherever possible so that all might be done for his 'profit'. Accounting officials were strictly supervised and were called to book if their performance was not up to standard. From the point of view of the highly centralised, efficient, professional administration it is difficult to see how things could have been arranged better. However, there were problems, some of which only really became apparent towards the end of the period. Macclesfield cattle farm, the only large 'enterprise', had to be run down because of the expense of running it, the unwillingness to invest in new stock and buildings, and its modest financial return; in particular, wage costs had risen to unprecedented heights. Rents as a whole were beginning to feel the effects of land surplus, although not, apparently, to any really serious degree. As Appendix II(a) shows, even in a lordship where the demesnes were being directly exploited, rents were the single most important source of revenue, only occasionally being overtaken by the judicial receipts. And signs of difficulty in letting holdings, however incipient, must have been very worrying for the future.

VI THE VALUE OF THE LORDSHIP

It is necessary, although fraught with danger, to say something about the variations in the value of Macclesfield over the whole period for which accounts are extant. The danger is aggravated by the fact that few of the pre-1347 accounts are particularly detailed or informative, and that the wealth of detail about actual administrative decisions is so much greater for the post-Black Death period. We are not, therefore, comparing like with like. However, it might be useful to compare the total figures derived from some of the representative accounts with the figure from the valor of 1376.

	£	s.	d.
1238/9	113	12	4[140]
1247–8	143	0	10
1298–9	118	17	4
1304–5	142	17	11
1329–30	169	1	0
1348–9	291	19	11
1363–4	274	6	10
1374–5	242	8	10
Valor of 1376	170	0	8[141]

Joining these figures up with a line on a graph and calling it a 'trend' would tell us virtually nothing about the financial administration of Macclesfield. There was no slump in 1376, for example; the valor was concerned with making a rough, conservative estimate of Macclesfield's ordinary revenue, while the other figures are all extremes. What is discernible, behind all the figures of Appendix II(a), are two rising trends over the whole period, one of which is earlier than the other but has a considerable degree of overlap with it. The first was the result of economic forces: that is, of the generations of Macclesfield peasants in the second half of the thirteenth and the early fourteenth centuries who took an empty landscape into cultivation. This great movement only petered out finally in the 1360s, and was what created the manor's rent roll. The other rising trend was the result of the more efficient exploitation of existing resources of tenants and land: this was more spasmodic, appearing in the train of the great exchequer reforms of the 1230s and 1240s, but being really marked only after the time of the Black Prince's coming of age. Only to a relatively small extent was this the result of the exploitation of the natural resources of the demesnes. Most of the increases were the product of courts of justice. If the overall revenue had to be raised, there was no other choice: rents were relatively stable, entry fines fixed by custom, and no other sources were capable of much improvement. This policy was a source of danger for the government in two main ways. The first, and most obvious, is that a falling population, faced with ever increasing 'tariffs' in its communal courts of justice, was tempted to respond by moving towards extremes of anti-government feeling and general discontent. This, in turn, as long as it fell short of any organised, communal approach, could have had the beneficent effect, from the government's point of view, of raising the yield from fines and amercements even further. The signpost at the end of this particular road, though, is plain to see. In a sense, the other response of an 'over-fined' population might, in the end, point along the same road. It is clear that frequently, if not always, fines rather than amercements or other types of judicial penalty were responsible for swelling the charges of the Macclesfield bailiffs. Fines, after all, were basically the 'buying off' of another penalty, were negotiated between the administration and the guilty party, and could be influenced, to a considerable degree, by considerations of patronage or by the desire to increase revenue. As the prince said to Robert Foxwist's ill-wishers in 1352, no fine was to be taken from them but 'judgement appropriate to the deed' was going to be rendered.[142] Does this mean, then, that when the temptation to take high fines because of financial need occurred justice was not going to be done? If so, then the increased revenue from Macclesfield in the later fourteenth century, difficult as it was to collect—although it was usually collected successfully—could well have been creating real problems as far as future governments were concerned. The £200 worth of cash liveries, or more, which the officials there managed to deliver in most years between 1349 and 1376 were bought at a higher price, perhaps, than was realised at the time.[143]

NOTES

[1] J. Tait (ed.), *The Domesday Survey of Cheshire*, Chet. Soc., New Series, LXXV (1916), p. 30.

[2] M. Sharp, thesis, appendix, pp. 156–7. See H. Johnstone, 'The Queen's Household', in *Tout*, V, pp. 231–89, for their administrative arrangements.

[3] *B.P.R.*, III, p. 92.

[4] In 1316 Isabella was allowed by the king to exercise jurisdiction over all felonies and trespasses committed within the hundred, and to take all profits of justice there. (*C.C.R.*, 1313–18, p. 373). Two years later she was granted, in addition, wardships, escheats, advowsons and other casual profits in all her dower lands, together with the liberty of return of writs and of taking all fines, ransoms and amercements imposed on her tenants, and the issues of lands which they forfeited. (*C.C.R.*, 1317–21, p. 202.) The first grant, in particular, caused friction between her own officials and those of her son in Cheshire. (*Tout*, V, p. 274.)

[5] S.C.6 787/2 m. 8.

[6] S.C.8 12/578. In 1351 the queen complained bitterly that many of her former Macclesfield officials still owed her considerable arrears, and she asked for the prince's help to compel them to disgorge. (*B.P.R.*, III, p. 29.)

[7] *C.P.R.*, 1272–81, p. 471, and 1307–13, p. 172, and 1324–7, pp. 226, 293.

[8] *B.P.R.*, I, p. 147. The manors exchanged were Mere and Fordington, and they were supplemented by the addition of £21 a year rent from the honour of Wallingford.

[9] *Chamb. Acc.*, p. 126.

[10] *B.P.R.*, I, p. 157. Similar investigations had taken place after the death of Queen Eleanor in 1290 into complaints about the behaviour of her officials (see *Tout*, V, pp. 271–2).

[11] S.C.6 802/4–8 and S.C.2 252. References to individual accounts will be found in Appendix II.

[12] *Ch. Pipe Rolls*, pp. 9, 12–13.

[13] *Ibid.*, pp. 35–6, 44, 51, 56, 65–6, 87, 92.

[14] E.372 146 rot. 34 m. 2.

[15] 1304–5 (S.C.6 1186/1); 1307–8 (E.372 164 rot. 34) 1329–31 (S.C.6 802/1 and 1297/1); 1347 (S.C.6 1297/2).

[16] In addition to the accounts listed above there exist three arrears accounts which relate to this manor: 1285–7 (S.C.6 1089/22), 1318–19 (S.C.6 1090/10), 1323 (S.C.6 1089/22) and also a file of memoranda relating to the 1331–2 account (S.C.6 1277/2).

[17] For example, in the early fourteenth century. (*Chamb. Acc.*, pp. 2, 16, 38.) This practice appears to have stopped after the 1320s.

[18] It cannot be definitely demonstrated that they were father and son, but it is likely. Thomas held office c. 1290 and 1296–1302 and Jordan c. 1325–6 and 1329–c. 1331. See the reference to 'Jordan son of Thomas Macclesfield' in 1309. (Ches. 29/21 m. 27.) For references to correspondence between Thomas and Queen Eleanor in 1290 see J. C. Parsons, *The Court and Household of Eleanor of Castile, in 1290* (1977), pp. 20–1.

[19] He studied civil and canon law and had still not proceeded to priest's orders as late as 1308, despite his tenure of the rectorship of Mottram. (A. B. Emden, *A Biographical Register of the University of Oxford to A.D. 1500*, (1958), II, p. 1200). Ches. 29/22 m. 33d.

[20] S.C.11 899.

[21] Legh was described as the principal keeper of the queen's forest of Macclesfield in 1346 when she asked for him to be excused from the earl of Lancaster's service (*C.P.R.*, 1343–5, p. 451). During the next thirty years he held the offices of deputy steward and riding forester of Macclesfield and justice of labourers in the hundred. (See S.C.2 252, *passim*.) In 1351 he was accused of misusing his office of deputy steward to deprive the prince of money due from a fine imposed on Sir John Arden. (*B.P.R.*, III, pp. 53, 90.)

[22] This was Robert Holewell, escheator of north Wales. (*B.P.R.*, I, p. 144.)

[23] *Ibid.*, p. 157. Other members of his council present were John Pirie (who had been chamberlain of Chester and then of north Wales in the 1330s and 1340s, and then promoted to receiver-general, for a few months, in 1346; *Tout*, V, pp. 62, 438; Sharp, thesis, appendix, pp. 14–15) and Sir William Shareshull (royal justice and prince's legal adviser).

[24] S.C.6 802/2; 802/4.

[25] S.C.6 802/4 m. 1. The halmote, portmote and hundred courts were normally held at least once a month.

[26] S.C.6 802/2 m. 1.

[27] S.C.6 802/4 m. 1d.

[28] Many heriots were not paid to Ferrers because the succeeding tenants claimed that they had never been customary in either forest or hundred (S.C.6 802/7 m. 3). An inquiry was held in the 1355 eyre of Macclesfield by John Delves, the lieutenant-justiciar, which found that heriots should be paid only from the goods of those tenants of the forest who had possessed live draught beasts ('averia viva') at their death (S.C.6 802/11 m. 1). See J. Hatcher, *Plague, Population and the English Economy, 1348–1530* (1977), pp. 21–30, for the problems of calculating death rates from such evidence.

[29] S.C.11 899. The document, which is in a mid-fourteenth century hand, is un-dated. A careful examination of all the names contained in it shows that it must fall within the dates specified. I hope to be able to discuss the date and contents of this rental in some detail on another occasion.

[30] S.C.6 802/4 m. 1d.

[31] Ches. 29/65 m. 9.

[32] S.C.6 802/2.

[33] *B.P.R.*, III, p. 166.

[34] S.C.2 252/6 m. 3; See Booth, thesis, pp. 100–2.

[35] See S. Pollard and D. W. Crossley, *The Wealth of Britain, 1085–1966* (1968), pp. 57–9, for a recent summary of the evidence.

[36] S.C.6 802/1 m. 1.

[37] For the various hypotheses connecting demography and economic history in the fourteenth century see Hatcher, *Plague, Population*, pp. 11–20.

[38] She received the manor back again the following year, and then held it until the exchange of 1347 (S.C.6 1297/2).

[39] S.C.6 802/6.

[40] *B.P.R.*, IV, p. 221.

[41] In 1370–1 John Trumpington paid the last instalment of a fine 'for the dis-charge of the composition for the goods and chattels which belonged to Thomas Ferrers, late justiciar of Chester' (S.C.6 772/7 m. 4).

[42] Ferrers relinquished his stewardship on 25 March 1351, 'from which date the bailiffs of the hundred, forest and borough are to account separately, by ordinance of the lord's council' (S.C.6 802/6).

[43] He did retain some: for example, licences to mine sea coal were granted in the halmote (S.C.2 252/4), and licences to smelt iron using charcoal were granted, and the collection of waifs and 'abstracts' throughout the whole hundred were farmed out, in the hundred court (S.C.2 252/6 m. 2). He presided over the election of reeve, catchpoll, and other officials in the portmote (S.C.2 155/86 m. 2) and confirmed the appointment of under-serjeants of the peace in the hundred court (S.C.2 252/4

m. 5). In 1353 Sir John Chandos was appointed steward of the manor, but this was a sinecure post, and Legh acted as his deputy (*B.P.R.*, III, pp. 95, 122).

[44] *B.P.R.*, III, p. 11.

[45] S.C.6 802/9 m. 4d.

[46] S.C.6 802/15 m. 5.

[47] See P. H. W. Booth, J. H. and S. A. Harrop (eds), *The Extent of Longdendale, 1360*, Cheshire Sheaf, Fifth Series (1976–7), item 57.

[48] See the earliest comprehensive list of Cheshire townships in the 1406 mise roll. John Rylands University Library of Manchester, Tatton MS 345, and the map p. xiii.

[49] They were Sutton, Hurdsfield, Pott Shrigley, Disley–Stanley, Yeardsley–Whaley, Rainow, Upton and Kettleshulme. Bollington had been granted by Queen Isabella to William Shirbourne rent-free and was not arrented with the others in 1351/2. (*B.P.R.*, III, p. 93.) See map, p. xiii.

[50] S.C.6 802/2.

[51] S.C.6 802/2.

[52] S.C. 11 899. They were called 'the demesne lands of Macclesfield, anciently' arrented'.

[53] *Ch. Pipe Rolls*, p. 56.

[54] Handley, Harrop and Midgely were leased while the park was agisted (S.C.6 802/4 m. 1).

[55] E.372 146 rot. 34 m. 2. It shared the stallion with the royal stud at Edale in the Peak.

[56] E.372 178. They were, again, borrowed, this time from Fotheringay (S.C.6 1277/2).

[57] S.C.6 802/4.

[58] This was also true of the other Cheshire demesnes. See Booth, thesis, pp. 205–6.

[59] S.C.6 802/7. It appears that the farm of Handley had had to be set at an unsatisfactorily low level (from the prince's point of view) to find a taker.

[60] *B.P.R.*, III, p. 142. According to the heading of his account he was appointed 'keeper and surveyor of the lord's stock within Cheshire, both of stallions, mares, oxen, cows and sheep and of any other livestock' with 'power to change that stock for the better, whenever necessary, with the advice of the chamberlain of Chester for the time being . . .' (S.C.6 802/9 m. 4).

[61] Hewitt, *Mediaeval Cheshire*, p. 52.

[62] S.C.6 802/9 m. 4.

[63] *B.P.R.*, III, p. 209.

[64] *Ibid.*, p. 187.

[65] S.C.6 802/13 m. 4.

[66] *B.P.R.*, III, p. 318.

[67] This lordship had just come into the prince's hands because of the minority of Edmund Mortimer, third earl of March. See G. A. Holmes, *The Estates of the Higher Nobility in Fourteenth Century England* (1957), p. 94.

[68] See Appendix II for references.

[69] For modern methods of agricultural accounting see A. G. Jeffrey, *Records and Accounts for Farm Management*, Ministry of Agriculture, Fisheries and Food Bulletin, 176 (1963), pp. 6–9. For a discussion of profit and company balance sheets and income statements see Richard G. Lipsey, *An Introduction to Positive Economics* (1966), pp. 247–60.

[70] Dorothea Oschinsky, *Walter of Henley* (1970), pp. 168–72, 179–82, 271 ff.; see above, pp. 18–19.

[71] Also as noted above (see p. 19), 'sales on the account' could represent auditors' surcharges.

[72] S.C.6 804/5 m. 3.

[73] S.C.6 802/2 m. 1; 802/4 m. 1; 802/6 m. 1; 802/7 m. 1.

[74] S.C.6 804/7 m. 1, m. 3.

⁷⁵ S.C.6 802/13 m. 4; 804/8 m. 5.

⁷⁶ S.C. 804/4 m. 2d. It is not at all clear what a 'villein' meant in the Macclesfield context. A. Curry suggests that the 'villeins' were those tenants of the manor who were liable to pay heriot, which sounds acceptable but conflicts with the definition agreed by John Delves in note 28 above (Curry, thesis, pp. 178–96). What the relationship was of these villeins to the 'bondmen' or 'neifs' of the manor, who are occasionally attested (*B.P.R.*, III, p. 162), is impossible to determine. It is clear that there were attempts at times to claim that all the Macclesfield tenants were of 'ancient demesne', which meant, in effect, that whatever their actual type of holding they were almost as good as free.

⁷⁷ The stock keeper alleged that the outbreak had led to fewer people wanting to buy the lactage of the prince's cows (S.C.6 803/3 m. 3).

⁷⁸ In that year William Oldfield bought a licence to assart four acres of waste in Sutton and Nicholas Downes paid £4 for a similar licence for land in Kettleshulme (S.C.2 252/10 m. 5d).

⁷⁹ When it was said that they could have yielded more except that they were 'in the lord's hands because of the pestilence from Whitsun because no one could take the farm' (S.C.6 802/4 m. 1).

⁸⁰ S.C.6 802/6 m. 1.

⁸¹ S.C.6 802/9 m. 1.

⁸² In only three years up to 1376 did the iron forge produce any revenue: 1358–9: £2 (S.C.6 802/15 m. 4); 1359–60: £5 (S.C.6 802/17 m. 1); 1360–1: £2 (S.C.6 803/3 m. 4d).

⁸³ Lessees of the right to mine sea coal paid 5s. 0d. in 1353–4 (S.C.6 802/9 m. 1); 6s. 8d. in 1354–5 (S.C.6 802/11 m. 1); 10s. 0d. in 1366–7 (S.C.6 803/13 m. 1) and 5s. 0d. in 1367–8 (S.C.6 803/15 m. 1). From 1368–9 there was no mining 'for lack of farmers'.

⁸⁴ S.C.6 804/4 m. 2d. Curry demonstrates that there was no recovery of either of these sources of revenue in the early fifteenth century (thesis, pp. 160–1).

⁸⁵ For details of the farms and issues of all the mills see Booth, thesis, p. 119.

⁸⁶ *D.K.R.*, 36, p. 303; S.C.6 803/15 m. 1.

⁸⁷ *B.P.R.*, III, pp. 336–7.

⁸⁸ *Ibid.*, p. 339. The two officials ordered the justices-in-eyre of Macclesfield forest to accept the community's claims to liberties without a fine, 'having regard to the great poverty of the town'.

⁸⁹ C. Stella Davies, *A History of Macclesfield* (1961), p. 8. For an election in the great portmote see S.C.2 252/6 m. 1. The mayor was an official of the community itself (probably originally of the gild merchant) and not of the earl. Consequently he had no financial responsibilities, and is never mentioned in the accounts and hardly at all in the court rolls. For the mayoralty in the fifteenth century see Curry, thesis, pp. 199–200.

⁹⁰ See pp. 163–4.

⁹¹ *Loc. cit.*

⁹² S.C.6 804/1 m. 2d.

⁹³ *B.P.R.*, III, p. 275.

⁹⁴ *Ibid.*, p. 336–7.

⁹⁵ See Appendix II (a).

⁹⁶ S.C.6 804/7 m. 2. The hundred court perquisites also included the issues of the bailiff's tourn, escapes of the forest, and trespasses of vert (presumably committed by residents of the hundred, and their beasts, going into the forest area). 'Issues of the eyre' also included the revenue from the three hundred courts held immediately after the eyre, to which pleas in the eyre were adjourned and, normally, fines for offences against the statute of labourers (although there were none this particular year).

⁹⁷ For the most recent discussion of this forest see the article by J. Green in *V.C.H.* (*Cheshire*), II, pp. 169–71, 178–84. Dr. Green does not mention the intimate con-

nection between manor and forest, nor does she note the list of townships in the forest in the 1406 mise roll.

⁹⁸ E.g. see the roll of fines in the 1348 eyre, E.101 120/29 m. 4. Such trespasses were sometimes presented in the halmote, portmote and hundred courts; S.C.2 252, *passim*.

⁹⁹ S.C.2 252/1 m. 3. Some gifts of timber from the forest were made by the prince after Poitiers. See Green, *op. cit.*, p. 183.

¹⁰⁰ S.C.6. 804/4.

¹⁰¹ See Chapter V, pp. 122–3.

¹⁰² E.g. the 1351 eyre (S.C.2 252/3 m. 4).

¹⁰³ In 1360–1 fines of 'workmen and servants' were made before Robert Legh and John Davenport, 'assigned by the lord's commission', when twenty-six fullers and weavers, eight reapers and sixty-two others were fined, the fines totalling £14 11s. 8d. (S.C.2 252/5 m. 8).

¹⁰⁴ S.C.6 802/13 m. 1, 1d.

¹⁰⁵ B.P.R., III, p. 342.

¹⁰⁶ Thomas Poker, the hundred bailiff, who was in Gascony too, also suffered from 'execution' at this audit (S.C.6 802/11 m. 2, 2d).

¹⁰⁷ B.P.R., III, p. 199.

¹⁰⁸ S.C.6 803/9 m. 1d, 2.

¹⁰⁹ S.C.6 803/10 m. 1d. For the importance of the instalment system in debt collection see the refusal of the magnates of England to agree to a royal suspension of instalments for crown debts in 1338, which the king had proclaimed on the grounds of financial emergency (E. B. Fryde, 'Parliament and the French War, 1336–40', in *Essays in Medieval History presented to Bertie Wilkinson*, ed. T. A. Sandquist and M. R. Powicke (1969), pp. 261–2).

¹¹⁰ S.C.6 1297/3. He performed homage and fealty to the prince in 1352 for the bailiwick which he held, as a grand serjeanty of the earl of Chester, in right of his wife, Ellen. (B.P.R., III, p. 54.)

¹¹¹ B.P.R., III, p. 199. In 1353 it was found that he had the right to take 4d. from every felon imprisoned in the gaol (Ches. 29/65 m. 9).

¹¹² S.C.11 899 m. 1, 1d. The total rent payable was 4s. 1d.

¹¹³ B.P.R., III, p. 167. He retained the township until 1369 (S.C.6 803/13 m. 1). Soty received a present from the prince of 37s. 8d. and two oaks from Lyme wood in 1358 (B.P.R., III, p. 316).

¹¹⁴ Ibid., pp. 335, 338.

¹¹⁵ S.C.11 899 m. 1d, 3, 3d.

¹¹⁶ S.C.6 802/4. Rent: 15s. 4d. a year.

¹¹⁷ S.C.6 802/9 and 802/15. Rent: £17 6s. 8d. a year.

¹¹⁸ B.P.R., III, pp. 56–7.

¹¹⁹ See pp. 127, 144.

¹²⁰ See also Booth, 'Taxation and Public Order', p. 27. He was fined £10 in the 1353 trailbaston sessions, S.C.6 802/13 m. 2.

¹²¹ Ches. 29/65 m. 3d.

¹²² Granted 9 July 1357 (D.K.R., 36, p. 355).

¹²³ B.P.R., III, p. 57.

¹²⁴ Ibid., p. 62.

¹²⁵ Ibid., p. 57.

¹²⁶ Ibid., p. 145. Foxwist then petitioned the prince, who ordered Delves to 'do what law and reason demand'.

¹²⁷ Ibid., pp. 78, 336.

¹²⁸ Ibid., p. 172; S.C.6 802/9 m. 3. The latter source, the hundred bailiff's account for 1353–4, records that the fine was imposed before Shareshull in his sessions, but there is no reference to it in the trailbaston roll (Ches. 29/65).

¹²⁹ Chamb. Acc., p. 233.

¹³⁰ B.P.R., III, p. 145. See also Green, *op. cit.*, p. 181.

[131] *Ibid.*, p. 172; S.C.6 802/9 m. 1.

[132] *Ibid.*, pp. 172-3.

[133] For Foxwist's outlawry see *Chamb. Acc.*, p. 225. His pledges thus had to pay his £40 fine. From 1354-5 the prince's council leased out the herbage of his lands for £1 a year and his corn was sold for £2 13s. 4d. (S.C.6 802/11 m. 1). In 1358-9 his house was dismantled and reassembled in Macclesfield town to be used as a court house and his grange was similarly removed to Midgley for the prince's stock there, *Chamb. Acc.*, p. 252. See also *B.P.R.*, III, pp. 316-17.

[134] *Ibid.*, p. 160.

[135] *Ibid.*, p. 258.

[136] *Ibid.*, p. 347.

[137] *D.K.R.*, 36, p. 355. For John Mottram's career see Curry, thesis, pp. 60-2.

[138] S.C.6 802/15 m. 3. See also David Postles, 'Problems in the administration of small manors: three Oxfordshire glebe-demesnes, 1278-1345', *Midland History*, IV (1977), pp. 8-12, for the difficulties of administering 'tenantless' properties.

[139] *B.P.R.*, IV, pp. 494-501.

[140] See Appendix II (a).

[141] C.47 9/57.

[142] See above, note 124.

[143] The only year of really low liveries, 1369-70, was the year of the death of the long-serving chamberlain John Burnham. The following year saw the deficit amply made up with over £380, demonstrating that the previous year's difficulties were due to the administrative changes in the Chester exchequer.

CHAPTER V

TAXATION AND THE SEARCH FOR REVENUE

Successive English governments of the thirteenth and fourteenth centuries expended a great deal of administrative effort and ingenuity in attempting to mobilise the country's resources in the interest, principally, of military policy. Taxation, and in particular parliamentary subsidies, with their important constitutional implications, has attracted the greatest attention from historians. It was not, however, just levies of cash which the government required of the king's subjects but also military and other types of personal service as well as supplies of food and other goods.[1] If mobilisation were to be successful, then realistic assessments of personal wealth had to be made and the obligation to part with some of that wealth enforced in ways that were both productive and acceptable to the community. The trouble was that as the government conducted its administration in ways which appeared increasingly oppressive to those affected, a reaction was provoked on the part of groups and individuals in defence of custom and tradition. At times of increased military activity this tension could reach the point of political crisis, as happened in 1294/7 and 1337/43, when fundamental constitutional questions about the relationship between the king and his subjects were raised.[2] Cheshire was certainly not excluded from these historical developments, but the county's unusual position in the English governmental system meant that the pressures and conflicts worked themselves out in ways which were rather different from those in ordinary counties.

I CHESHIRE, PARLIAMENT AND TAXATION

It was not until late in the fourteenth century that Cheshire's exemption from liability to contribute to subsidies granted in the English parliament became an established principle. This privilege was affirmed in 1379 and 1380 on the grounds that the county did not send representatives to the House of Commons, although this was not held to remove the overriding obligation to contribute to the cost of national defence. As a result, the community had the duty to assemble at the monarch's requirement, and make an appropriate grant.[3] Naturally, respectably ancient roots had to be found for such a doctrine and so, by the middle of the fifteenth century, the myth was being propagated that Cheshire had possessed its own parliament from before the time of the Norman conquest and that this body had always had full powers to make laws and grant subsidies.[4] Even shorn of its obvious anachronism, this theory does not do justice to the complex history of taxation and representation within the county in the thirteenth and fourteenth centuries. There are significant parallels between Cheshire's development in this respect and that of the principality and march of Wales.[5] As far as taxes on laymen were concerned, Cheshire seems to have been liable to at least some of those granted in parliament up to 1292. Subsequently, for no obvious reason, this obligation was allowed to lapse by the crown. Between 1292 and 1346 there are no records of any taxes being imposed on Cheshire laymen. From the latter date, therefore, the county administration was faced with the task of devising, and imposing, a wholly new system of taxation, one which lasted until the sixteenth century.

The story begins twenty years before the period now under discussion. In 1253, the year before he gave the county to his son, the lord Edward, King Henry III levied a feudal aid on his military tenants in England which also included those who held lands in Cheshire.[6] Obviously, then, those Cheshire men who held by knight-service were obliged to contribute aids to their feudal overlord on the customary occasions. In 1276/7 another feudal levy, that of scutage, was assessed on the county only to be later remitted on the grounds that the tenants had done their service, and more than was due, in the Welsh war.[7] Moreover, tallages had been imposed on the comital demesnes within the county in 1240[8] and 1250/4,[9] and this may be the only tax which has a continuous history from the days of the Norman earls.[10] In 1275 Edward I held his first general parliament, at which he received a grant of a fifteenth of the movable goods of laymen throughout England. On 24 October[11] assessors of this tax were appointed for Cheshire, but there must have been some objection to the directive because, on 3 November, the king had to request the county to grant the fifteenth like the rest of the realm.[12] There is no record of any response to this demand, but it is clear that the county did agree to pay the tax, since it was subsequently collected through Cheshire's own financial machinery.[13] Edward's second tax on movables, a thirtieth, was imposed in 1283, apparently without Cheshire being compelled to contribute.[14] In 1290 the king was granted his third levy of this type, another fifteenth, which was at first to apply only to England but was extended to Wales, the Welsh march and Ireland in the following year.[15] It was the year after this, 1292, that Cheshire was finally persuaded to contribute despite the fact that its sister county, Flintshire, had already agreed to make a grant of £464.[16] England was now about to enter a period of intensive taxation unparalleled in its previous history. In each of the four years between 1294 and 1297 taxes on movables were levied, but neither Wales nor Cheshire was included. In the case of Wales this was probably because of the state of rebellion and civil disorder which was one of the reasons for the taxes being requested in the first place. With Cheshire the reason is not obvious, especially when it is realised that although the principality of Wales contributed to two further parliamentary taxes on movables, in 1300 and 1318, Cheshire did not and was never, as far as we know, required to pay such a tax again.[17] Early in 1311 the government ordered an investigation into the county's tax liability, since it had by now been forgotten, apparently, whether national taxes had ever been paid there.[18] This must surely mean that the records which had been made to further the assessment and collection of the subsidies of 1275 and 1292 had been kept locally instead of being forwarded to the royal exchequer, and had either been lost or destroyed. One possible explanation for this *de facto* exemption from taxes in the last years of the thirteenth century is that the government regarded Cheshire as being, under Sir Reginald Grey's leadership, more important as a military bulwark against the Welsh than as a source of revenue. Whatever the reason, the county paid no taxes at all until 1346 except for two subsidies on the clergy in 1333 and 1338.[19]

The new system of taxation, developed in the county during the Black Prince's time, was based on two different types of levies. One was the common fine, a payment made by the county community in return for the grant either of a charter of liberties or of a pardon for specified offences. The second was a straightforward grant, a *subsidium* or *donum*, which, like the parliamentary subsidy, was made not in return for favours received (as was the case with the common fine) but as an expression of public obligation to the lord of the county. Whatever the levy was called, it could still be collected using the same assessment of taxable wealth. It has usually been held that this system had its origin in the Welsh marcher lordships in the fourteenth century.[20] More recently it has been suggested that what occurred in the principality, the march and Cheshire in that century was a parallel development of a new taxation system.[21] It is probable that the roots of this 'marcher system' should be sought not so much in Wales itself as in the financial difficulties of the English crown in the first part of the fourteenth century and the *ad hoc* methods which were adopted to try and solve them. Particularly important here is the attempt to reconcile the administration of justice with financial profit, a strategy which already had a long, if not honourable, history in England.

As far as Cheshire was concerned the story resumes in late 1340 when Edward III returned from campaigning in France and set in hand a purge of his government, which he blamed for being both inefficient in supplying him with money and oppressive in ruling the country in his absence.[22] Searching judicial inquiries into alleged abuses of power were authorised the following year, as a result of which large fines were imposed.[23] The king decided, moreover, to ignore the fact that Cheshire was in the hands of the earl of Chester, his infant son, and in February 1341 he ordered Hugh Berwick to take over the administration of the county from the justiciar, Sir Henry Ferrers. Berwick proceeded to hold a judicial inquiry within the county, nominally acting under a commission of the earl of Chester but in actual fact carrying out a royal policy which was being applied to the whole of England. Although no records of his sessions survive, the financial results are very clear in the fines that resulted, most of which were payable in instalments over six years and which together totalled more than £900. A special collector had to be appointed to cope with them, and this resulted in the introduction of Master John Burnham the younger into the Cheshire administrative service and the beginning of a long career which ended only when he died holding the office of county chamberlain nearly thirty years later. Burnham's account as special receiver for 1342–3 (which also covers the 'last part' of 1341–2) shows that he paid over to the keeper of the earl's wardrobe, Peter Gildesburgh, more than £400 of the fines and associated revenue during that time.[24] This was a powerful combination of large yield and successful collection that must have appeared attractive to the earl's council. When the Black Prince came of age in the mid-1340s, with all the new expenses that this implied, it was a precedent which must have weighed very heavily with them.

In 1346 there occurred the first outright grant of taxation by the men of Cheshire to their lord since the fifteenth of 1292. As with the thirteenth century subsidies, it was inspired by the imposition of a levy throughout England. This was Edward III's feudal aid, exacted from his military tenants at the rate of 40s. od. a knight's fee, on the traditional basis of making his eldest son, the Black Prince, a knight.[25] The only advantage of such an aid was that it did not require parliamentary consent. The orders went out in July that year, and in the same month the community of Flintshire was asked by the prince to grant him an aid to assist him with the expenses of the forthcoming military expedition which was to be the occasion of his assumption of knighthood.[26] This could not be a feudal aid, since that would only be payable to the prince when his own son was knighted. There can be no doubt that a similar request was made to Cheshire, although there is no record of it, because we find the prince's officials complaining in April 1347 that, although the community of the county had 'lately granted freely' an aid of £1,000 to the prince, none of it had been collected. The negotiations for the grant had been carried out by Peter Gildesburgh and Sir William Shareshull.[27] Both the feudal aid in England and the Cheshire grant proved extremely difficult to collect. It is very likely that the Cheshire tax was a failure, since, although it was theoretically payable within two years, and two instalments were charged in the 1347–8 chamberlain's account there is no evidence that any of it was ever collected.[28]

The contrast, in financial terms, between the yields of Hugh Berwick's sessions and of the 1346 grant was striking. It is not surprising, therefore, that the prince's administration decided to abandon the idea of direct grants for twenty years and returned to the policy of making the most of the profits of justice. Consequently, in December 1347 an eyre of the Cheshire forests was set in motion. Sir Richard Stafford and Peter Gildesburgh, the lay and clerical heads of the prince's central administration, were the chief justices, while one of their associates was Shareshull, a key figure in the development of financial policy in the royal government as well as in the prince's administration during these years. As a royal councillor and justice of the court of Common Pleas Shareshull had been a victim of the 1341 purge but had been rehabilitated and in 1344 was appointed chief baron of the exchequer, in which office he may well have had a hand in setting up the prince's central exchequer round about that time. From 1350 until his retirement in 1361 he held the office of chief justice of the court of King's Bench. He was the principal architect of the 1349/51 labour legislation and, in G. L. Harriss's view, was responsible for effecting, by this and other means, an alliance between the crown and the 'parliamentary commons' against the lower orders.[29] Shareshull's policy was dominated by two interconnected strategies: the enforcement of the criminal law, which would be a good thing in itself, but a policy by which the government would also be enabled to raise large sums of money. To achieve this he used the King's Bench or specially commissioned courts of criminal justice, nicknamed 'trailbastons'. Financially, at least, there is no doubt of the success of his policy. His trailbaston sessions in Cornwall and Devon in 1354/5 yielded over £2,500.[30] On occasions his activities became even more overtly taxational in nature, when a community was allowed to 'buy off' the holding of a court by the payment of a large sum of money. This was of advantage in the sense that if no 'ransom' money were forthcoming, then the court in question could be held and fines levied from the convicted parties in the usual way. Its disadvantages were, first, that financial considerations tended to swamp judicial ones and, secondly, it was tempting to elicit a common fine by administering justice in what the leaders of local communities considered an oppressive way. The employment of a third type of court, the general eyre, is a good example. Although the crown's right to hold general eyres was unquestioned, the court had fallen out of regular use in the late thirteenth century. Moreover, the eyre was not just a law court but a general inquiry into maladministration and abuse of power, and thus was liable to incur the dislike of communal leaders. Common fines to buy off threatened general eyres had been imposed on Durham and Kent in 1333 (1,000 marks apiece) and on Kent alone in 1348 (£1,000).[31] Likewise, there is no doubt that the Cheshire forest eyre of 1347 was held primarily to raise money. This court was previously unknown in the county and would have been opposed on that score alone, but it had the advantage of applying only to part of Cheshire, the area under forest law, and would provoke only limited opposition. The bitterness of the resistance to this eyre was, however, probably unforeseen by the prince's council, and its financial results were hardly impressive.[32] More important than immediate profits was the fact that it had been firmly established that a forest eyre could be held in Cheshire, and English forest customs were beginning to be imported into the county.[33]

In 1353 Cheshire witnessed what was probably the most thorough elaboration of Shareshull's grand design, which, in this instance, took place during the Black Prince's state visit to the county.[34] The plan was for Shareshull and Roger Hillary to hold a general eyre at Chester from 19 August. Hillary had once been chief justice of Common Pleas, and was to be again in the future.[35] Shareshull had already held general eyres for the Black Prince in the principality of Wales in 1346 and 1347 (and was to hold another in the lordship of Denbigh in 1362).[36] The court of King's Bench had previously been precluded from entering Wales, the march and Cheshire, and so there was an additional reason for employing the eyre in those regions. Originally a Cheshire forest eyre was to be held simultaneously, but that was postponed to 1357 on the grounds that insufficient time had elapsed since the last one. However, before the general eyre could start it was bought off, very likely as the result of a bargain between the county magnates (that is, the wealthier knights) and the prince, who received, in return, a huge common fine of 5,000 marks, payable within four years. As part of the bargain no general eyre was to be held for at least thirty years, and the county received other concessions: the Cheshire 'Magna Carta' was confirmed, some oppressive legal customs were abolished, rights were given to prisoners and condemned felons, and certain practices in connection with lawsuits over land were outlawed.[37] The agreement between the prince and his council and the community of the county was recorded in a charter of liberties which he granted them on 10 September 1353, almost certainly at a public session of his great council. This occasion was a 'Cheshire parliament' in all but name, and one of the items included in the charter, the abolition of the custom of thwertnic, was ordained by the prince 'at the request and with the assent of the community', an expression which has a distinct flavour of the terminology of parliamentary legislation. In substitution for the general eyre the prince gave Shareshull and Hillary a new commission, to hold sessions of trailbaston, starting on 20 August. Again this was probably part of the 'package deal' between the two sides. The justices then proceeded to try a large number of criminal cases, with every appearance of judicial thoroughness, and, as a result, fines were imposed which totalled well over £1,000.[38]

The sums of revenue produced in 1353 have no parallel in Cheshire's medieval history. Payment of the common fine of 5,000 marks was to be made by all in accordance with their wealth in 'lands, goods and chattels', with the exception of the church's spiritualities and of anyone who was worth less than 20s. 0d. Instructions were sent out to the effect that the lesser folk were not to be overrated, as had happened previously, which is presumably a reference to the 1346 grant.[39] Possibly the assessment was made in the same way as the Tudor subsidies, and was based on personal wealth (either land revenue or movable goods). The large sums realised in this year have to be judged in context, however: first, England as a whole was contributing to a triennial parliamentary subsidy (from which Cheshire was exempted) and, second, the trailbaston fines were imposed, without any doubt, on genuine evildoers.

In 1357 the forest eyre which had been postponed from 1353 met at Chester and Macclesfield under the presidency of Sir Richard Willoughby, Sir Richard Stafford and John Delves. Resistance by the forest communities was now largely broken. Two of them proffered communal fines, payable over five years: Wirral (£1,000) and Mara-Mondrem (£2,000).[40] Firm government and aggressive administrative methods were seen to be paying off. Such methods depended, however, on a victory in the battle between the county government's determination to raise revenue and the solidarity of the communities' leaders reinforced institutionally by local self-policing and self-administration of justice through the system of juries and sworn inquisitions. At one stage the prince's business manager, Sir John Wingfield, was afraid that the whole 1357 forest eyre was going to be subverted by a 'great confederacy' among those living in the forests to ensure that presentments for forest offences were not made.[41] A certain amount could be done to counter such resistance through the administration's spies,[42] but overall it was a straightforward trial of strength. Macclesfield forest community, despite pressure, refused to pay a communal fine, and this certainly paid off, since the individual fines imposed in the eyre amounted to only £63-odd, of which no more than £23 had been collected as late as 1361.[43] The reason for Macclesfield forest being able to make such a stand was that its community, unlike those of the other two forests, was socially and institutionally cohesive. Macclesfield forest and manor were more or less identical, and through the manorial courts, which possessed a considerable measure of independence from county administration, this community could hold out against the government's revenue drive.[44]

The reason for the exaction of the large common fines of 1353 and 1357/8 was undoubtedly the expenses connected with the prince's Aquitainian expedition of 1355/7. It is difficult to discern how taxation policy developed in the following ten years because of a gap in the chamberlains' accounts coupled with the complete lack of the prince's central accounts. In 1368 there was a return to the tactic of asking for outright grants from the county, first a *subsidium* of 2,500 marks (payable within two years), which was followed by a *donum* of 3,000 marks in 1373.[45] No information survives to give any background to the negotiation of these two grants. The 1368 subsidy was unusual in that it was granted during a long period of peace in the war between England and France, and its only justification, therefore, was as a subvention for the prince's career as prince of Aquitaine.[46]

To assess the impact on Cheshire society of the various levies which have been mentioned it is necessary to consider the size and frequency of the various instalments as they fell due (Table 6). There is, as has been emphasised many times, a world of difference between charging the community with revenue and actually collecting it. Most of the 1353 common fine was paid over within the stipulated time limits; and so were the trailbaston fines of the same year. Despite the very large charges added to John Burnham's account as county chamberlain, his remainder at the end of the financial year 1356–7 was only just over £176.[47] By the end of 1361–2, however, the year of the last term of payment for the forest common fines, his remainder had risen to £1,117 12s. 6¼d., of which over £300 was respited.[48] It will be remembered that the chamberlain's account at this time consists largely of the charges of *liveries* from subordinate accounting officials, the only exceptions being those revenue items for which the chamberlain was personally responsible and for which he was charged in the usual way. Consequently, the forest fines must have been almost wholly responsible for the considerable increase in remainder. At Burnham's death in 1370 or early 1371 his accumulated remainder had been reduced to £668-odd, but this was large in comparison with the figure of fourteen years earlier.[49] By Michaelmas 1374, at the end of the last surviving chamberlain's account from the Black Prince's time, the remainder had been further reduced to something over £300.[50] It is apparent, therefore, that although there were difficulties in collecting this new 'taxation' they were eventually overcome. This was an administrative achievement of the highest order. If Sir William Shareshull originally devised the plan, and the main responsibility for administering it can be laid at the door of John Delves, the actual execution of it must be credited to John Burnham, the self-effacing civil servant.

TABLE 6

LEVIES CHARGED UPON CHESHIRE, 1346/76

1346–7	£500	Free gift or mise of 1346
1347–8	£500	
1353–4	£833	
1354–5	£833	Common fine of 1353
1355–6	£833	
1356–7	£833	
1357–8	£600	
1358–9	£600	
1359–60	£600	Common fines of Wirral and Mara-Mondrem forests
1360–1	£600	
1361–2	£600	
(1362/8	Gap in accounts)	
1368–9	£833	*Subsidium* of 1368
1369–70	£833	
1373–4	£666	
1374–5	£666	*Donum* of 1373
1375–6	£666	

It can be seen from the above sketch that the 'mise', in the later sense of a 'tallage of recognition', was not a feature of Cheshire's taxation scheme in the fourteenth century. Two of the levies, those of 1346 and 1353, were, indeed, called 'mises' in contemporary documents, but the term there had its general meaning of 'imposition'.[51] What small amount of evidence there is suggests that the 'mise at the creation of a new earl' was a late development in Cheshire's history, its first definite occurrence being in 1463.[52] Why it should have been imported into the county's fiscal system at that time, and whether its genesis is to be sought in Wales and the marches (as D. L. Evans thought) or in the English custom that the king was entitled to seek financial aid from his subjects towards the expenses of securing his kingdom (the view of G. L. Harriss) will perhaps never be known.[53]

The major difficulty with the various levies we are concerned with here is to estimate the severity with which they fell on local communities and individuals. The earliest assessment list is dated 1406 and was produced in connection with the common fine of 3,000 marks made by the county in return for a charter of pardon for offences arising out of Henry Percy's rebellion of 1403.[54] It is a simple list of all the townships within the county, grouped together under the several hundreds, with the proportion of the fine each had to pay, together with a note of the fraction that applied personally to the lord of the township in question. On the face of it, this looks to be a 'fossilised assessment list' along the lines of the national lay subsidy which became 'frozen' at the levels of 1334. It is not known when this Cheshire assessment was originally made. There is good evidence to suggest that it antedates 1353, and, at the justiciar's eyre held at Macclesfield on 5 October 1349, a man was found guilty of illegal recovery of a distraint levied by the poker of the hundred for non-payment of the mise due from Northenden.[55] Consequently, the distribution of personal wealth revealed by the 1406 assessment may well be that of Cheshire before the impact of the Black Death, although no firm conclusions can be drawn from such a supposition.[56]

Historians of Cheshire have normally regarded the Black Prince's financial policy towards the county as being little short of extortionate. Such an opinion has, however, to be evaluated by comparing the financial demands on the people of Cheshire with those made by the king on neighbouring counties.[57] During the reign of Edward III Cheshire paid 'taxes' in sixteen financial years at least, the sums demanded ranging between £500 and £833. In the same period ordinary lay subsidies were levied in England in twenty-two years,[58] not counting the ninth of 1340 and the feudal aid of 1346. In 1334 Shropshire's contribution to the subsidy was fixed at £644, Staffordshire's at £578.[59] No case can be made, therefore, for saying that Cheshire's treatment was greatly different in this respect from that of comparable English counties. What, then, of R. R. Davies's view that what he terms the 'casual revenue' of the Welsh marcher lords, which was so similar to the post-1346 Cheshire 'taxation', bore more heavily on the inhabitants of those lordships than parliamentary subsidies did on their fellows in England?[60] It has to be said that, on the basis of the evidence put forward, the case has not been made. The principal example which he gives is that of the lordship of Chirkland, which paid its lord £87 a year 'casual revenue', on average, between 1340 and 1350. On the other hand, the same lordship contributed only £67 to the parliamentary subsidy of 1291/2. In fact, this is not as compelling a comparison as it seems to be, since the tax of 1291/2 was collected so incompetently in both Wales and Cheshire that a royal investigation into the negligence of its assessors and collectors was ordered.[61] The best measure of the impact of taxation, moreover, is gained not by pondering overall figures but by discovering, if possible, how much local communities and individual households were likely to have to pay. This can be done in the case of at least part of Cheshire in respect of the 1353 common fine. In the accounts for the St. Pierre estates, which were largely situated in the south-west of the county, there is given the proportion of the fine which was payable by each manor. In Caldecott, for example, the lord's part was 1s. 9d. for one year, while in the larger manor of Peckforton, the estate's administrative head-quarters, it was 6s. 8d., in comparison with a total charged (net) manorial revenue of £21 2s. 1d.[62] A contribution of 1½ per cent of total revenue, by the landlord, does not appear excessive by any standards. In Bickley, however, the lord's part was higher, amount-ing to more than 3 per cent of the annual revenue but, nevertheless, still not what could reasonably be called 'extortionate'. What about the common people? Bickley had fifty tenants in 1353–4, which meant that the average tenant household paid 9d. to the instalment of the common fine of that year.[63] There is no way of knowing anything about the wealth of more than a very small number of Cheshire peasants at that time. On the other hand, the most relevant comparison as far as contemporaries were concerned would be with the amount of rent a tenant would have to pay for his holding. Unfortunately, no detailed extents or rentals from the St. Pierre lands are extant. Perhaps a comparison could be made, therefore, with the episcopal manor of Farndon, which is about eleven miles away on the west side of Bickley and which was surveyed in detail in the late thirteenth century, when the customary holding of a tenant attracted 1s. 10d. a year rent.[64] If the Bickley tenant were paying rent of similar magnitude, which we have no real way of knowing, then we might suggest that the burden of Cheshire taxa-tion on the more substantial tenants was heavy but probably not oppressive.

II   INVESTMENT IN LAND REVENUE

Taxation was not the only way in which the lords of Cheshire could increase the county's financial yield. It has been seen that during the years between 1272 and 1327 there was a tendency for the revenue first to shrink and then to be collected with difficulty.[65] Financial administration during the lordships of Edward I and Edward II was firmly subordinated to political considerations. Also there was a policy of granting the estates of the earldom to royal relatives. Under the royal earls, much more reliant as they were upon the county's revenue, there was a tendency for more active attention to be paid to financial policy. Even so, leasing of both estates and offices remained usual under Edward of Caernarfon and probably under Edward of Windsor also. It was only during the thirty years of the Black Prince's maturity that serious efforts were made to exploit all possible sources of revenue.

It was 1346 that marked the watershed in Cheshire's financial history. In that year leasing of the justiciarship of Chester was abandoned for ever, taxation was reintroduced, and a period of unprecedentedly active management was inaugurated. In so far as this affected the prince's landed estates within the county the change has already been examined in some detail elsewhere.[66] During this time two substantial estates were added to the prince's properties: the first being the newly created manor of Drakelow (comprising two districts, Rudheath, to the south-east of Northwich, and Overmarsh, between Churton and Farndon, on the western border of the county), the second the landed inheritance of Sir John St. Pierre of Peckforton. The manner of their acquisition, and the way they were subsequently administered, illustrates the ruthlessness of the administrators' activities in this phase of the county's history and also the problems which such ruthlessness engendered.

Rudheath and Overmarsh were the 'secular sanctuaries' of the earl of Chester and, as a result, all assarting and reclamation had long been prohibited in them. Nonetheless, by 1300 the inhabitants of near-by villages had already ploughed up over 1,500 acres of Rudheath when the necessity for having the sanctuaries as recruiting bases for armies against Wales had receded.[67] In the early decades of the fourteenth century it looked as if the earl's rights over these two areas were being forgotten.[68] In 1342, however, there was a revival of interest, although nothing further was done for another four years.[69] Then, in 1346, the administration decided to take positive action and at judicial sessions presided over by Sir William Shareshull and Peter Gildesburgh the 'recovery' of Rudheath and Overmarsh was engineered.[70] It is interesting to note one of the methods used in bringing this about. Five years later the abbot of Chester claimed that the prince's council had promised that if he were to put up no legal defence at the sessions, so as to set an example to other tenants of Rudheath lands, he would not lose by it.[71] The formal re-establishment of the prince's rights was just the first step in a long and complicated process which continued with the perambulation of the boundaries, the measurement of the recovered lands, and the taking of decisions about their future status. In the year 1347–8 the first revenue was being paid to the prince from Rudheath while Overmarsh yielded nothing because it was waiting to be surveyed.[72] Before the exercise could be completed, and the full financial benefits realised, the Black Death supervened, presenting the prince's administrators with some of the most difficult managerial problems they had to deal with.

A rental and an extent of Rudheath lordship survive, both of which postdate the pestilence, and the latter is incomplete.[73] There is no extant survey for Overmarsh. The rental indicates that 1,287-odd Cheshire acres of land had been recovered in Rudheath, equivalent to 2,723 statute acres. Of this, 150 acres was formed into the demesne of a newly created manor called Drakelow (which was situated in western Rudheath), divided into three fields of approximately equal size to be managed on a three-field system.[74] It is significant that the newly recovered areas (despite being separated by a good many miles) were to be organised as a conventional manor, with manor house, demesnes, court, and tenant land. The remainder of Rudheath was made up of 185 tenancies, some held by single tenants, others by groups of people, yielding a total annual rental of over £50.[75] Of their original landlords, those who were laymen were allowed to retain only those lands in the heath which they held in demesne, while the tenants, and their rents, were transferred to the prince. The ecclesiastical lords, that is, the abbeys of Chester and Dieulacres, were given preferential treatment in that they were allowed to retain both their demesnes and under-tenants, being obliged to pay rent to the prince for both of these.[76] A minority of the tenants were to hold 'in fee', but the majority were described as 'termors'.

This, of course, is the picture which emerges after the onset of the Black Death. In the summer of 1349 nearly seventy-five Rudheath tenants died without leaving anyone to take over their holdings, while in Overmarsh over 173 acres of arable land were left unploughed.[77] The net charged receipts for the whole manor fell to less than £11 in 1348–9. In contrast with the rest of the earldom's estates, there was no subsequent smooth transition to normality, presumably because administrative control over the manor had been so recently established. In 1349–50 a reduction of one third in the rents, which had been fixed at between 1s. 0d. and 2s. 0d. an acre, had to be conceded to the Rudheath tenants, otherwise they would have abandoned their holdings.[78] Overmarsh fared even worse, since no inducements could prevent a mass desertion of tenancies which resulted in some 215 acres of arable land lying unploughed. In the whole manor the decasus of rent reached £30.[79] The Black Prince's officials were, without doubt, tenacious of their employer's financial rights but they could be realists when the occasion demanded it. Rudheath's rents were established at their reduced level, where they remained practically unaltered for nearly twenty years. Overmarsh proved to be a much more intractable problem. As late as November 1351 no agreement had been reached on what rents the tenants there should pay. They were unwilling to offer more than 6d. an acre (8d. at the outside) and, in addition, wanted to hold their lands in fee. Ferrers and Burnham were advised that these demands were unacceptable and ordered to seize the tenancies and let them for pasture.[80] By the following June a compromise must have been agreed, because Overmarsh's rent roll was established at £19 17s. 0¼d., with all the tenants holding for twelve years.[81] Despite this settlement the situation remained unhealthy. The charged rents gradually declined until they reached just over £11 in 1370–1, when ninety-three and a half acres in Overmarsh could find no takers at all.[82] At first the Drakelow demesnes were managed directly by the earl's officials, and in 1349–50 the crop of corn and legumes was sold for some £14, and forty-five acres were sown for the following year.[83] This experiment did not survive the poor weather and bad harvest of 1354–5, after which the demesnes were leased to the bailiff, William Dyseworth, at an annual rent of £6 13s. 4d.[84] It was no longer possible for the administration to undertake expensive capital outlay in the hope of a long-term return, especially as the Aquitainian expedition meant that cash in large quantities was immediately required.[85] This freezing of investment was intensified in 1356, when it was necessary to find extensive sources of patronage to reward those followers who had helped the prince to victory at Poitiers. In that year the Drakelow demesnes, plus £40 annually out of the Rudheath rents, were assigned to Sir John Chandos for life.[86] By then the administrative link between Rudheath and Overmarsh had become redundant, and the two lordships were finally given separate bailiffs in 1362.[87] This withdrawal from active exploitation was completed in 1365 when Roger Page, one of the prince's archers, was made bailiff of Drakelow and Rudheath for life.[88] It was still necessary to keep an accurate check on land holding within the lordships, and so a new extent of Rudheath was made in 1370.[89] This was obviously the product of a thoroughgoing overhaul, since, as a result, the Rudheath rent roll was increased to nearly £50, not far short of what it had been at the outbreak of the Black Death over twenty years before.[90]

If the 'recovery' of Rudheath and Overmarsh represented the forcible resuscitation of old rights, the complicated story of the acquisition of the St. Pierre inheritance in 1353 tells of the acquisition of completely new property. Sir John St. Pierre II, its landlord, was then about forty-five years old, the owner of a considerable landed estate mostly in the south-western quarter of the county, an estate which comprised one quarter of Malpas barony and portions of other Cheshire baronies. His principal residence and administrative headquarters were at Peckforton, where he had a game park. Sir John was, in contemporary terms, a county 'magnate', his lands being worth well over £100 a year, and he had undertaken considerable military service in the past. When his son married, in 1351, the Black Prince had given the boy a present of 100 marks.[91] Moreover his importance in county society was magnified by the fact that as co-holder of Malpas barony he was also hereditary joint master-serjeant of the peace for Cheshire.[92] His career was, it would seem, that of a successful county knight whose main ambition in life, one would expect, would have been to increase his wealth and social standing and hand them both on, intact, to his eldest son. Why he should have decided to remove himself from Cheshire to Anglesey and transfer all his lands to the Black Prince is, then, somewhat difficult to account for.

The transfer took place in two stages. In April 1353 Sir John sold the reversion to his Cheshire property to the prince in return for £1,000 in cash plus the keepership of Beaumaris castle and the associated fee of £40 a year.[93] On 29 September, during the prince's visit to the county, he made a second grant, which either replaced or supplemented the first, whereby the life interest in his estates was made over to the prince in return for lands in Anglesey worth £100 a year.[94] Later evidence suggests that this second arrangement was in substitution for the first, and that Sir John expected his lands to return to his family in the future. There are two possible explanations for the exchange, and both of them imply that St. Pierre was subjected to considerable pressure by the prince and his officials. The first is based on the undoubted fact that Sir John's title to his lands was a weak one. It came down to him through his great-grandfather, Sir Urian St. Pierre, who had died in 1295 after performing distinguished service to King Edward I.[95] It was very likely as the result of royal favour that Sir Urian had obtained, at some time before 1281, the hand in marriage of Idony, one of the daughters and co-heiresses of the Cheshire landowner David of Malpas. This David, however, was only the illegitimate son of William of Malpas and had obtained possession of his father's half of that barony by ousting his uncle Philip, the legitimate heir.[96] It is possible, therefore, that Sir John's defective title was being waved in front of his eyes in order to compel him to decide that it was preferable to receive compensation in land and offices in Anglesey rather than run the risk of a lawsuit. Once the lands were in the prince's hands their title was immune from challenge in the Cheshire courts. The other explanation arises out of Sir John's involvement in a violent feud with the Maistresson family in the early 1350s, which led to his serjeanty of the peace being seized by the county officials.[97] This could have been used as an inducement to leave the county.

Whatever the pretext, there is no doubt that the prince's interest in the St. Pierre estates was financial. The return of Macclesfield manor to the prince's hands, the recovery of Drakelow, and the acquisition of the St. Pierre lands, all indicate a policy of investment in land revenue in a concentrated form in Cheshire in these years. Both revenue and capital were available to be exploited. The St. Pierre estate was placed under the administration of receivers who made liveries to the chamberlain, twelve of whose accounts survive for the years between 1353 and 1371.[98] Over £155 was delivered to the chamberlain by the receiver in 1354–5, and in the *valor* of 1365/6 the yield was estimated at £138 12s. 7½d.[99] On 5 July 1354 the decision was announced to dispose of the inheritance's most valuable asset, all the wood (except for the 'great oaks') growing in Peckforton park.[100] The following November, Wingfield ordered Delves and Burnham to sell the wood 'as profitably as possible', but the actual felling did not take place until the next summer.[101] The timber was bought by a consortium of eleven men who paid 800 marks, due in instalments within five years.[102] The oaks which remained were even more valuable. Thirty-three grants of oaks for timber from the park to the prince's followers are recorded between 1357 and 1362, mostly to soldiers who took part at the battle of Poitiers. Similar, though fewer, grants were made from the wood attached to Bickley, another St. Pierre manor.[103] In 1357 it was reported by Delves and Burnham that £900 had been offered for the Peckforton oaks, although no sale seems to have been concluded.[104] The stripping of the park's assets both before and after Poitiers is an example of successful revenue raising but indicates clearly that this was being done at the expense of future profits.

In 1363 a legal action was undertaken in connection with the St. Pierre estates which, given the very best interpretation, reveals the prince and his ministers as acting in a devious and suspiciously hasty way. The date itself is significant: it was the year the prince left to begin what was virtually his new career as prince of Aquitaine. The repayment of his obligations to his soldiers in the currency of Peckforton timber had come to an end the year before.[105] On 2 June, while he was in the prince's company at Plympton helping to arrange his embarkation, John Delves, who was now his business manager as well as lieutenant-justiciar of Chester and north Wales, obtained his master's licence to sue in the county court, by writ of right, for the recovery of one quarter of the St. Pierre portion of Malpas barony. Delves was acting on behalf of his second wife, Isabel (*née* Egerton, *alias* Malpas).[106] Isabel's claim was based on descent from Philip of Malpas, the legitimate uncle of the bastard David.[107] To make this 'parting gift' even sweeter, the prince gave orders that the trial of the action in the county court (of which, of course, Delves was still co-president) was not to be hindered by 'protections, essoins or other subtleties of law'.[108] St. Pierre, who was at that time living at Beaumaris as keeper of the castle, was warned, that same day, to be at the session of the Chester county court which was to take place just over a month later. As he had no legal advisers to whom he could turn, he had to seek help from the prince's officials, and so he asked the prince's auditor, William Cranewell to take a message to John Burnham begging for a postponement. Burnham, as it happens, was by then the sole remaining feoffee of the estate and thus the nominal defendant in the action. A postponement was granted to the county court of 12 December, but St. Pierre later claimed that he was told about this so late that it had not left him sufficient time to ride to Chester to help defend the suit. Consequently, Delves and his wife were victorious, provoking Sir John to complain, in the bitterest terms, that 'he never thought he would have seen his lands lost while they were in the prince's hands'.[109] The prince, ironically enough, had lost nothing, since when he had granted the licence to proceed in the action it had been on condition that he was not to be the loser by the result. Delves, therefore, was not to receive any profit from his victory until after the prince's death, although he leased the lands from Michaelmas 1364 to 2 April 1366.[110] As it happened, Delves died before the prince, in 1369, whereupon the recovered portion of the barony was given to his widow by decision of the prince's council on the grounds that her right of inheritance could not be affected by a promise made by her husband, since he had the management of her lands only during his life.[111]

Sir John St. Pierre, without any doubt at all, felt that he had been the victim of sharp practice. Whatever the truth of the matter, the case illustrates the importance in the fourteenth century of what might be termed 'anti-patronage': that is, that the grace and favour afforded by a 'good lord' to his friends had its reverse side. Underlying the whole affair was, once again, the urgent need of the prince for money to finance his overseas career. This had led him in the first place to invest in the St. Pierre estates and then to realise their assets in a somewhat profligate way. It was John Delves's responsibility to provide the ready cash from the English and Welsh estates that the prince's Gascon subjects proved so reluctant to part with.[112] Delves was also anxious to establish himself firmly in that level of society to which the prince's service had raised him. Already he had acquired considerable land and rents, but only from grants for life.[113] Consequently it was only through his marriage that he could expect to acquire property to pass on to his descendants, and this fact may well explain why the lady Isabel's lawsuit was so ruthlessly prosecuted. This episode and, indeed, the whole saga of the prince's tenure of the St. Pierre lands made sense in terms of short-term needs, but it boded ill for the future. In particular, the manipulation of the county court in a matter which touched so closely the interests of the Cheshire landlords as did the right to real property must have made it clear to the community that the prince's government's favour was not just a prerequisite of advancement but a necessity for holding on to what they already had.

III POLICIES AND CONSEQUENCES

In 1291–2 Cheshire's financial 'yield' to its lord had been just over £485. Sixty-two years later, in 1353–4, it was nearly £3,000. The latter figure is almost six times the former. Nearly everything that has been said in the foregoing pages has tried to show that no firm conclusions can be drawn from the juxtaposition of such bald figures. First of all, such sums of money need to be scrutinised in detail to see whether they are comparable, and, in the example given, it must be stated that they are not.[114] Secondly, changing figures, however reliable, are but inadequate guides to changes in financial policy. In order to arrive at any overall assessment of Cheshire's financial administration between the accession of Edward I and the death of his great-grandson we have to ask what successive groups of administrators were attempting to do in the financial sphere, to examine the consequences in terms of the raising of revenue, and then to provide an explanation linking the two. Immediately we are faced with the difficulty that has beset all students of medieval financial administration, namely that the evidence is unevenly distributed. As a result, the study undertaken here must fall into two very unequal parts: a long prologue of some seventy years from 1272 to 1346, leading up to a thirty-year period for which really detailed information has survived.

Any investigation of policy has to start by asking whether the year 1346 was really as much of a watershed as it appears. In other words did the policies pursued by Peter Gildesburgh, John Wingfield and John Delves from the 1340s to the 1360s in any way follow on from what had gone before? There is no evidence, it is true, that before 1346 any lord of Cheshire, or his officials, had ever given such energetic consideration to exploiting the county's revenue as was the case in the thirty years subsequent to that date. Of course, there is no source of information before 1346 to compare in richness of detail with the two volumes of the *Black Prince's Register* which relate to Cheshire affairs. On the other hand, it was only during the short principate of Edward of Caernarfon, between 1301 and 1307, that the administrative machinery was both designed for, and capable of, a policy of close financial control and exploitation. It is indicative, though, that at this earlier time there appears to have been no attempt to impose taxation on the county or to increase the yield of judicial revenue, as was the case forty years later. In the administrative sense, therefore, 1346 does represent a discontinuity. Administration is not the same as government, however, and radically different administrative methods can be used to achieve the same governmental ends. In a deeper sense there are signs of a persistent tendency in governmental policy which was expressed in

Cheshire financial administration, and it is this which bridges the gap between the two periods. It is an oversimplification to call this a drift away from bureaucratic efficiency towards feudal decentralisation. It was more a tendency for government in the interests of external policy to predominate at the expense of government in the interests of those who were governed. If a medieval monarch was a person who combined the attributes of a war leader with those of a dispenser of justice, then to be successful he had to keep both in rough balance. There was always liable to be tension between these two sides of government, between 'home' and 'foreign' policy, in fact, but I have argued elsewhere that during the Black Prince's two visits to the county, in 1353 and 1358, signs were already apparent that the needs of war were predominating, at the expense of those of justice.[115]

On the surface, the Black Prince's rule of Cheshire could not have been more different from that of Edward I. Under the latter, it has been shown, hardly any revenue at all went from Cheshire to London. This was not because either the will or the administrative expertise was lacking to administer the county revenues 'profitably'. Edward I, after all, liked and was used to getting his own way. As his *quo warranto* campaign demonstrates, he believed in using the full power and authority of the crown, admittedly while not wanting to change traditional methods of government or social relations. It is not surprising, therefore, to find that financial policy with regard to Cheshire in his reign was 'feudal' in that it relied on the delegation of power and authority to Sir Reginald Grey, as payment for the crucial role he played both in the Welsh campaigns of the 1280s and 1290s and in the reorganisation of the newly conquered country. Yet in Grey's first term as justiciar of Chester, between 1270 and 1274, an inquiry had been held into allegations of his oppressive conduct. He was deprived of the office in the following year, and it may be a significant indicator of the quality of his first ministry that Chester castle was handed back by him in a 'ruinous' state.[116] His reinstatement corresponded with the second and, as it turned out, the decisive Welsh war of 1282. He was rewarded in the classic 'feudal' way with the gift of what became the marcher barony of Ruthin, and his grip over the administration of Cheshire was strengthened. In his last years he was dominant in the councils of the king's heir-apparent, the first English Prince of Wales. There are striking parallels between his rise to power and wealth and that of John Delves in the following century. Delves was (acting) justiciar of Chester and then climbed upwards through his prince's central counsels. In some ways, he acquired even more power and authority in Cheshire than his predecessor. What is striking about the Delves era, however, is the extent of centralisation of the administration. By the 1360s this was apparent rather than real: the main 'foreign policy' requirement was for large and regular sums of money to pay for the English armies (and, later, English administration) in France. Delves's undoubted ascendancy over Cheshire government and society was granted in return for the successful fulfilment of this aim. It is clear, then, that underneath the superficial differences there is a close similarity of aims between the two periods.

Having said that, there can also be no doubt that the Black Prince's ministers were faced with unprecedented demands for revenue in the years between 1346 and 1371. As P. J. Morgan has pointed out, this hit Cheshire particularly hard because of the very leniency with which the county had been treated since the end of the Welsh wars.[117] Although the prince's involvement in the war against the French was financed to a considerable extent by the English government, even at an early stage in the conflict his estates were charged with heavy financial responsibility.[118] Loan-finance had to be raised to bridge the gap between immediate cash needs and the collection of future revenue. In 1346 and 1347 there were severe cash flow problems arising out of the failure to collect the 1346 Cheshire mise which meant that £1,000 had to be borrowed from a merchant to supply the prince's 'great need'.[119] Side by side with the increase in the demand for both money and patronage which was engendered by foreign war, there occurred operational changes in revenue collection in Cheshire. This is most clearly apparent in the employment of the device of 'assignment', which was imported from the king's government. It enabled the prince's retainers and others to collect annuities from his local officials, and gave them some security of payment.[120] The first assignment on the chamberlain's account appears in 1349–50, the second the following year.[121] After the battle of Poitiers there was the first big rise in the number of assigned annuities on this account, and by 1356–7 they totalled £357.[122] Growth continued upwards until a ceiling was reached in 1369–70, when, out of a total charge on the chamberlain's account of some £2,500, over £1,500 was assigned for annuities[123] This was exceptional in that it was a result of the renewal of war between England and France in 1369, and by 1373–4 the figure had fallen to £850.[124] Assignments were also made on the accounts of other Cheshire officials. In 1351 the prince granted the earl of Arundel an annuity of £200 for life, of which £100 was to be the fee farm of Chester (payable by the city sheriffs) while the rest to come out of the revenue of the Dee mills.[125]

Assignment of revenue is, in itself, a sign only of competition for resources and not of any strain in collection of revenue. As far as Cheshire was concerned it meant that the assignees' representatives collected particular items of revenue instead of the prince's officials.[126] Likewise with borrowing: credit was essential if large-scale military expeditions were to be mounted overseas.[127] There is no doubt, however, that the magnitude of the sums required and the urgency with which, at times, they needed to be collected did result in severe strain on the administrative machinery. For example, the assignment of all the revenues of Cheshire and Cornwall to the expenses of the prince's household between 1352 and 1355 showed that even in relatively normal times the prince was finding it difficult to live within his means, and this measure was designed to result, among other things, in stringent control over local expenditure.[128] By the late spring of 1358 the prince's finances were in such desperate straits that Wingfield ordered Delves and Burnham to come to London without delay, telling the chamberlain (Burnham) to bring with him all the money in the county treasury and not to pay any further assignments that year. Those who came to claim assigned revenues were to be told that no further payments could be made because the money had all been spent. Similar instructions were given to the chamberlains of north and south Wales and the receiver of Cornwall. So damaging would the knowledge of this diplomatic lie have been to the prince's credit that strict secrecy had to be enjoined on all the officials in question.[129] In June the following year the chamberlains of Chester and north Wales were told to be sure to collect all the revenues due that midsummer on time because of the prince's 'great need of money for his next overseas expedition'. That this need was both great and difficult to meet is confirmed by the loan of 20,000 marks which Sir John Wingfield had negotiated at that time on the prince's behalf. The creditors included Wingfield himself and others of the prince's friends, and the whole of the prince's appanage in England and Wales was pledged to the loan's repayment.[130] There is no doubt that his credit was now somewhat threadbare. Then again in 1369–70, there followed a partial 'stop' on those annuities assigned to the chamberlain's account: of the twenty-seven payable (worth over £1,500), sixteen were reduced by half, although all the arrears were paid the following year.[131]

Thus a financial straitjacket was put on Cheshire finances in these years which made husbanding of resources very difficult indeed and investment for the future all but impossible. The demands of patronage also entailed the granting of official positions as a reward for service, often for the lifetime of the holder. By 1371 the offices of justiciar, of constable of Chester castle, of steward of Macclesfield and of Longdendale, of bailiff of Drakelow, and hayward of Frodsham had all been disposed of in this way. Moreover a completely new and, as far as can be judged, wholly unnecessary office of 'master forester and surveyor of the Cheshire forests' had been created in 1353 simply to be granted to Sir John Chandos at an annual fee of £53 13s. 4d.[132] Chandos was so well endowed with offices, lands and revenues in Cheshire that he was able to dispense patronage in his turn.[133] A clear example of the subordination of administrative efficiency to the needs of military expenditure and patronage is the case of the lordship of Longdendale. This property comprised two manors, Mottram and Tintwistle, situated on the north-eastern extremity of the county. It had been taken into the prince's hands by the autumn of 1357, probably as the result of an alienation without licence earlier in the century. He retained possession until 1374, when it was restored to the heiress's husband, Sir John Lovel of Titchmarsh. In the decade between 1346 and 1355 we should expect the prince's officials to have made the most of this 'windfall' through vigorous administration and the exploitation of all possible sources of revenue within the lordship. By the early 1360s this was no longer possible. In the receiver's account for 1359–60 Longdendale's total charge was nearly £40, of which only just over £30 was delivered to the chamberlain.[134] In 1361 the lordship was granted on lease to Sir William Carrington, a local knight who had been one of the prince's indentured retainers since 1355. Five years later this lease was cancelled on account of Carrington's 'slowness of payment', an allegation which is fully borne out by the accounts.[135] Despite this, the lease was restored to him for life in 1368, although the payments continued to be just as slow as before.[136]

It is easy to be censorious about the actions of those men, public and private, who have lived in the past. We know so much more about the results of what they did that it is tempting to feel we could have done far better than they. We can see, in startling clearness, that the government of Cheshire was encountering serious problems during the last two decades of the Black Prince's life, problems which came to fruition during the reign of his son, Richard II. I have argued that the roots of this deterioration have to be sought in the wars of Edward I's reign and the political breakdown during that of Edward II. What happened in Cheshire was, in effect, only an extreme case of the problems experienced by the rest of England. Under Edward I the county was still resilient, in that its aggregate wealth based on land was still growing, as was also, presumably, its population. By the time of the Black Prince this was no longer the case, and the financial burdens that were placed on the county must have begun to weigh more heavily on both individuals and their families. Demands for military service were heavy throughout the whole period. During the wars of Welsh conquest it was not uncommon for 1,000 to 2,000 infantry to be required from Cheshire for the king's army.[137] It has long been thought that the reputation which the county's soldiers, particularly the archers, won at this time led them to being employed in such an important role in the Black Prince's French campaigns.[138] It is likely, although difficult to demonstrate, that Cheshire's involvement in warfare over such a long period of time had a deleterious effect on good government, particularly relating to the problem of the behaviour of repatriated soldiers. The behaviour alleged of the anonymous criminal gangs from the county in the parliamentary petitions of Richard II's reign does suggest a close parallel with the activities of the Free Companies which ravaged France in the later fourteenth century, some of the most important of which are known to have had strong Cheshire connections.

Could the royal lords of Cheshire, kings and earls, have adopted different policies from the ones they did? It is difficult to see how they could, given the social and political constraints within which they had to operate. The terrible example of the fate of King Edward II is sufficient to explain why Edward III and his son pursued such a vigorous and expensive foreign policy requiring military involvement. In other words, a king was either a successful war leader or was liable to lose his throne. The history of the revenues of Cheshire directly witnesses to this simple fact. As far as the manor of Macclesfield was concerned, the changes which resulted have been examined in some detail. The rent roll of this lordship grew considerably between 1241 and the end of the century, although the manor's net charge remained stable at about £100 to £110 a year because as rents went up judicial receipts came down.[139] From at least the time of the Black Death, and probably earlier, it was no longer possible to increase rents substantially, and so, as financial pressure increased, success could be achieved only by increasing the judicial revenue. As the net charge rose to figures of between £200 and £250 a year the manor's profits of justice also increased, to between £80 and £110. This was not done by raising entry fines, or through other administrative actions, but by increasing the overall level of fines for serious offences, the only real source that was open to manipulation by the prince's officials. Such increases can have been achieved only by a 'sale' of the prince's judicial authority parallel to the sale of *dominium* which resulted from the leasing of demesnes and the predominant use of patronage in appointments to offices.[140]

Other sources of county revenue show the same factors in operation. In Drakelow manor, for example, its court was charged to yield up to £2 10s. 0d. between 1348 and 1356. In 1359–60 the charge increased to over £3 and reached a peak of nearly £6 in 1361–2, a time when Macclesfield judicial revenue was also high. Other lordships show high points for court receipts: Middlewich's was between 1358 and 1364, Shotwick's between 1360 and 1363. Frodsham manor was leased *en bloc* from 1361 to 1363, but after it came back in hand its judicial profits reached a level, in 1365–6, which was twice as high as the previous maximum.[141] It cannot be mere coincidence that these increases came about at a time when, between the end of the Poitiers expedition and the establishment of the principality of Aquitaine, the prince's need for money was very great indeed.

Naturally, the raising of revenue on this scale depended to a great degree on the acquiescence of the community. It was possible, however, for strong government, stimulated by great financial need, to overstep the mark. The history of Mara-Mondrem forest is probably the best example of how thing could go wrong. This forest's revenue came largely from the earl's demesne pastures and woods within its boundaries, where the local inhabitants could obtain pannage, agistment and supplies of wood. Certain forest townships had customary rights in these areas for which they paid fixed rents, but there was always a demand for the demesnes over and above that.[142] In the early years of the fourteenth century the forest was charged to yield about £60 in a good season.[143] From at least Michaelmas 1349, when the detailed accounts begin, it was the practice to lease the pannage and agistment of the forest, and the result was a total net charge of between £44 and £55. This was collected, as the livery profile shows, quickly and efficiently. By the late 1350s pressure to raise the yield of all revenue sources in Cheshire was very strong, and, in the summer of 1357, Delves and Burnham persuaded Wingfield that much more could be raised from Mara-Mondrem if the leasing of the pannage and agistment were abandoned. They proposed to replace it by putting a legal prohibition on all 'escapes' into the demesnes, and 'escaped' animals found there were to be rounded up by the foresters and taken to a specially constructed pound where they could be redeemed, for a fine, by their owners.[144] This was, in fact, done, but with financially disastrous results. The forest dwellers refused to co-operate, and revenue fell sharply. Consequently the administration had to admit defeat and, in 1359, reverted to the former system.[145] As it was not possible to use the normal forest court (or regard), which was only held, theoretically, every three years, to bolster the ordinary revenue of the forest (the forest eyre was a different matter which has been discussed in the context of taxation), the only alternative left was to raise money from the sale of timber. This could be done in two ways, by selling the prince's own wood (which had previously been almost wholly used for repairs to his own properties) and by granting licences to other landowners in the forest to sell theirs. The survey of 1337 suggests that wood in Mara, but especially in Mondrem, was coming to be in short supply.[146] Sales began to rise in value in the mid-1350s, reached a peak in 1361–2, and then began to decline somewhat, although they remained high in most years. Licences to sell wood were first authorised in the summer of 1361, for which the prince had to be paid one third of the price for which the timber was sold. This expedient was intended to realise large sums of money—£51 was charged in 1364–5—but the sellers put up a spirited resistance to paying for the licences, and so the scheme had to be largely abandoned. Despite such failures, there was a short-term success in that the forest's revenue went up from round £50 in the early 1350s to between £70 and £80 in the 1360s and 1370s. Nevertheless, the social price that had to be paid was high. Stiff communal resistance among the forest inhabitants was provoked, fraud was encouraged among the forest officials (who were already notoriously so inclined), and the low stocks of timber were further depleted.[147] Moreover, as has already been seen with the St. Pierre estates, timber was also much in demand for gifts for the prince's soldiers after Poitiers. Even more serious than all these factors, the tables of revenue in Appendix II show that the attempts to increase the yield gravely damaged the mechanism of collection. Towards the end of the price's life, more and more of the charge of Mara-Mondrem was falling into arrears. In 1373–4, of the total amount paid over by the master forester to the chamberlain, £39 was current issues, £28 was arrears.

Strangely enough, the most important judicial revenue of all within the county, the profits of the county court and the hundred eyres, did not quite conform to the above pattern. The annual sum from these sources, which were collected by the county sheriff, could range widely. It was over £250 in 1302–3 but only £90-odd in 1305–6, for example. The normal range between 1347 and 1374 was from £150 to £250 a year. Charged receipts were, admittedly, on the higher side of this range, between 1357 and 1361, but the peak of over £320 was reached late, in 1371–2.[148] The bulk of this revenue comprised fines before the justiciar 'for releasing the earl's suit', that is, payable by those convicted of serious offences, and such penalties were obviously subject to administrative pressure to increase the revenue. Nevertheless, the supply of captured or repentant criminals may well have been the determining factor here, and that was obviously less amenable to detailed governmental control. The most spectacular rise of all sources of revenue occurred not in the judicial sphere, as it happens, but in the yield of the county's escheator's account. In the early fourteenth century his office had been producing some £60 to £70 a year. This, of course, was the revenue from those landed properties which had been 'seized' by the escheator and were being either leased or managed directly.[149] Between 1349 and 1373 charged escheat revenue rose ninefold. In 1349–50 it was nearly £55, by 1358–9 it had reached £240, and it had broken through to just over £482 in 1372–3.[150] These figures suggest that Delves and Burnham, who were given complete control over the disposal of escheated lands in 1359, were taking literally the injunction to sell them 'as profitably as possible'.[151] In doing so they undoubtedly transformed the administration of escheats and replaced the usual emphasis on patronage with their drive for 'profit'. As wardship, marriages and so on were the main source of general middle-range patronage, it meant that the only way to advancement in the Cheshire of the 1360s was through the prince's military or financial service. There were, moreover, considerable difficulties in collecting the swollen revenues of the sheriff and escheator's offices. Although, in 1373–4, the escheator's total current charge was some £451, the remainder from the previous year was over £400. The remainder on the sheriff's account that year was also high, at £285.[152]

When the late prince's administrators estimated that Cheshire's financial service. There were, moreover, considerable difficulties in were obviously being conservative, since the county had realised twice as much as that, and more, within living memory. Perhaps, though, they were also being realistic. By the end of the fourteenth century Cheshire's finances were on a definite downward trend, a trend which was halted, and even then only temporarily, with the renewed need to help finance the war of Welsh re-conquest of 1403/8.[153] In the short term the prince's financial policies were very effective, but they were ominous for future development, partly because of a shrinking economic base but also because the policies themselves were geared to immediate gain. In August 1359 virtually all capital expenditure on Cheshire was forbidden, although, as we have seen, investment in both government and estates had been small enough in previous decades.[154] Any body of medieval administrators had to subordinate their ideas and policies to those of their employer. The Black Prince's public life was dominated first by the French war and then by the need to hold on to Aquitaine. When he died his policy was in ruins and he and his officials had become the prisoners—not of failure, but of their own administrative success.[155]

NOTES

[1] Michael Prestwich, *War, Politics and Finance under Edward I* (1972), p. 282.

[2] G. L. Harriss, *King, Parliament and Public Finance in Medieval England to 1369* (1975), pp. 49–74, 231–52.

[3] See the writs addressed to Cheshire in August 1379 and July 1380 (*C.C.R.*, 1377–81, pp. 322, 472).

[4] H. D. Harrod, 'A Defence of the Liberties of Chester, 1450', *J.C.N.W.A.S.*, New Series, VIII (1902), pp. 28–32.

[5] Joseph R. Strayer and George Rudishill junior, 'Taxation and Community in Wales and Ireland, 1272–1327', *Speculum*, XXIX (1954), pp. 410–16; Keith Williams-Jones (ed.), *The Merioneth Lay Subsidy Roll, 1292–3*, Univ. of Wales Board of Celtic Studies, History and Law Series XXIX (1976); T. B. Pugh (ed.), *The Marcher Lordships of South Wales, 1415–1536*, Univ. of Wales Board of Celtic Studies History and Law Series XX (1963); Llinos Smith, 'The Arundel Charters to the Lordship of Chirk in the Fourteenth Century', *Bulletin of the Board of Celtic Studies*, 23 (1968–70), pp. 153–66; R. R. Davies, *Lordship and Society in the March of Wales, 1282–1400* (1978), pp. 183–7, 266.

[6] *Ch. Pipe Rolls*, pp. 101–2.

[7] *Ibid.*, pp. 127–8. An earlier scutage, levied in 1186–7, applied only to the

knights of the honour of Chester who held land outside Wales and Cheshire (*ibid.*, pp. 18–19).

[8] *Ibid.*, p. 58.

[9] *Ibid.*, pp. 93, 100. The second period may represent two tallages, one levied in 1250 (applying to Chester, Frodsham, Middlewich, Northwich and Macclesfield) and the other between 1250 and 1254 (applying to all the demesnes except for Frodsham, Darnhall, Over, Weaverham and Rushton, which were pardoned.

[10] See Barraclough, 'Earldom', p. 36.

[11] *C.C.R.*, 1272–9, pp. 250–1.

[12] *C.P.R.*, 1272–81, p. 108.

[13] James F. Willard, 'The Taxes upon Movables of the Reign of Edward 1', *E.H.R.*, XXVIII (1913), p. 518; *Ch. Pipe Rolls*, p. 120. No assessment records for Cheshire survive. In 1281 the justiciar and William Perton were ordered to audit the accounts of the collectors of the fifteenth in Cheshire (*C.P.R.*, 1272–81, p. 434). The audit apparently took place at the abbot of Chester's house in Chester, E.159/55 m. Id.

[14] Willard, *op. cit.*, p. 519.

[15] Williams-Jones, *Merioneth Lay Subsidy*, p. viii; Strayer and Rudishill, 'Taxation', p. 410.

[16] *Ch. Pipe Rolls*, p. 171; *C.P.R.*, 1292–1301, p. 109. Over £200 of the 'fifteenth of the county of Chester' was charged in the account of the keeper of the wardrobe for 1294–5 (Fryde, ed., *Prests*, p. 215).

[17] Strayer and Rudishill, 'Taxation', p. 410.

[18] *C.C.W.*, p. 339.

[19] *C.C.R.*, 1333–7, p. 48; *C.C.R.*, 1337–9, p. 392. A papal tenth was levied on the clergy of the county in 1274 (*C.C.R.*, 1272–9, p. 128), and Cheshire was certainly included in the 1291 valuation of church property known as the Taxation of Pope Nicholas. Moreover, some at least of the county's clergy were included in the grant of a moiety of benefices to the king in 1294 (*C.P.R.*, 1292–1301, p. 123).

[20] Pugh, *Marcher Lordships*, pp. 145–9.

[21] Davies, *Lordship and Society*, pp. 183–7, 266.

[22] Natalie M. Fryde, 'Edward III's Removal of his Ministers and Judges, 1340–1', *B.I.H.R.*, XLVIII (1975), p. 149.

[23] Harriss, *King, Parliament*, pp. 283–4.

[24] *Chamb. Acc.*, pp. 114–18 (supplemented by the original, S.C.6 771/14).

[25] Harriss, *King, Parliament*, pp. 410–6.

[26] *B.P.R.*, I, p. 34; 1,000 marks was granted; D. L. Evans (ed.), *Flintshire Ministers' Accounts, 1328–53*, Flintshire Historical Society, Record Series, 2 (1928), pp. lvii–lviii.

[27] *Ibid.*, p. 67.

[28] *Chamb. Acc.*, p. 122. B. E. Harris in 'The Palatinate 1301–1547', *V.C.H. (Cheshire)*, II, p. 23 suggests that the money from the 1346 grant 'began to flow in' in 1347–8. The account in question is an incomplete draft (see the original, S.C.6 771/15), contains no liveries of money, and cannot be used, therefore, to support such a statement.

[29] For his career see B. H. Putnam, *The Place in Legal History of Sir William Shareshull* (1950); Harriss, *King, Parliament*, pp. 342–3.

[30] Putnam, *Shareshull*, p. 39.

[31] W. N. Bryant, 'The financial dealings of Edward III with the county communities, 1330–1360', *E.H.R.*, LXXXIII (1968), pp. 761–4; J. G. Edwards, 'Taxation and Consent in the Court of Common Pleas', *E.H.R.*, LVII (1942), pp. 473–82. The main difficulty the crown faced in attempting to impose levies of taxation upon individual English counties was that the assembly of the *communitas comitatus*, either in the county court or elsewhere, could not bind those who were not present at its meetings. This problem never seems to have arisen with Cheshire.

[32] Fines totalling £184 were imposed in Wirral forest, £178 in Mara-Mondrem

(*B.P.R.*, III, pp. 8–10; *Chamb. Acc.*, p. 121). The actual collection of the fines proved very difficult.

³³ J. Green, 'Forests', *V.C.H. (Cheshire)*, II, pp. 169–70.

³⁴ For a detailed discussion of the events of this year see P. H. W. Booth, 'Taxation and Public Order: Cheshire in 1353', *Northern History*, XII (1976), pp. 16–31.

³⁵ E. Foss, *The Judges of England*, III (1851), pp. 443–4.

³⁶ Putnam, *Shareshull*, pp. 40, 67.

³⁷ C.53 162 m. 11. The city of Chester made a separate grant of 500 marks in return for a new charter (*Chamb. Acc.*, p. 213).

³⁸ *Chamb. Acc.*, pp. 210–12.

³⁹ *B.P.R.*, III, p. 115. The prince's cousin, the duke of Lancaster, was pardoned the proportion of the common fine pertaining to his Cheshire estates (*Chamb. Acc.*, p. 213).

⁴⁰ *Chamb. Acc.*, p. 247.

⁴¹ *B.P.R.*, III, p.278.

⁴² See pp. 99, 104.

⁴³ S.C.6 802/17 m. 5d.

⁴⁴ For the structure of Macclesfield see above, pp. 92–3.

⁴⁵ S.C.6 772/5 m. 3; S.C.6 772/9 m. 2. Separate grants were again made by the city of Chester, of 201 marks (1368) and 300 marks (1373).

⁴⁶ Harriss, *King, Parliament*, pp. 466–508; P. J. Morgan, 'Cheshire and the Defence of the Principality of Aquitaine', *T.H.S.L.C.*, 128 (1979), pp. 143–4.

⁴⁷ S.C.6 771/21. This account is misdated in *Chamb. Acc.*, pp. 237–43.

⁴⁸ S.C.6 772/3 m. 5, 5d.

⁴⁹ S.C.6 772/5 m. 5d.

⁵⁰ S.C.6 772/10 m. II(1)d.

⁵¹ *Chamb. Acc.*, p. 163.

⁵² Harris, 'Palatinate', p. 24.

⁵³ Evans, *Flintshire Ministers Accounts*, pp. lviii–lix; Harriss, *King, Parliament*, p. 40.

⁵⁴ John Rylands University Library of Manchester Tatton MS 345.

⁵⁵ Harris, 'Palatinate', p. 24; S.C.2 252/1 m. 5.

⁵⁶ It is just about possible, though very unlikely, that the assessment was based on the vanished thirteenth century lay subsidy rolls. There are two possibilities therefore: first, that a new assessment was made for the collection of the grant of £1,000 in 1346; second (and I incline to this), that the list was not made for any specific grant of taxation but was a general county assessment to be used whenever a common payment of any kind had to be raised e.g. for the common fine when a judgement of the county court was reversed on a writ of error in the court of King's Bench, or for the 'mise' for the repair of the Dee bridge, or for the payment known as sheriff's stuth (Ches. 29/37 m. 10; *Sheaf*, Third Series, XVI, 3775; the connection between sheriff's stuth and the assessment is suggested in the figures given in S.C.6 783/1).

⁵⁷ Booth, 'Taxation and Public Order', pp. 23–5.

⁵⁸ James F. Willard, 'The Taxes upon Movables of the Reign of Edward III' *E.H.R.*, XXX (1915), pp. 69–74.

⁵⁹ *Loc. cit.*

⁶⁰ *Lordship and Society*, p. 187.

⁶¹ *C.P.R.*, 1292–1301, p. 109; Williams-Jones, *Merioneth Lay Subsidy*, pp. xxxi–xxxii.

⁶² S.C.6 783/1 m. 2.

⁶³ S.C.6 783/2 m. 4d. *Cf.* the figures for incidence of taxation on particular estates in the late thirteenth century in Edward Miller, 'War, taxation and the English economy in the late thirteenth and early fourteenth centuries', in *War and economic development*, ed. J. M. Winter (1975), pp. 15–16.

⁶⁴ Staffordshire Record Office D(W) 1734/J 2268.

⁶⁵ See above, pp. 57, 61.

⁶⁶ P. H. W. Booth, '"Farming for profit" in the fourteenth century: the Cheshire estates of the earldom of Chester', *J.C.N.W.A.S.*, 62 (1979), pp. 73–90.

⁶⁷ Ches. 33/1 m. 12d.

⁶⁸ *C. Inq. Misc.*, II, pp. 31, 296; *C.P.R.*, 1330–4, p. 191.

⁶⁹ When Sir Thomas Ferrers was granted a lease of the justiciarship it was declared that his rent did not include 'the moors of Rudheath, Overmarsh, Ravensmoor and Hoole Heath and all other places which could be recovered for the lord's soil' (S.C.6 1268/3 No. 5).

⁷⁰ *B.P.R.*, I, p. 37. Nothing worth exploiting seems to have been found at Hoole Heath (near Chester) or Ravensmoor (near Nantwich).

⁷¹ *B.P.R.*, III, p. 32. Moreover, a certain William Boydell was awarded 20 marks for unspecified 'good service' to the prince at the sessions (*ibid.*, p. 37).

⁷² *Chamb. Acc.*, p. 122. Letters dated 5 June 1348 authorised the payment of measurers of Rudheath and Overmarsh, while the riders of the bounds had been paid earlier (2 February 1348) (*Chamb. Acc.*, pp. 125–6).

⁷³ S.C.11 900, 894.

⁷⁴ S.C.11 894 m. 1.

⁷⁵ S.C.11 900 m. 5; S.C.6 801/3 m. 1.

⁷⁶ *B.P.R.*, III, pp. 16, 19.

⁷⁷ S.C.6 801/3 m. 1. Heriots produced a herd of over fifty head of cattle.

⁷⁸ S.C.6 801/4 m. 2. This reduction was granted 'usque mundus melioretur', and was confirmed in 1351 (*B.P.R.*, III, p. 4).

⁷⁹ S.C.6 801/4 m. 1.

⁸⁰ *B.P.R.*, III, p. 48.

⁸¹ S.C.6 784/4 m. 1. The Rudheath tenants in fee also paid no rents until the autumn of 1351, because, it seems, their tenure was in doubt (S.C.6 783/17 m. 6, 6d; *B.P.R.*, III, p. 48). The majority of the Rudheath tenants were, from 1351–2, described as 'tenants-at-will'.

⁸² S.C.6 787/2 m. 1d.

⁸³ S.C.6 801/4 m. 1.

⁸⁴ S.C.6 784/7 m. 8.

⁸⁵ For the financial significance of the leasing of the demesnes see Booth, 'Farming for profit', pp. 88–90.

⁸⁶ *B.P.R.*, III, p. 231.

⁸⁷ S.C.6 785/5 m. 5. £4 6s. 8d. of Overmarsh's rent was alienated to Sir Richard Stafford for life.

⁸⁸ *B.P.R.*, III, p. 473. He was still bailiff twenty-two years later.

⁸⁹ S.C.6 787/4 m. 3d. The extent is lost, but the account shows that the number of tenants in fee was increased while the 'tenants-at-will' were given sixteen-year leases in return for a fine of two years' additional rent.

⁹⁰ A. E. Curry, in 'The Demesne of the County Palatine of Chester in the early Fifteenth Century', Manchester Univ. M.A. thesis (1977), pp. 114–23, shows that although Rudheath seemed to be going against the financial trend in the 1370s a decline set in shortly afterwards which led to the *decasus* reaching 25 per cent early in the following century.

⁹¹ In 1329 he helped bring Cheshire levies back from the Midlands, where they had been deployed by the justiciar, Sir Oliver Ingham, against the rebellious Henry of Lancaster (*C.P.R.*, 1327–30, p. 347). Three years later he was on military service for the king under the earl of Salisbury's command (*C.C.R.*, 1330–3, p. 510; *C.P.R.*, 1330–4, p. 375). In 1347 he served overseas with the earl of Lancaster (*B.P.R.*, I, p. 118).

⁹² Ches. 29/12 m. 6.

⁹³ *B.P.R.*, III, p. 96.

⁹⁴ *Ibid.*, p. 123.

⁹⁵ *C.F.R.*, 1272–1307, p. 350; *C.C.R.V.*, p. 372; *C.Ch.R.*, 1257–1300, p. 279; *C.C.R.*, 1279–88, p. 202.

[96] See Ormerod, *History of Cheshire*, III (1882), p. 522.

[97] *B.P.R.*, III, pp. 61, 69, 71, 98.

[98] S.C.6 783/1–14. For the form of these accounts see above, p. 38.

[99] S.C.6 783/12 m. 1.

[100] *B.P.R.*, III, p. 170.

[101] *Ibid.*, p. 184; S.C.6 783/4 m. 4. A previous attempt at sale had been stopped because the administration had put a reserve price of 1,000 marks on the wood and this could not be achieved (*B.P.R.*, III, p. 175).

[102] S.C.6 783/4 m. 4.

[103] *B.P.R.*, III, pp. 503, 553 (under 'Bickley' and 'Peckforton').

[104] *Ibid.*, p. 273.

[105] *Tout*, V, p. 373.

[106] *B.P.R.*, III, p. 457. Delves's action was against the prince's feoffees-to-uses, to whom the property had been transferred some time earlier.

[107] Ormerod, *History of Cheshire*, III, p. 522. The account given here differs on a number of important points from what is otherwise known from record sources.

[108] *B.P.R.*, III, p. 457.

[109] The progress of the case is recorded in a group of six letters copied on a piece of paper which was inserted into volume III of the Cheshire register (*B.P.R.*, III, pp. 487–8).

[110] S.C.6 786/5 m. 7d; S.C.6 783/12. The lease was granted on preferential terms, presumably as compensation for his delay in receiving the benefits of the judgement.

[111] S.C.6 783/14 m. 1.

[112] Morgan, 'Cheshire and the defence of Aquitaine', pp. 143–5.

[113] See *B.P.R.*, III, p. 368; *B.P.R.*, IV, p. 421; S.C.6 786/9; *C.C.R.*, 1364–8, p. 378.

[114] See above, pp. 67–70.

[115] Booth, 'Taxation and Public Order', pp. 28–31.

[116] *C.P.R.*, 1272–81, p. 6; *C.C.R.*, 1272–9, p. 141.

[117] 'Cheshire and the defence of Aquitaine', p. 144.

[118] Harriss, *King, Parliament*, pp. 332–3.

[119] *B.P.R.*, I, pp. 4, 66, 122.

[120] See Harriss, *King, Parliament*, p. 217, and 'Preference at the Medieval Exchequer', *B.I.H.R.*, XXX (1957), pp. 17–40. Assignment of an annuity to Sir Robert Crevequer, Reginald Grey's agent and Constable of Beeston castle between 1279 and 1301, was made on the Dee mills in 1289, and was paid until 1301, thus showing that this practice was not unknown in thirteenth century Cheshire (*C.P.R.*, 1281–92, p. 328).

[121] *Chamb. Acc.*, pp. 129, 166.

[122] *Ibid.*, p. 153.

[123] S.C.6 772/5 m. 5.

[124] S.C.6 772/9 m. 3; J. W. Sherbourne, 'The Cost of English Warfare with France in the later Fourteenth Century', *B.I.H.R.*, L (1977), pp. 135–50.

[125] *B.P.R.*, III, p. 52. A later grant to the earl was a conditional one as security for the performance of the marriage settlement between the prince's stepson and Arundel's daughter (*ibid.*, pp. 480–1). In 1356 the revenue from the Drakelow demesnes and £40 of the rent of Rudheath was assigned to Sir John Chandos for life (*ibid.*, p. 231), while two years later Sir Richard Stafford was granted Northwich town for life, together with the lordship of Hopedale in Flintshire and £7 6s. 8d. a year rent from Overmarsh, (*ibid.*, pp. 323–4). Finally, Middlewich was granted for life to two of the prince's esquires in 1370 (S.C.6 787/2 m. 1).

[126] See E. B. Fryde, 'Materials for the study of Edward III's credit operations, 1327–48, Part III', *B.I.H.R.*, XXIII (1950), pp. 8–9.

[127] It is all but impossible to quantify the extent of the prince's borrowings between 1355 and 1371 because of the loss of his household financial records. The

earl of Arundel appears to have been his largest creditor and to have furnished him with at least £5,500 between 1359 and 1365 (*B.P.R.*, III, pp. 354, 449; *B.P.R.*, IV, p. 550; K. B. McFarlane, *The Nobility of later Medieval England* (1973), pp. 88–91). Very many loans are recorded to the prince in *B.P.R.*, IV, and in the 1350s the lenders ranged from the king to ordinary merchants.

[128] See above, pp. 65, 76.

[129] *B.P.R.*, III, p. 301. The background to this 'stop' of assignment was the military expedition of 1359–60 which was being planned, and which led to a second visit by the prince to Cheshire in the autumn of 1358 with the same declared intention as in 1353 (i.e. of restoring order to the county). *Ibid.*, pp. 307–23.

[130] *Ibid.*, p. 438; *B.P.R.*, IV, p. 326. Edward III had to do the same, when particularly badly in need of money (E. B. Fryde, 'Materials . . . Part I', *B.I.H.R*, XXII (1949), p. 121.)

[131] S.C.6 772/5 m. 5.

[132] S.C.6 772/6 m. 1d; 787/2 m. 1d; 772/5 m. 4d; 787/2 m. 1d, 4, 4d.

[133] *B.P.R.*, III, p. 473.

[134] S.C.6 802/17 m. 5.

[135] P. H. W. Booth, J. H. and S. A. Harrop (eds), *The Extent of Longdendale, 1360*, Cheshire Sheaf, Fifth Series (1976–7), item 57. By 1365–6 Carrington's arrears were nearly £30 (S.C.6 803/12 m. 3).

[136] S.C.6 804/1 m. 3d. Carrington was to pay himself his retaining fee of £26 13s. 4d. out of his farm and hand over the rest to the chamberlain.

[137] J. E. Morris, *The Welsh Wars of Edward I* (1901), pp. 96, 128, 131, 209; H. J. Hewitt, *Cheshire under the three Edwards* (1967), p. 99.

[138] Hewitt, *Edwards*, pp. 101–3. It is a less well known fact that considerable numbers of troops from Cheshire were required to serve in Scotland: 1298 (1,000 men), 1300, 1308 (400 men), 1317 (500 men), 1322 (1,000 men), 1332 (300 men), 1333 (500 men). *Ibid.*, p. 99, and *C.C.R.*, 1313–18, p. 563, *C.P.R.*, 1321–4, p. 177, *C.P.R.*, 1330–4, p. 359, *C.C.R.*, 1333–7, p. 23.

[139] See Appendix II (a).

[140] See above, pp. 77. P. H. W. Booth, 'Taxation and Public Order', pp. 28–9, and 'Farming for Profit in the Fourteenth Century', pp. 89–90.

[141] See Appendix II (d).

[142] J. Green, 'Forests', *V.C.H.* (*Cheshire*), II, pp. 175–8. See Appendix II (c).

[143] *Chamb. Acc.*, pp. 2–4.

[144] *B.P.R.*, III, p. 273.

[145] S.C.6 787/4 m. 2.

[146] S.C.12 22/96.

[147] Richard Ercall, the prince's master carpenter, was responsible for selling the prince's timber and was unable to resist the temptation to convert some of the profit to his own use (S.C.6 786/1 m. 4).

[148] S.C.6 787/4 m. 4, 4d.

[149] *Chamb. Acc.*, pp. 3, 17, 39.

[150] *Chamb. Acc.*, p. 156, S.C.6 785/3 m. 4, S.C.6 787/5 m. 6–7d. Flintshire escheats, in fact, added very little to these totals.

[151] See above, p. 79.

[152] S.C.6 787/7 m. 4–5.

[153] Curry, thesis, p. 175.

[154] *B.P.R.*, III, p. 365.

[155] See J. R. Maddicott, *The English Peasantry and the Demands of the Crown, 1294–1341*, Past and Present, Supplement 1, Oxford, 1975, for, a recent statement of the relationships between government policy and the economic history of the first half of the fourteenth century.

APPENDIX I

CHIEF ACCOUNTANTS OF CHESHIRE, 1270/1374

(Justiciars in capitals and chamberlains in lower-case)

Name of accountant	Term of office	Accounts	References	Type of payment	Total charge £ s. d.
SIR REGINALD GREY (1)	June 1270–16 Oct. 1274	1. 1272–3	Ch.P.R., pp. 108–10	F	533 6 8
		2. 1273–4	"	F	799 15 10¼
SIR GUNCELIN BADLESMERE	16 Oct. 1274–14 Nov. 1281[1]	1. 1274–5	pp. 111–14	I	774 6 4
		2. 1275–6	pp. 116–20	I	695 11 2
		3. 1276–7	pp. 121–7	I	728 14 4
Leo / Leo's son	c. 1276/ c. 1281[2]	4. 1277–8*	pp. 133–6	I	706 7 6
		5. 1278–9*	"	I	682 18 10
		6. 1279–80*	"	I	
		7. 1280–1	ACCOUNT MISSING	–	
SIR REGINALD GREY (2)	14 Nov. 1281–22 Oct. 1299	1. 1281–2	Ch.P.R., pp. 145–6	(F)	(666 13 4)[3]
		2. 1282–24 June 1283	"	(F)	(Half-year)[3]
		3. 24 June 1283–Mich. 1283	pp. 148–50	(F)	(Half-year)[4]
		4. 1283–4	pp. 150–1	F	(666 13 4)[5]
		5. 1284–5[6]	"	F	523 13 4
		6. 1285–6[6]		F	"
		7. 1286–7[6]	pp. 153–7	F	"
		8. 1287–8[6]	"	F	"
		9. 1288–9[6]		F	"
		10. 1289–90[6]		F	"
		11. 1290–1[6]		F	"
		12. 1291–2[7]		F	485 1 4
		13. 1292–3[7]		F	"
		14. 1293–4[7]		F	"
		15. 1294–5[7]	pp. 159–72	F	"
		16. 1295–6[7]	"	F	"
		17. 1296–7[7]		F	"
		18. 1297–8[7]		F	"
		19. 1298–9[8]		F	"
SIR RICHARD MASCY	22 Oct. 1299–12 April 1301	1. 1299–1300	pp. 175–8	F	666 13 4
		2. 1300–12 Apr. 1301	"	F	(333 6 8)[9]

In king's hands (note against the Grey (2) accounts group)

Name of accountant	Term of office		Accounts	References	Type of payment	Total charge £ s. d.
William Melton	12 April 1301–1304	In earl's hands	1. 12 Apr. 1301–Mich. 1301	Ch.P.R., pp. 193–216	I	999 14 4¼[1]
			2. 1301–2	Ch.A., pp. 1–14	I	1,198 15 8[10]
			3. 1302–3	,, pp. 15–27	I	1,282 16 4
			4. 1303–4	,, pp. 38–46	I	1,113 6 3¼[11]
Hugh Leominster	1304/c. 1307		1. 1304–5	ACCOUNT MISSING	(I)	–
			2. 1305–6	Ch.A., pp. 76–77	I	977 12 7
			3. 1306–7	ACCOUNT MISSING	–	–
SIR ROBERT HOLLAND (1)	1307/24 Oct. 1309	In King's hands	1. 1307–8	,,	F	666 13 4[12]
			2. 1308–9	,,	F	,,
SIR PAYN TIPTOFT	24 Oct. 1309–26 Dec. 1311		1. 1309–10	,,	F	666 13 4[13]
			2. 1310–11[14]	,,	F	,,
SIR ROBERT HOLLAND (2)	26 Dec. 1311–Nov. 1312		1. 1311–12	,,	F	(666 13 4)[15]
Stephen Cheshunt	Dec. 1312–June 1315	In earl's hands	1. Dec. 1312–1313	Ch.A., pp. 78–82	I	864 7 0[16]
			2. 1313–14	ACCOUNT MISSING	(I)	–
			3. 1314–June 1315	,,	(I)	–
(Walter) Fulborn	June 1315–Mich. 1315		1. June 1315–Mich. 1315	Ch. A, pp. 83–8	I	668 2 8¾
(William Burstow)	1315–26 May 1320		1. 1315–16	ACCOUNT MISSING	(I)[17]	–
			2. 1316–17	,,	(I)[17]	–
			3. 1317–18	,,	(I)[17]	–
			4. 1318–19	,,	(I)[17]	–
			5. 1319–26 May 1320	,,	(I)[17]	–
Richard Bury	26 May 1320/c. 1324[18]		1. 26 May–Mich. 1320	Ch.A., pp. 89–94	I	450 5 4¾
			2. 1320–1	ACCOUNT MISSING	I	–
			3. 1321–2	,,	(I)	–
(SIR OLIVER INGHAM (1))	30 March 1322[19]–May 1325		4. 1322–3	E.159 106 m. 130d	–	–
			5. 1323–4	ACCOUNT MISSING	–	–

Escheator / keeper	Period of office		Account year	Reference		£	s.	d.
William Easington	c. 1324/ 17 Dec. 1326	*In king's hands*	1. 1324–5	ACCOUNT MISSING	–	–	–	–
			2. 1325–6	*Ch.A.*, pp. 95–9	I	–	–	–
			3. 1326 Mich.–17 Dec.	S.C.6 1268/4 (file two), E.159 106 m. 130d	I	–	–	–
John Paynel (1)	17 Dec. 1326–		1. 17 Dec. 1326–7	E.372 174 rot. 44	I	1,188	8	5
Thomas Blaston	7 Mar. 1328		2. 1327–13 Mar. 1328	,, ,,	I	313	1	3¼
	7 Mar.–29 Nov. 1328		1. 7 Mar.–Mich. 1328	E.372 174 rot. 47	I	923	19	4¼
			2. Mich.–29 Nov. 1328	,, ,,	I	83	7	6
SIR OLIVER INGHAM (2)	29 Nov. 1328–		1. 29 Nov. 1328–1329	ACCOUNT MISSING	F[19]	666	13	4
Simon Rugeley (1)	23 Oct. 1330		2. 1329–23 Oct. 1330	,, ,,	F	666	13	4
	23 Oct.– 25 Dec. 1330		1. 23 Oct.–25 Dec. 1330	E.372 176 rot. 50	I	–	–	–
John Paynel (2)	25 Dec. 1330–		1. 25 Dec. 1330–1331	E.372 177 rot. 41	I	1,085	11	8
Simon Rugeley (2)	17 Sep. 1332[20]		2. 1331–17 Sep. 1332	*Ch.A.*, pp. 109–10	I	689	15	10½
	17 Sep. 1332–		1. 17 Sep. 1332–1333	ACCOUNT MISSING	(I)[21]	–	–	–
	17 Sep. 1335		2. 1333–4	,, ,,	(I)	–	–	–
			3. 1334–17 Sep. 1335	,, ,,	(I)	–	–	–
John Paynel (3)	17 Sep. 1335– 1336	*Revenue for king's sons' use*	1. 17 Sep.–Mich. 1335	*Ch.A.*, pp. 111–13[22]	I	314	11	1½
SIR HENRY FERRERS (1)	1336–15 March 1341[23]		2. 1335–6	,, ,,	F	1,097	2	0¾
			1. 1336–7	S.C.6 1268/3 (No. 3)	F	1,200	0	0
			2. 1337–8	,,	F	,,	,,	,,
			3. 1338–9	,,	F	,,	,,	,,
			4. 1339–40	,,	F	(600	0	0)[24]
			5. 1340–14 Feb. 1341	,,	F	(,,)		
(Cheshire seized into the king's hands, 15 March 1341–31 March 1342)								
SIR HENRY FERRERS (2)	31 Mar. 1342– 1343[26]	*In earl's hands*	1. 31 Mar. 1342–1343	S.C.6 1268/3 (No. 3)	F	1,333	6	8[25]
SIR THOMAS FERRERS	1343[26]– 18 July 1353		1. 1343–4	S.C.6 1268/3 (No. 5)	F	1,333	6	8
			2. 1344–5	,,	F	,,	,,	,,
			3. 1345–6	,,	(F)	(,,)		[27]

Name of accountant	Term of office		Accounts	References	Type of payment	Total charge £ s. d.
Master John Burnham, jr	c. 1346/70		1. 1346-7	ACCOUNT MISSING	(I)	–
			2. 1347-8	Ch.A., pp. 119-27[28]	I	–
			3. 1348-9	ACCOUNT MISSING	(I)	
			4. 1349-50	Ch.A, pp. 128-31	I	(£1,018 11 8½)[29]
			5. 1350-1	", pp. 159-70	I	£1,404 16 11[30]
			6. 1351-2	ACCOUNT MISSING	(I)	–
			7. 1352-3	ACCOUNT MISSING	I	–
			8. 1353-4	Ch.A, pp. 206-19	I	(£2,943 2 10)[31]
			9. 1354-5	", pp. 220-31	I	£2,744 12 0
			10. 1355-6	ACCOUNT MISSING	(I)	–
			11. 1356-7	Ch.A., pp. 237-43	I	(£2,522 5 5)[32]
			12. 1357-8	ACCOUNT MISSING	(I)	–
			13. 1358-9	Ch.A., pp. 244-57	I	£2,556 15 2[33]
			14. 1359-60	", pp. 258-76	I	£2,397 18 1½
		In earl's hands	15. 1360-1	S.C.6 772/1, 2	I	£2,180 16 10
			16. 1361-2	S.C.6 772/3, 4	I	£2,378 4 8
			17. 1362-3	ACCOUNT MISSING	(I)	–
			18. 1363-4	"	(I)	–
			19. 1364-5	"	(I)	–
			20. 1365-6	"	(I)	–
			21. 1366-7	"	(I)	–
			22. 1367-8	"	(I)	–
			23. 1368-9	"	(I)	–
			24. 1369-70[34]	S.C.6 772/5	I	(£2,026 11 1)[35]
Robert Paris	1370/17		1. 1370-1	S.C.6 772/6, 7	I	£1,417 0 11
			2. 1371-2	ACCOUNT MISSING	I	–
			3. 1372-3	S.C.6 772/8	I	(£1,766 16 8)
	July 1374		4. 1373-17 July 1374	S.C.6 772/9	I[36]	

John Wodehouse	17 July 1374–3 June 1394	In earl's hands		S.C.6 772/10	I[36]
			1. 17 July 1374–Mich. 1374	ACCOUNT MISSING	(I)
			2. 1374–5	" "	(I)
			3. 1375–6	" "	(I)
			4. 1376–7	" "	(I)

Key
* Revenue assigned to Vale Royal
Ch.P.R. Ch. Pipe Rolls
Ch.A. Chamb. Acc.
F FARM
I ISSUES

NOTES

[1] In January 1311 reference was made to the possibility that Sir Bartholomew Badlesmere should account for the time when his father, Guncelin, was justiciar of Chester. If he should not do so, the royal exchequer rolls were to be inspected to see what Guncelin's annual charge had been, and to see whether a fourteenth or fifteenth had been levied at that time and how much it had yielded. (*C.C.W.*, p. 339.) At the end of his account for 1276–7 Guncelin had left a 'debet' of £363 12s. 1d. In April 1277 Ralph de Basages (king's clerk) claimed that Guncelin had paid him 500 marks by letters patent, plus a further 200. (*C.P.R.*, 1272–81, p. 190; *C.A.C.W.*, pp. 67–8.) In October 1274 he had been granted the sum of £66 13s. 4d. as a fee out of the issues of his bailiwick (*C.P.R.*, 1272–81, p. 60).

[2] In December 1277 Edward I ordered all the issues of Cheshire up to 1,000 marks (a year) to be paid to the abbey of Vale Royal, and on 10 January 1278 Leo son of Leo was granted the chamberlainship for this purpose. (*Ch. Pipe Rolls*, p. 137.) In 1315 it was reported that Leo had acted as chamberlain in the sixth, seventh, eighth and tenth years of Edward I (1277–80, 1281–2). (*C.C.R.*, 1313–18, p. 158.)

[3] When his accounts for 1283–4 were audited, Grey claimed that he should not have to account for his farm for Michaelmas 1281–24 June 1283 because of the Welsh war, and as a result he had the king's permission to account in the wardrobe as approver. His approver's accounts survive as follows:

1. *1281–2.* E.101 505/32 m. 1 (Part One): total charge, £661 3s. 4d.; net charge, £169 3s. 4d.
2. *1282–24 June 1283.* E.101 505/32 m. 1 (Part Two): total charge, £284 5s. 2d.; net charge appears to have been nil.

[4] Grey also accounted for this half-year as approver (*Ch. Pipe Rolls*, pp. 147–50). Total charge, £292 0s. 0d.; net charge, £257 13s. 4d.

[5] Grey's farm was reduced to 785½ marks (£523 13s. 4d.) a year because of various losses. Of this, he paid £724, including arrears, over for the building works at Vale Royal.

[6] By far the greatest part of Grey's farm in these years (over 2,600 marks in all) was spent on the Vale Royal works, plus £800 on works at Chester castle. At the end of this period he had a *superplusagium* of £361-odd. On 17 November 1281 he had been ordered to pay his farm to the abbot of Vale Royal, for works, until further notice. (*C.P.R.*, 1279–81, p. 465.) This assignment was repeated in October 1283 (*C.P.R.*, 1281–92, p. 82). In 1285 a respite of all Grey's debts was ordered (E. 159/58 m. 10).

[7] Grey's farm was further reduced by £38 12s. 0d. a year 'in eight out of nine years' because of reduction in revenue. (*C.P.R.*, 1281–92, p. 172.) In the period 1291–8 £451 was spent on Vale Royal, while £400 was delivered to the exchequer (*not* £4,000, as in *Ch. Pipe Rolls*, p. 173). War provisions accounted for a considerable part of the rest of his charge. On 16 April 1292, Grey had been ordered to pay up to £1,000 out of his farm to the works of Vale Royal (*C.C.R.*, 1288–96, p. 227). By 1305 £549 had still not been paid, and the exchequer assigned it elsewhere because of the grant of the county to Prince Edward (*C.C.R.*, 1302–7, p. 247).

[8] At the end of his period of office Grey's 'debet' was £594 19s. 0½d. In 1300 he was allowed to pay this off at £20 a year, and one cancelled payment is charged in the 1301–2 chamberlain's account (it is omitted in the published text, but see S.C.6 771/1 m. 1). No subsequent payment of this attermination is recorded, and it looks as if Grey was pardoned (*C.F.R.*, 1272–1307, p. 426). The particulars of Grey's account for this year are in S.C.6 1268/3 (roll one). But see E. 159/80 m. 8d.

[9] This half-year's farm appears in the first account of William Melton, as chamberlain of Prince Edward (*Ch. Pipe Rolls*, p. 193). Masey still owed £19 8s. 11½d. arrears of the farm of the justiciarship in 1338 (*C.P.R.*, 1338–40, p. 31).

[10] Receipts of Flintshire, foreign receipts and arrears excluded henceforth.

[11] Melton's last account left him with a 'debet' of £424 12s. 2¼d.

[12] S.C.6 1268/3 (2) may possibly be Holland's account for 1307–8. Only expenses can be read, and there is no balance or liveries. He was appointed farmer, 1 October 1307 (C.F.R., 1307–19, p. 5). In June 1309 £200 of Holland's arrears and farm were assigned to the Circuli Albi of Florence (C.P.R., 1307–13, p. 121).

[13] C.F.R., 1307–19, p. 50. On 19 December 1311 Holland was granted 1,000 marks out of the farm of Cheshire in recompense for his loss of the justiciarship: it seems that this grant may not have taken effect. (C.P.R., 1307–13, p. 411.)

[14] In the exannual roll of the exchequer for 1338–9 Tiptoft is recorded as owing £161 14s. 7½d. arrears of his farm of the justiciarship of Chester for Michaelmas–26, December 1311 (E.207 2/3). Tiptoft's farm was increased to £1,000 a year on 19 December 1311 (C.F.R., 1307–19, p. 121) but it is unlikely that this order took effect.

[15] C.F.R., 1307–19, p. 122. Holland's farm was increased to £1,000 a year on 23 January 1312 (ibid., p. 124). It was remitted to him, 'for good service', on the same day (C.C.R., 1328–30, pp. 508–9). In a report made in 1337 on the king's debts in Cheshire it was stated that Holland had owed unspecified arrears of his farm of the justiciarship for 1307–8, 1308–9 and 1311–12 (C.260 48/39), and in the enrolment version of this same report these debts are given as £333 11s. 11¼d. (C.P.R., 1338–40, p. 31). Holland served a third term as justiciar, but not as farmer, c. 1319–c. January 1322.

[16] It is not clear whether this figure includes arrears (S.C.6 771/7 m. 1).

[17] Burstow rendered issues for at least part of this period, since he later complained that the lord Edward's auditors had unjustly charged him with £4 1s. 7¼d. (Ches. 29/35 m. 3). A royal exchequer inquiry, January 1321, found that he owed £190–odd (E. 159/94 m. 96d). Later proceedings reduced this further, to £110 (E. 159/95 m. 70, 70d, 71) and the debt was finally pardoned.

[18] Bury was pardoned the arrears of his account as chamberlain, for good service, March 1330 (C.P.R., 1327–30, p. 505).

[19] Ingham was appointed justiciar (but not farmer) 28 February 1328 (C.P.R. 1327–30, p. 242). On 29 November he was made farmer, for life (C.F.R., 1327–37, p. 113). He had already served one term as justiciar (1322/5). It is unlikely that he ever accounted as farmer, as demonstrated by the exchequer Bille file (E.207 2/3), where, on the basis of the pipe rolls of 1348–9 and 1345–6, it was stated that he owed £2,978 3s. 6d. arrears of the farm of the justiciarship of Chester from before 1333 and, on the basis of the 1336–7 pipe roll, that he owed 5,000 marks arrears of the same farm for 29 November 1328–1333 (at 1,000 marks a year). This last sum is confirmed by the report on the king's Cheshire debts of 1337 (C.160 48/39 and C.P.R., 1338–40, p. 31). As there are extant chamberlains' accounts for the years 1330/3, it is possible that Ingham also farmed the county between 1322 and 1325. He was pardoned all his debts due to the king, including those as justiciar, 15 July 1337 (C.P.R., 1334–8, p. 467), and this pardon was confirmed by the Black Prince in respect of Ingham's heirs in 1351, when £1,058 8s. 4d. was still outstanding. (B.P.R., III, p. 32.)

[20] At the end of his term Paynel claimed to have a superplusagium of £137 8s. 4d. on his account. In 1337, in the list of king's debts, he was charged with a 'debet' of £393 0s. 0¼d. as chamberlain, and as a result his rectory of Rostherne was sequestered. (C.260 48/39; C.P.R., 1338–40, p. 31.) This 'debet' was confirmed by a scrutiny of the accounts which was made in 1342, based on the Memoranda Roll of Trinity, 1332; however, as Paynel had made liveries of £601 3s. 6d. on the visus of his account, he actually had a superplusagium, as stated above, for which he said he had received satisfaction from the Lord Edward. (C.260 53/27.) A further scrutiny in the rolls revealed two other 'debets' of his:

1. Remainder of his account, 17 December 1326–13 March 1328: £47 15s. 2d.
2. Victuals bought for Flint castle: £13 19s. 8½d.

See also *Rot. Parl.*, II, p. 316.

[21] *C.F.R.*, 1327–37, p. 326.
[22] See also original, S.C.6 771/13 m. 2.
[23] The king ordered the seizure of Cheshire on 14 February 1341 (*C.F.R.*, 1337–47, p. 214) and the seizure was actually made good on 15 March 1341. The county was returned to Ferrers at Easter (31 March) 1342. (S.C.6 1268/3 No. 3.)
[24] Ferrers's account for 1336–15 March 1341 was rendered, after his death, by his executor, Sir Thomas Ferrers, through the latter's attorneys, John Pirie and John Goloneys (king's clerk). Pirie had been chamberlain, 1337/41 and had 'received the prince's debts when Henry Ferrers was farmer' (*B.P.R.*, I, p. 134). Liveries were made on this account as follows:

1. 1336–7   £1,000
2. 1337–8   £1,000
3. 1338–9   £1,000
4. 1339–40   £750
5. 1340–14 February 1341 £500

£300 of the subsequent arrears of £1,150 was pardoned and, after various other allowances £405 12s. 0½d. remained.
[25] During this year John Burnham junior (possibly already chamberlain) accounted as receiver of the issues of the fines and debts not included in Ferrers's farm (*Chamb. Acc.*, pp. 114–8). His total charge was £385 19s. 11½d. (see S.C.6 771/14 m. 1). This second account for Ferrers's farm was rendered, once again, by Thomas Ferrers as his executor (S.C.6 1268/3 No. 5).
[26] It is not clear exactly when Sir Thomas succeeded Sir Henry as justiciar-farmer of Chester. Sir Henry was dead by 16 September 1343 (*C.F.R.*. 1337–47, p. 324).
[27] The last of Sir Thomas's accounts as farmer to survive is a *visus* which covers the period up to Christmas 1345 (S.C.6 1268/3 No. 5). A note at the end of this *visus* states that he retained the farm until Michaelmas 1346, when he rendered it into the prince's hands, and, while he retained the post of justiciar, John Burnham junior subsequently accounted for the issues, as chamberlain.
[28] This account, although in good condition, is incomplete and is probably only a draft. It contains no heading, total receipts, liveries or final balance.
[29] Includes issues of Flintshire.
[30] See also S.C.6 771/17. The total charge has been calculated by subtracting Cheshire and Flintshire arrears and Flintshire receipts from the total charge.
[31] This figure has been calculated by subtracting both foreign and Flintshire receipts (S.C.6 771/18 m. 7). Very likely it includes arrears.
[32] Calculated as in note 31. Liveries to the receiver-general totalled £1,899 11s. 11d. (S.C.6 771/21 m. 5d). The date of this account has been ascertained by comparing figures with the Macclesfield account for 1356–7 (S.C.6 802/13).
[33] Calculated from S.C.6 771/22. Liveries to the receiver-general totalled £2,233 3s. 1¾d.
[34] Burnham's last account is decayed. It is not clear when he died, but as his last recorded livery was on 22 February 1371 it is likely that his death occurred between that date and the annual audit, which probably took place in the spring.
[35] Calculated by deducting Flintshire receipts from sum total, and thus it includes Cheshire and Flintshire arrears.
[36] In these two accounts it is not possible to distinguish arrears from current receipts. By subtracting the Flintshire receipts and arrears from the total for the two years, the sum £2,258 2s. 10d. is calculated, which includes Cheshire arrears.

APPENDIX II

(a) MACCLESFIELD REVENUES, 1182/1376
(Fractions of pence are ignored in these tables)

Year of account	1182-3	1183-4	1184-5	1237-8 (Aug.–Aug.)	1238-9 (Aug.–Aug.)	1239-40 (Aug.–Jan.)	1240 (Mar.–Dec.)	1240-1 (Dec.–Dec.)
	£ s. d.	£ s. d.	£ s. d.	£ s. d.	£ s. d.	£ s. d.	£ s. d.	£ s. d.
Assize rents	19 14 0 (farm)	20 0 0 (farm)	20 0 0 (farm)	20 15 1	21 2 1	(13 1 4)	(21 14 7)	22 6 6
Mills (farms)				12 13 4	13 6 8	(6 13 4)	(14 6 8)	15 6 8
Market and fair tolls				6 3 0	6 0 2	(7 0 4)	(15 16 1)	10 4 1
Demesne pastures				8 17 10	8 14 0	(4 6 2)	(31 7 4)	21 12 6
Judicial revenue				45 11 11	46 7 3	(6 5 2)	(34 2 2)	22 5 8
Miscellaneous (including sale of stock)				16 0 0[1]	18 2 2[2]	(1 5 1)	(2 11 5)	2 11 5
Net charge				110 1 2	113 12 4	(38 11 5)	(119 18 3)	94 6 10
Liveries of money	—	—	—	—	—	—	—	—
References	Ch. Pipe Rolls p. 9	Ibid., p. 12	Ibid., p. 13	Ibid., pp. 35–6	Ibid., p. 44	Ibid., p. 51	Ibid., p. 56	Ibid., pp. 65–6

Year of Account	1245–6 (Oct.–Oct.)	1247–8	1286–7	1296–7	1297–8	1298–9	1304–5
	£ s. d.	£ s. d.	£ s. d.	£ s. d.	£ s. d.	£ s. d.	£ s. d.
Assize rents			—	57 19 0	57 19 0	58 10 5	58 0 6
Decasus			—	(0 15 6)	(0 6 4)	(0 2 6)	
Mills (farms)	104 14 7 (farm)	143 0 10 (farm)		23 6 8	23 6 8	23 6 8	34 13 4
Market and fair tolls				5 4 4	7 12 6	9 14 3	31 13 8
Demesne pastures				4 5 1	11 6 0	5 17 4	11 3 7
Judicial revenue			—	10 2 6	9 8 6	29 16 6	5 6 10
Miscellaneous (including sale of stock)			—	23 10 0[3]	15 8 5[3]	7 10[3]	2 0 0
Net charge			—	99 14 3	104 12 11	118 17 4	(142 17 11)
Expenses				(23 17 11)	(20 1 10)	(23 13 2)	
Liveries of money			110 0 0	—	—	—	—
References	*Ibid.*, p. 87	*Ibid.*, p. 92	S.C.6 1089/22	E.372	146 rot.	33 m. 1, 2.	S.C.6 1186/1

Year of Account	1307–8			1329 (Aug.–Sep.)			1329–30			1330–1[6]			1347 (Sept.–Dec.)			1348 (Mar.–Mich.)			1348–9		
	£	s.	d.	£	s.	d.	£	s.	d.	£	s.	d.	£	s.	d.	£	s.	d.	£	s.	d.
Assize rents	65	6	0	(60	16	7)	77	19	9	77	19	11	(2	11	6)	(76	2	5)	84	6	0
Decasus		–		(3	3	7)	(2	18	9)	(3	3	3)		–		(1	1	6)	(2	10	1)
Mills (farms)	34	6	8	(8	5	0)	35	13	4	35	13	3		–		(30	17	4)	30	17	4
Market and fair tolls	10	4	5		–		9	18	0	5	1	6	(1	1	0)	(6	7	6)	6	12	3)
Demesne pastures	8	5	8	(17	0	0)	12	0	11	11	0	3	(6	1	7)	(23	13	4)	35	8	6
Judicial revenue	17	18	4	(0	1	0)	20	2	5	5	1	0	(8	7	5)	(144	0	3)[7]	162	15	4[9]
Miscellaneous (including sale of stock)	4	7	0		–		18	9	4	28	6	8	(1	0	0)		–		22	17	0[10]
Net charge	131	3	6	(82	9	10)[5]	169	1	0	115	6	3	(13	5	4)	(244	3	7)	291	19	11
Expenses	(9	4	7)	(0	9	1)	(2	4	0)	(44	3	1)	(5	16	1)[8]	(35	15	9)[8]	(48	6	5)
Liveries of money		–			–			–			–		(4	0	0)		–		121	1	7[11]
References	E.372 164 rot. 34			S.C.6 802/1			S.C.6 802/1			S.C.6 802/1; 1297/1			S.C.6 1297/3			S.C.6 802/2			S.C.6 802/4		

Year of Account	1350–1[11]			1353–4			1354–5			1356–7			1358–9			1359–60[19]			1360–1			1361–2		
	£	s.	d.	£	s.	d.	£	s.	d.	£	s.	d.	£	s.	d.	£	s.	d.	£	s.	d.	£	s.	d.
Assize rents	86	1	10	82	3	8[14]	78	19	11	79	1	1	79	19	0	80	14	5	80	19	7	↓		
Decasus	(4	2	11)	(3	3	7)	(1	14	10)	(1	11	2)	(1	9	10)	(←		)	(1	10	10)	(0	17	2)
Mills (farms)	21	18	10	20	13	4[14]	→			→			↓			21	6	8	21	11	8	↓		
Market and fair tolls	5	5	6	10	7	9[15]	13	14	5	11	7	7	11	0	4	16	10	9	13	9	7	10	2	0
Demesne pastures	21	14	2	19	12	4	17	5	4	14	13	4	9	0	0	9	11	8	9	14	8	9	16	8
Judicial revenue	81	6	0	117	12	1[16]	112	0	3	85	2	6	56	2	10	58	5	3	80	8	8	84	19	7[20]
Miscellaneous (including sale of stock)	12	13	4	18	10	0	24	0	0	3[18]	11	8	36	3	4	45	3	6	29	0	11	74	16	10
Net charge	200	16	0	202	4	9	250	3	2	197	10	5	179	19	11	206	15	6	205	8	2	263	8	0
Expenses	(24	0	9)[13]	(63	10	9)[17]	(14	5	6)	(23	4	11)	(31	19	1)	(23	6	11)	(27	6	10)	(18	1	2)
Liveries of money { Arrears	277	15	9	88	11	2	41	2	5	22	5	10	35	14	9	30	7	5	45	3	5	40	1	0
Current				149	19	4	209	18	11	145	10	10	146	17	8	159	10	1	163	1	10	216	10	0
References	S.C.6 802/6; 802/7			S.C.6 802/9			S.C.6 802/11			S.C.6 802/13			S.C.6 802/15			S.C.6 802/17			S.C.6 803/3			S.C.6 803/5		

Year of Account	1362–3	1363–4	1364–5	1365–6	1366–7	1367–8	1368–9	1369–70	1370–1
	£ s. d.	£ s. d.	£ s. d.	£ s. d.	£ s. d.	£ s. d.	£ s. d.	£ s. d.	£ s. d.
Assize rents	→	81 2 8	81 13 8	81 2 4	81 3 7	81 17 1	→	86 14 1[21]	Account decayed
Decasus	(0 16 8)	(0 16 8)	→	(1 8 0)	(1 12 0)	(1 13 0)	(1 15 0)	(1 15 0)	
Mills (farms)	21 6 3	21 6 3	22 18 4	30 18 4	24 18 4	25 1 10	25 0 0	24 16 8	
Market and fair tolls	17 5 11	24 1 5	16 3 3	17 18 3	12 2 7	13 6 2	11 2 0	14 15 11	
Demesne pastures	10 0 0	→	→	→	→	→	10 0 0	10 0 0	
Judicial revenue	110 4 10	83 10 0	86 0 11	80 12 7	55 16 4	60 8 6	66 17 9	59 15 11	
Miscellaneous (including sale of stock)	→	→	→	→	↓	↓			
Net charge	31 8 1	77 15 3	66 19 7	65 12 0	76 2 10	45 16 3	68 7 8	25 10 3	
Expenses	244 1 11	274 6 10	256 4 7	259 16 3	233 4 6	209 19 6	236 16 5	194 13 6	
Liveries of money { Arrears	(26 11 6)	(22 12 1)	(26 14 6)	(24 19 3)	(25 7 2)	(24 17 4)	(24 13 1)	(25 4 6)	
Current }	224 7 7 } 208 4 11	84 5 7 } 216 5 6	64 18 11 } 210 3 10	23 1 7 } 210 3 10	26 4 0 } 258 1 3	26 4 0 } 190 12 3	} 229 9 2	10 17 5 } 31 6 3[22] 120 11 10[23]	265 8 4
References	S.C.6 803/7	S.C.6 803/9	S.C.6 803/10	S.C.6 803/12	S.C.6 803/13	S.C.6 803/15	S.C.6 804/1	S.C.6 804/2	

Year of Account	1371–2 £ s. d.	1372–3 £ s. d.	1373–4 £ s. d.	1374–5 £ s. d.	1376 valor £ s. d.
Assize rents	↓	↓	86 14 5	86 15 11	
Decasus	(12 16 0)	(3 4 5)	(3 4 5)↓	(2 19 5)	
Mills (farms)	23 19 8	22 0 0	24 0 0 →	24 0 0	
Market and fair tolls	16 13 7	9 0 6	11 1 4	8 2 9	
Demesne pastures	20 7 11	20 0 0	20 0 3	20 0 0	
Judicial revenue	82 2 3	65 12 1	51 19 3	115 15 11[25]	
Miscellaneous (including sale of stock)	44 6 8	30 9 10	57 1 6	30 19 2	
Net charge	234 8 4	194 8 4	212 12 0	242 8 10	170 0 8
Expenses	(26 19 10)	(36 3 10)[24]	(33 0 4)	(40 5 6)	
Liveries of money { Arrears	} 206 5 0	} 219 2 9	17 4 4 } 164 3 5	} 163 16 4	
{ Current					
References	S.C.6 804/4	S.C.6 804/5	S.C.6 804/6	S.C.6 804/7	C.47 9/57

NOTES

[1] Including aid of manor, £10; aid of borough, £4.

[2] Including aid of manor, £7 6s. 8d.; aid of borough, £4.

[3] Including wardship of Cheadle and Adlington.

[4] The farm of Macclesfield and Overton appears in the chamberlain's accounts for 1301–2 (£220), 1302–3 (£232), 1303–4 (£240); *Chamb. Acc.*, pp. 2, 16, 38.

[5] Allowances of £84 18s. 4d. were discharged from the accounts for 1329 (August–September), 1329–30 and 1330 (September–December) but it is not possible to assign sums to particular years.

[6] Amalgamation of two accounts.

[7] Eyre of Macclesfield, £130 16s. 5d.

[8] Including £16 12s. 3¼d. expenses of Thos. Ferrers for holding the eyre when he was receiver of Macclesfield.

[9] Fines before the justiciar, £139 9s. 3d., including £9 12s. 3d. for fines before the justice of the forest.

[10] Two forges, £17 10s. 9d.; 'profit of merchants' on the price of 127 oxen and six cows bought by the bailiff, £5 6s. 3½d.

[11] Which left £424 7s. 3¼d. still undischarged (arrears and issues).

[12] Amalgamation of two accounts.

[13] Including exoneration of £56 17s. 9¾d., of which over £40 (arrears) was transferred to the succeeding account.

[14] Henceforward excludes rent of Bollington (and its mills) which are granted to William Soty for no render.

[15] Including, henceforward, rent of the common oven.

[16] Of which nearly £60 comprises fines of Macclesfield men in Shareshull's sessions.

[17] £38 15s. 11½d. spent on the enclosure of Macclesfield park.

[18] Of which £13 4s. 4d. was a sum paid to the stock keeper by the chamberlain and other accountants for the expenses of his office.

[19] The forest eyre fines were accounted for by special collectors, who delivered £23 to the chamberlain in 1359–60 and £27 9s. 0d. in 1360–1.

[20] Including fines before the justices of labourers, and in subsequent accounts.

[21] Including farm of Bollington and mills, £5 6s. 8d., henceforward.

[22] Adam Mottram, as forest collector, made a livery of only £6 out of his current receipts (the net charge for which was £129 18s. 5d.).

[23] Figures supplied from chamberlain's account, S.C.6 772/6 m. 1.

[24] An annuity of £20 charged on the forest collector's account is deducted here from expenses and added to the current livery.

[25] £51 14s. 11d. from fines and amercements of Macclesfield residents imposed in the county court and charged in the poker's account.

APPENDIX II

(b) MACCLESFIELD LIVERY PROFILES

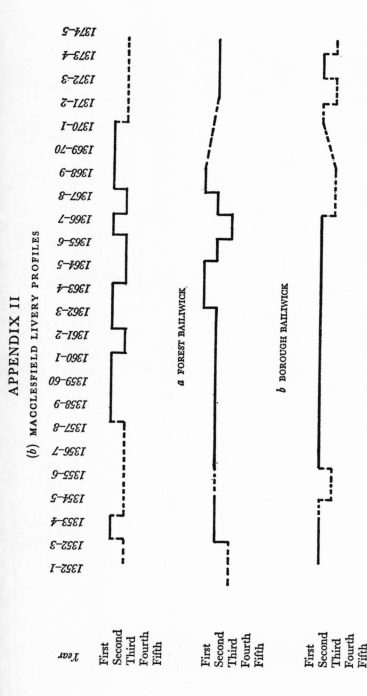

a FOREST BAILIWICK

b BOROUGH BAILIWICK

c HUNDRED BAILIWICK

These tables are constructed so that the line ('profile') shows when the current net receipts for each financial year (plotted on the horizontal axis) had been paid over in full (or nearly so). On the vertical axis are the actual years of payment. 'First years' indicates the *end* of the year of the actual account, 'second year' (and so on) the ends of subsequent accounting years. Thus, in the borough bailiwick, the revenue arising from the year 1366-7 was all paid to the chamberlain by the end of the third year, that is: 1369-79 (i.e. by Michaelmas 1370).

APPENDIX II

(c) MARA–MONDREM REVENUES, 1349/74

Year of Account	1349–50 £ s. d.	1350–1 £ s. d.	1351–2 £ s. d.	1352–3 £ s. d.	1353–4 £ s. d.	1354–5 £ s. d.	1355–6 £ s. d.	1356–7 £ s. d.	1357–8 £ s. d.	1358–9 £ s. d.	1359–60 £ s. d.
Rents	21 0 4	20 0 0	↓	↓							
Pannage and agistment	26 13 4	↓	↓	↓	22 13 4	25 6 8	26 13 4	↓	0 6 8[2]	–	24 4 0[5]
Regard of forest	–	–	–	–	–	–	–	–	–	–	–
Wood { Sales	1 12 3	4 12 9	1 8 4	5 5 1	5 0 5	)[1] 7 6 8	7 6 8	8 15 0	3 19 10	7 4 6[4]	10 0 6
{ Licences to sell	–	2 11 4	–	–	–	(0 13 4)	0 13 4	–	–	5 8 5	–
Miscellaneous	1 3 4	↓	2 0 0	48 5 5	48 14 1		0 13 4	–	9 3 1[3]	5 17 1[3]	1 17 4[3]
Net charge	50 9 3	49 7 9	44 8 8	48 5 5	48 14 1		55 13 8	56 8 8	34 9 11	39 10 4	56 12 2
Expenses	–	–	–	–	–		–	7 6 8	–	–	–
Liveries { Arrears	–	–	15 2 7	4 13 4	–		–		2 4 2	5 3 8	2 5 9
of money } Issues	22 6 3	34 11 1	39 15 4	48 5 5	48 13 8	(28 18 10)	48 7 0	54 3 8	28 13 0	34 13 1	56 12 2
References	Chamb. Acc., pp. 147–9	Ibid., pp. 201–2	S.C.6 783/17 m. 1d	S.C.6 784/2 m. 1d	S.C.6 784/3 m. 1d	S.C.6 784/5 m. 1d	S.C.6 784/7 m. 1	S.C.6 784/10 m. 1	S.C.6 785/1 m. 1d	S.C.6 785/3 m. 1, 1d	S.C.6 785/5 m. 2d

Year of account	1360-1			1361-2			1362-3			1363-4			1364-5			1365-6			1366-7			1367-8			1368-9			1370-1		
	£	s.	d.	£	s.	d.	£	s.	d.	£	s.	d.	£	s.	d.	£	s.	d.	£	s.	d.	£	s.	d.	£	s.	d.	£	s.	d.
Rents	↓			↓			↓			↓			↓			↓			↓			↓			↓			↓		
Pannage and agistment	32	0	0	↓			↓			↓			↓			33	0	0[8]	33	6	8	↓			↓			↓		
Regard of forest	0	5	4[4]	–			–			0	8	6	–			–			–			–			–			–		
Wood { Sales	6	6	0	31	16	6	7	12	7	13	16	8[7]	21	15	4	1	10	4	10	19	4	13	0	2	3	6	0	12	11	8
Licences to sell	–			–			0	8	9	1	4	3	51	0	5	1	15	4	16	19	5	8	5	8	–			0	13	4
Miscellaneous	4	11	6	–			–			–			0	3	0	–			–			–			–			–		
Net charge	64	3	2	84	16	10	61	1	8	68	9	9	125	19	1	57	6	0	82	5	9	75	12	10	57	13	0	67	12	0
Expenses	–			–			–			–			–			–			–			–			–			–		
Liveries of money { Arrears	3	3	9	9	9	6	21	8	6	25	17	11	23	2	4	21	6	5	36	10	4	23	17	4	(73	10	10)	42	14	5[9]
Issues	54	13	8	63	5	4	34	15	0[6]	39	10	0	65	10	1	50	5	8	48	12	6	54	14	11				28	9	6
References	S.C.6 785/8 m. 3, 3d			S.C.6 785/9 m. 1d			S.C.6 786/1 m. 4			S.C.6 786/3 m. 4d			S.C.6 786/5 m. 2d			S.C.6 786/6 m. 3			S.C.6 786/7 m. 3			S.C.6 786/8 m. 3			S.C.6 786/10 m. 2d			S.C.6 787/2 m. 2, 2d		

Year of account	1371-2	1372-3	1373-4
Rents	↓	↓	↓
Pannage and agistment	↓	30 6 8	↓
Regard of forest	–	–	–
Wood { Sales	4 13 4	14 11 9	6 3 0
Wood { Licences to sell	–	–	–
Miscellaneous	–	–	2 13 4
Net charge	57 13 8 (1 6 8)[10]	65 18 9	60 3 4
Expenses	–	–	–
Liveries of { Arrears	80 1 0	16 15 8	28 0 0
Liveries of { Issues money		38 6 4	39 12 11
References	S.C.6 787/4 m. 2	S.C.6 787/5 m. 2	S.C.6 787/7 m. 2

[1] Part of membrane torn away.

[2] Pannage and agistment not farmed this year; all beasts found in the forest to be captured as 'escapes', so that more profit can be obtained for the lord.

[3] Escapes.

[4] Forest eyre.

[5] Pannage, 4s. 0d.; £24 0s. 0d. part of £32 0s. 0d. farm of herbage, agistment, escapes, fisheries and pannage from Christmas 1359 for six years.

[6] Of the unpaid charge, £22 5s. 4d. was attributed to the farmers of the pannage and agistment.

[7] By a writ dated 29 July 1361 the sale of wood and underwood within the forest (i.e. on other men's holdings) was to be permitted by licence of the earl, at a price of one third of the sale value of the wood sold. This sum therefore consists of £13 6s. 8d. for wood sold without licence and, therefore, forfeited (the rest of the sum of £25 16s. 8d. for the same is charged in the chamberlain's account). It was not possible to collect the one third payments for licence to sell £71 8s. 0d. worth of wood because 'no execution could be made'.

[8] Including £8 for the last term of the 1359/65 lease and £25 for the new lease (£33 6s. 8d. a year) from Christmas 1365.

[9] Including one whole year's rent (£33 6s. 8d.) for the farm of the pannage and agistment.

[10] Tithe (presumably wood sales or pannage/agistment).

APPENDIX II

(d) DRAKELOW-RUDHEATH-OVERMARSH REVENUES, 1348/76

Year of Account	1348–9 £ s. d.	1349–50 £ s. d.	1350–1 £ s. d.	1351–2 £ s. d.	1352–3 £ s. d.	1353–4 £ s. d.	1354–5 £ s. d.	1355–6 £ s. d.	1356–7 £ s. d.	1357–8 £ s. d.	1358–9 £ s. d.
Assize rents: Rudheath	51 4 0	↓	51 4 4[1]	45 14 3	↓	46 2 2	↓	↓	↓	↓	↓
Overmarsh	4 3 4	–	1 12 3	1 12 6	10 14 9	19 17 0	↓	↓	↓	↓	↓
Decasus	(13 0 9)	(30 14 1)	(25 13 10)[2]	(3 6 0)	(1 4 6)	(1 2 5)	(1 14 5)	(7 2 5)	(10 10 2)	(4 7 4)	(3 6 5)
Sale of corn and stock	0 17 6	15 11 7	23 5 4	25 0 2	22 2 0	12 2 1	1 11 0 11	36 5 7 · 6 13 4[4]	nil[5]	–	–
Judicial revenue	0 6 6	0 3 5	1 1 10	1 3 4	1 3 1	1 19 9	2 9 5	1 3 9	3 18 9	2 6 6	1 8 7
Miscellaneous	–	2 17 8	3 10 11	6 15 6	1 16 1	3 16 5	1 14 7	5 17 0	3 2 0	1 12 3	2 1 0
Net charge	10 8 9	23 16 9	(...)	52 2 6	58 4 10	62 12 9	55 13 1	95 17 11	60 16 10	64 0 6	64 18 7
Expenses	(33 1 9)	(15 5 10)	(...)	(24 17 7)	(22 0 10)	(20 2 1)	(23 16 8)[3]	(12 18 6)	(1 12 11)	(1 10 1)	(1 3 9)
Liveries of money { Arrears { Issues	–	23 16 0	(...)	37 14 5	10 0 0 · 44 16 1	48 5 9	16 19 8 · 48 2 3	2 12 0 · 80 3 1	4 12 3 · 63 16 4	63 18 10	57 17 3
References	S.C.6 801/3	S.C.6 801/4	Chamb. Acc., pp. 193–9	S.C.6 783/17 m. 6	S.C.6 784/2 m. 10	S.C.6 784/4 m. 1	S.C.6 784/5 m. 12	S.C.6 784/7 m. 8	S.C.6 784/10 m. 7	S.C.6 785/1 m. 9	S.C.6 785/3 m. 3

Values are given in £ s. d. (pounds, shillings, pence). A downward arrow (↓) indicates the value is subsumed in a later column; "–" indicates none/dash.

Year of Account	1359–60	1360–1	1361–2	1362–3[7]	1363–4	1364–5	1365–6	1366–7	1367–8	1368–9
Assize rents: Rudheath	↓	↓	↓	46 6 8	↓	↓	↓	46 15 8	46 11 2	46 11 2
Overmarsh	↓	↓	↓	19 17 0	↓	16 13 1	( )[8]	14 16 0	7 8 0[9]	15 0 0
Decasus	(2 19 1)	(2 0 7)	(2 4 11)	(1 19 6)	(2 6 10)	(0 6 11)	(0 6 11)	(0 6 11)	(0 5 11)	(0 6 11)
Sale of corn and stock	–	–	–	–	–	–	–	–	–	–
Judicial revenue	3 4 6	0 9 6	5 19 6	0 11 4	1 9 4	2 15 4	(1 11 1)	0 10 1	0 14 5	2 15 3
Miscellaneous	2 8 8	5 14 6[6]	2 10 5	3 1 3	2 10 6	4 9 6	(5 8 4)	5 2 9	(4 13 2)	6 15 6
Net charge	68 6 7	69 15 11	71 7 6	67 0 0	67 0 0	68 6 2	(49 8 4)	63 10 1	(55 14 10)	64 19 4
Expenses	(0 6 8)	(0 6 8)	(0 16 8)	(0 16 8)	(0 16 8)	(1 11 6)	(3 10 10)	(3 7 6)	(3 6 0)	(5 15 8)
Liveries of money { Arrears	0 7	}	3 10 6	1 0 0	1 18 0	–	–	2 10 4	4 16 8	1 3 5
{ Issues	64 11 10	67 3 1	69 10 0	64 4 6	66 19 5	65 11 7	(49 6 4)	58 16 9	55 14 8	58 6 0
References	S.C.6 785/7 m. 5	S.C.6 785/8 m. 4d	S.C.6 785/9 m. 2d	S.C.6 786/1 m. 3, 3d	S.C.6 786/3 m. 3d, 4	S.C.6 786/5 m. 2	S.C.6 786/6 m. 2	S.C.6 786/7 m. 2	S.C.6 786/8 m. 2, 2d	S.C.6 786/10 m. 2, 2d

Year of Account	1370-1 £	s.	d.	1371-2 £	s.	d.	1372-3 £	s.	d.	1373-4 £	s.	d.
Assize rents:												
Rudheath	41	9	5	52	12	3[11]	58	12	3	49	12	0
Overmarsh	11	10	9	↓			15	0	0[12]	15	0	0
Decasus	(0	6	11)	—			—			—		
Sale of corn and stock	—			—			—			—		
Judicial revenue	2	12	2	5	1	7	2	16	7	0	7	10
Miscellaneous	4	19	5	5	3	4	2	5	4	2	6	6
Net charge	56	17	4	70	18	11	75	8	3	64	2	6
Expenses	(3	7	6)	(3	9	0)	(3	5	11)	(3	3	10)
Liveries of money { Arrears	23	2	0	} 83 13 10			—			19	17	0
Issues	27	3	4[10]				57	10	0	52	0	9
References	S.C.6 787/2 m. 1d, 2			S.C.6 787/4 m. 3d			S.C.6 787/5 m. 1d, 2			S.C.6 787/7 m. 1d		

[1] £5 6s. 8d. is charged for this year at the end of the 1351-2 account for the rent of free tenants.

[2] £12 17s. 3d. *decasus* of lands of tenants dead in the pestilence and which were not taken by anyone else; £12 16s. 7d. *decasus* at the lord's will; i.e. rents of Rudheath tenants who are receiving one-third remission.

[3] Some post-sum total allowances and exonerations cannot be read.

[4] Lease of demesne lands.

[5] Demesnes and £40 of Rudheath rent are granted to Sir John Chandos.

[6] Of this, £5 10s. 6d. is from the perquisites of the court of Overmarsh (of which £3 8s. 0d. is for nine heriots).

[7] From this year onwards the bailiffs of Drakelow and Rudheath accounted separately. This and the remaining tables consist of figures taken from two accounts.

[8] Overmarsh account is incomplete.

[9] No Overmarsh account for the whole year survives.

[10] £20 annuity which should have been granted to Richard Hampton was respited.

[11] Including £9 1s. 9½d. duplication of termors' rent, for their new sixteen-year lease.

[12] Farm of Overmarsh lordship.

APPENDIX III

VALOR OF THE LANDS OF THE LATE BLACK PRINCE, 1376 (SUMMARISED) (C.47 9/57)

1. *Commissioners appointed to make the valor*

Executors of the prince's will (i - v)

  i. John Harewell, bishop of Bath and Wells
     Chancellor of Aquitaine and constable of Bordeaux in the 1360s.

  ii. William Spridlington, bishop of St. Asaph
     Chief auditor of the prince's estates, *c.* 1353/69.

  iii. Sir Hugh Segrave
     Steward of the prince's lands, *c.* 1372/6.

  iv. Alan Stokes
     The prince's receiver-general, 1372/6.

  v. John Fordham
     The prince's secretary, *c.* 1370/*c.* 1374.

  vi. Richard Stokes
     One of the prince's auditors, 1359/76.

  vii. Richard Fillongley
     (One of) the auditors of the prince in Aquitaine, *c.* 1362/*c.* 1370.

  viii. William Skipwith
     Justiciar of north and south Wales, 1374/6.

  ix. Hugh Young
     Chamberlain of south Wales in 1376.

  x. David Cradok
     Chamberlain of north Wales in 1373.

  xi. John Wodehouse
     Chamberlain of Chester, 1374/94.

(References are given in *Tout*, VI, pp. 58–72, and scattered throughout *Tout*, V.)

2. *Summary of the valor*[1]

  i. North Wales   £3,041 7 6¼
                              (less justiciar's fee: £40)

ii. South Wales   £1,830   4   11¼
(less £110 granted to Sir Richard
Bere for life and £50 justiciar's fee)

iii. Cheshire

a. City of Chester	104	0	0
b. Middlewich town	64	0	0
c. Dee mills	240	0	0
d. Drakelow manor	50	0	0
e. Overmarsh manor	15	0	0
f. Mara forest	51	7	0
g. Northwich	66	0	0
h. Shotwick manor	30	14	1
i. Frodsham manor	56	13	4
j. Office of sheriff	124	7	4
k. Perquisites of the county court, before the justiciar	180	0	0
l. Office of escheator	100	0	0
Total	1,082	1	9

iv. Flintshire   442   19   5

v. Macclesfield lordship

a. Macclesfield borough	31	0	0
b. Macclesfield hundred	31	14	0
c. Bailiwick of Macclesfield forest	88	0	0
d. On the account of the Macclesfield stock keeper	13	6	8
e. Macclesfield park	6	0	0
Total	170	0	8

Total of Cheshire, Flintshire and Macclesfield

     1,695²   1   10
(less £61 6s. 6d. ancient alms
granted by the earls of Chester, and
£129 granted to Sir Richard
Stafford before the princess's
marriage)

vi. County of Cornwall   2,219   7   9½
(of which £1,016 1s. 4d. is for
coinage of tin)

vii. Devon   273   19   5¾
(less deductions from Cornwall and
Devon: £20 fee farm of Exeter
granted to John Sully, £120 14s.
11d. from certain manors granted to
Sir Neil Loring)

viii. England

a.	Wallingford lordship	340	0	0
b.	Watlington manor	40	0	0
c.	Risborough manor	83	0	0
d.	Byfleet manor	27	15	2
e.	Shoreham manor	15	0	0
f.	Whitchurch manor	20	0	0
g.	Berkhamsted lordship	93	0	0
h.	Rising lordship	90	0	0
i.	Lynn tolbooth	26	13	4
j.	Coventry lordship	139	16	0
k.	Goscote hundred	8	0	0
l.	Repingdon	3	0	0
m.	Nettlebed	3	0	0
n.	The wardrobe in London (beyond reprises)	10	0	0
o.	Kennington manor	13	6	8

Total   922 11 2

(of which the third part: £307 10s. 4½d.)

Grand total (of gross figures)   £9,982   12s.   8¾d.

NOTES

[1] The detailed breakdown of the total figures for each heading is given here only for Cheshire, Macclesfield lordship and 'England'. In the original document the sub-headings are broken down further into 'rents' and 'other profits', and the portions of rents due at the different terms are indicated.

[2] £1,595 1s. 10d. in the original document, although S.C.12 22/97 suggests that the figure confirmed by addition is correct.

LIST OF SOURCES

A. MANUSCRIPT SOURCES

i. Public Record Office

Chancery
C.47 (Chancery Miscellanea)
C.53 (Charter Rolls)
C.81 (Chancery Warrants)
C.260 (Chancery Files)

Exchequer, Queen's Remembrancer
E.101 (Various Accounts)
E.143 (Extents and Inquisitions)
E.153 (Escheators' Files)
E.159 (Memoranda Rolls)
E.163 (Miscellanea)
E.207 (*Bille* Files)

Exchequer, Office of the Auditors of Land Revenue
L.R.12 (Receivers' Accounts: Series III)

Exchequer, Lord Treasurer's Remembrancer's and Pipe Offices
E.352 (Chancellor's Rolls)
E.368 (Memoranda Rolls)
E.372 (Pipe Rolls)

Exchequer, Treasury of the Receipt
E.36 (Miscellaneous Books)

Palatinate of Chester
Ches. 2 (Enrolments)
Ches. 3 (Inquisitions Post Mortem)
Ches. 17 (Eyre Rolls)
Ches. 19 (Sheriff's Turn Rolls)
Ches. 24 (Gaol Files, Writs, etc.)
Ches. 25 (Indictment Rolls)
Ches. 29 (County Plea Rolls)
Ches. 33 (Forest Proceedings)
Ches. 34 (Quo Warranto Rolls)
Ches. 38 (Miscellanea)

Special Collections
S.C.1 (Ancient Correspondence)
S.C.2 (Court Rolls)
S.C.6 (Ministers' and Receivers' Accounts)
S.C.8 (Ancient Petitions)
S.C.11 (Rentals and Surveys: Rolls)
S.C.12 (Rentals and Surveys: Portfolios)

ii. British Library

Add. MS 22,923 (Account of the treasurer of Prince Edward's wardrobe, expenses only, 1306/7)
Add. Roll 26,593 (Roll of fines and atterminations of Lancashire and Cheshire made in the royal exchequer, 1331/2)
Harleian MS 5001 (A 17th century transcript of Add. MS 22,923, made when the latter was complete)

iii. Duchy of Cornwall Office

Jornale of John Henxteworth, the prince's controller in Gascony, 1355/6

iv. Eaton Hall, Cheshire

Eaton Hall Charters, 321 (Cheshire Divers Ministers' Accounts, 1353–4)

v. Staffordshire Record Office

D(W)1734/J2268 (Extents of the manors of the bishopric of Coventry and Lichfield, 1298)

vi. John Rylands University Library of Manchester

Tatton MS 345 (Mise Book, 1406)

B. PRINTED SOURCES

Unless otherwise stated, the place of publication is London

1. Those directly relating to Cheshire

Bennet, M. J., 'The Lancashire and Cheshire clergy, 1379', *T.H.S.L.C.*, 124 (1973), pp. 1–30.
Booth, P. H. W., and Harrop, J. H. and S. A. (eds.), *The Extent of Longdendale, 1360*, Cheshire Sheaf, Fifth Series, 1976–7.
Brownbill, J. (ed.), *The Ledger-Book of Vale Royal Abbey*, Rec. Soc., 68, 1914.
Calendar of Chancery Warrants, 1244–1326, 1927.
Calendar of Charter Rolls, 4 vols., 1908–16.
Calendar of Close Rolls, 1272–1377, 1892–1913.
Calendar of Deeds, Inquisitions and Writs of Dower on the Chester Plea Rolls, Henry III–Edward III, Reports of the Deputy Keeper of the Public Records, 26, 27 and 28, Appendices, 1865–7.
Calendar of Fine Rolls, 1272–1377, 1911–24.
Calendar of Inquisitions Post Mortem, II–XIV, 1906–52.
Calendar of Memoranda Rolls, 1326–7, 1969.
Calendar of Miscellaneous Inquisitions, I–III, 1916–37.
Calendar of Patent Rolls, 1272–1377, 1891–1916.
Calendar of Recognizance Rolls of the Palatinate of Chester to the end of

the Reign of Henry IV, Report of the Deputy Keeper of the Public Records, 36, Appendix II, 1875.

Calendar of Various Chancery Rolls, 1277–1326, 1912.

Christie, R. C. (ed.), *Annales Cestrienses*, Rec. Soc., 14, 1886.

Evans, D. L. (ed.), *Flintshire Ministers' Accounts, 1328–53*, Flintshire Historical Society Record Series, 2, 1928.

Hopkins, A. (ed.), *Selected Rolls of the Chester City Courts in the late Thirteenth and early Fourteenth centuries*, Chet. Soc., Third Series, 2, 1950.

Jones, Arthur (ed.), *Flintshire Ministers' Accounts, 1301–28*, Flintshire Historical Society, 3, 1913.

Lyons, P. A. (ed.), *Two 'Compoti' of the Lancashire and Cheshire manors of Henry de Lacy, earl of Lincoln, XXIV and XXXIII Edward*, Chet. Soc., 112, 1884.

Register of Edward the Black Prince, Part I, 1346–8; Part Two, Cornwall, 1351–65; Part III, Palatinate of Chester, 1351–65; Part IV, England, 1351–65, 1930–33.

Stewart-Brown, R. (ed.), *Accounts of the Chamberlains and other Officers of the County of Chester, 1301–60*, Rec. Soc., 59, 1910.

— (ed.), *Calendar of County Court, City Court and Eyre Rolls of Chester, 1259–1297, with an Inquest of Military Service*, Chet. Soc., New Series, 84, 1925.

— and Mills, Mabel (eds), *Cheshire in the Pipe Rolls, 1158–1301*, Rec. Soc., 92, 1938.

Tait, James (ed.), *The Domesday Survey of Cheshire*, Chet. Soc., New Series, 75, 1916.

— (ed.), *The Chartulary or Register of St. Werburgh's Abbey, Chester*, Chet. Soc., New Series, 79, 82, 1920–2.

Wilson, K. P. (ed.), *Chester Customs Accounts, 1301–1565*, Rec. Soc., 111, 1969.

2. Other printed sources

Armitage-Smith, S. (ed.), *John of Gaunt's Register, 1371–5*, Camden Third Series, XX, XXI, 1911.

Beachcroft, G., and Sabin, A., *Two Compotus Rolls of St Augustine's Abbey, Bristol, for 1491–2 and 1511–12*, Bristol Record Society, IX, 1938.

Blackley, F. D., and Hermansen, G., *The Household Book of Queen Isabella of England, 1311–12*, Alberta, 1971.

Briggs, Helen M., *Surrey Manorial Accounts: A Catalogue and Index of the Earliest Surviving Rolls down to the year 1300*, Surrey Record Society, XXXVII, 1935.

Byerly, B. J. and C. R. (eds), *Records of the Wardrobe and Household 1285–6*, 1977.

Chibnall, Marjorie (ed.), *Select Documents of the English Lands of the Abbey of Bec*, Camden Third Series, LXIII, 1951.

Denney, A. H. (ed.), *The Sibton Abbey Estates: Select Documents, 1325–1509*, Suffolk Records Society, II, 1960.

Edwards, J. G. (ed.), *Calendar of Ancient Correspondence concerning Wales*, University of Wales Board of Celtic Studies, History and Law Series, II, 1935.

Emmison, F. G. (ed.), *Account Roll of the Manor of Clapham Bayeux, 1333–4*, Bedfordshire Historical Record Society, XIV, 1931.

Farr, M. W., *Accounts and Surveys of the Wiltshire Lands of Adam de Stratton*, Wiltshire Archaeological and Natural History Society, Records Branch, 1959.

Fryde, Natalie M., *List of Welsh Entries in the Memoranda Rolls, 1282–1343*, Cardiff, 1974.

Hall, Hubert, *A formula book of English historical official documents*, Part I (diplomatic documents), Part II (ministerial and judicial records), Cambridge, 1908–9.

Hall, Hubert (ed.), *The Pipe Roll of the Bishopric of Winchester, 1208–9*, 1903.

Harvey, P. D. A. (ed.), *Manorial Records of Cuxham, Oxfordshire, c. 1200–1359*, Oxfordshire Record Society, 50, 1976.

Hilton, R. H. (ed.), *Ministers' Accounts of the Warwickshire Estates of the Duke of Clarence, 1479–80*, Dugdale Society, 1952.

Holt, N. R. (ed.), *The Pipe Roll of the Bishopric of Winchester, 1210–11*, Manchester, 1964.

Jack, R. I. (ed.), *The Grey of Ruthin Valor: the Valor of the English Lands of Edmund Grey, Earl of Kent, drawn up from the Ministers' Accounts of 1467–8*, Bedfordshire Historical Record Society, 46, 1965.

Johnstone, Hilda (ed.), *Letters of Edward, Prince of Wales, 1304–5*, Roxburghe Club, 1931.

Kirk, R. E. G. (ed.), *Accounts of the Obedientiars of Abingdon Abbey*, Camden Society, New Series, LI, 1892.

Lewis, E. A., 'The Account Roll of the Chamberlain of West Wales from Michaelmas 1301 to Michaelmas 1302', *Bulletin of the Board of Celtic Studies*, II, (1925), pp. 49–86.

— 'The Account Roll of the Chamberlain of the Principality of North Wales from Michaelmas 1304 to Michaelmas 1305', *ibid.*, I, (1923), pp. 256–75.

Lodge, E. C., and Somerville, R. (eds.), *John of Gaunt's Register, 1379–83*, Camden Third Series, LVI, LVII, 1937.

Lumby, J. R. (ed.), *Chronicon Henrici Knighton*, Rolls Series, 2 vols., 1889, 1895.

Midgley, L. M. (ed.), *Ministers' Accounts of the Earldom of Cornwall, 1296–7*, Camden Third Series, LXVI, LXVIII, 1942, 1945.

Mills, Mabel (ed.), *The Pipe Roll for 1295: Surrey membrane*, Surrey Record Society, XXI, 1924.

Page, F. M. (ed.), *Wellingborough Manorial Accounts, 1258–1323*, Northamptonshire Record Society, VIII, 1936.

Pugh, R. B., 'Ministers' Accounts of Norhamshire and Islandshire', *Northern History*, XI (1975), pp. 17–26.

Pugh, T. B. (ed.), *The Marcher Lordships of South Wales, 1415–1536: Select Documents*, University of Wales Board of Celtic Studies, History and Law Series XX, 1963.

Rhys, Myvanwy (ed.), *Ministers' Accounts of West Wales, 1277–1306*, I, (Text and Translation), Cymmrodorion Record Series, 13, 1936.

Sabin, A. (ed.), *Some Manorial Accounts of Saint Augustine's Abbey, Bristol, . . . for 1491–2 and 1496–7*, Bristol Record Society, XXII, 1960.

Salzman, L. F. (ed.), *Ministers' Accounts of the Manor of Petworth, 1347–53*, Sussex Record Society, LV, 1955.
Saunders, H. W. (ed.), *An Introduction to the Obedientiary and Manor Rolls of Norwich Cathedral Priory*, Norwich, 1930.
Sayles, G. O. (ed.), *Select Cases in the Court of King's Bench*, Selden Society, 82, 1965.
Stitt, F. B., *Lenton Priory Estate Accounts, 1296–8*, Thoroton Society, Record Series, XIX, 1959.
Styles, Dorothy (ed.), *Ministers' Accounts of the Collegiate Church of St Mary, Warwick, 1432–85*, Dugdale Society, XXVI, 1969.
Tupling, G. H. (ed.), *South Lancashire in the Reign of Edward II*, Chet. Soc., Third Series, I, 1949.

G. SECONDARY SOURCES

1. Those directly relating to Cheshire
Alexander, J. W., 'New Evidence on the Palatinate of Chester', *E.H.R.*, LXXXV (1970), pp. 715–29.
Barraclough, Geoffrey, 'The Earldom and County Palatine of Chester', *T.H.S.L.C.*, 103 (1951), pp. 23–57.
Bennett, M. J., 'A County Community social cohesion amongst the Cheshire gentry, 1400–25', *Northern History*, VIII (1973), pp. 24–44.
— 'Sources and problems in the study of social mobility: Cheshire in the later Middle Ages', *T.H.S.L.C.*, 128 (1979), pp. 59–95.
Bird, W. H., 'Taxation and Representation in the County Palatine of Chester', *E.H.R.*, XXX (1915), p. 303.
Booth, P. H. W., and Jones, R. N., 'Burton in Wirral: from Domesday to Dormitory, Part Two', *Cheshire History*, 4 (1979), pp. 28–42.
— ' "Farming for Profit" in the Fourteenth Century: the Cheshire Estates of the Earldom of Chester', *J.C.N.W.A.S.*, 62 (1980), pp. 73–90.
— 'Taxation and Public Order: Cheshire in 1353', *Northern History*, XII (1976), pp. 16–31.
— 'The Financial Administration of the Lordship and County of Chester, 1272–1377', Liverpool University M.A. dissertation, 1974.
— and Dodd, J. Phillip, 'The Manor and Fields of Frodsham, 1315–74', *T.H.S.L.C.*, 128 (1979), pp. 27–57.
Curry, Anne E., 'Cheshire and the royal demesne, 1399–1422', *T.H.S.L.C.*, 128 (1979), pp. 113–35.
— 'The Demesne of the County Palatine of Chester in the Early Fifteenth Century', Manchester University M.A. thesis, 1977.
Davies, C. Stella, *A History of Macclesfield*, Manchester, 1961.
Davies, R. R., 'Richard II and the Principality of Chester', in *The Reign of Richard II: Essays in Honour of May McKisack*, ed. F. R. H. Du Boulay and C. M. Barron, 1971.
Driver, J. T., *Cheshire in the Later Middle Ages, 1399–1540*, Chester, 1971.
Gillespie, James L., 'Richard II's Cheshire Archers', *T.H.S.L.C.*, 125 (1974), pp. 1–39.
Harrod, H. D., 'A Defence of the Liberties of Chester, 1450', *J.C.N.W.A.S.*, New Series, VIII (1902), pp. 28–32.
Hewitt, H. J., *Cheshire under the Three Edwards*, Chester, 1967.

— *Medieval Cheshire: An Economic and Social History of Cheshire in the Reigns of the Three Edwards*, Chet. Soc., New Series, 88, 1929.

King, Daniel, *The Vale-Royal of England*, 1656.

Morgan, P. J., 'Cheshire and the defence of the Principality of Aquitaine', *T.H.S.L.C.*, 128 (1979), pp. 139–60.

Ormerod, G., *History of the County Palatine and City of Chester*, second edition (revised and enlarged by T. Helsby), 1882.

Sharp (*née* Tout), Margaret, 'Comitatus Palacii', *E.H.R.*, XXXV (1920), pp. 418–19.

— 'Contributions to the History of the Earldom and County of Chester, 1237–1399, Historical, Topographical and Administrative, with a Study of the Household of Edward the Black Prince and its Relations with Cheshire', Manchester University Ph.D. thesis, 1925.

Stewart-Brown, R., 'The Avowries of Cheshire', *E.H.R.*, XXIX (1914), pp. 41–5.

— 'The Cheshire Writs of Quo Warranto in 1499', *E.H.R.*, XLIX (1934), pp. 676–84.

— 'The End of the Norman Earldom of Chester', *E.H.R.*, XXV (1920), pp. 27–54.

— 'The Exchequer of Chester', *E.H.R.*, LVII (1942), pp. 289–97.

— 'The Royal Manor and Park of Shotwick', *T.H.S.L.C.*, 64 (1912), pp. 82–142.

— *Serjeants of the Peace in Medieval England and Wales*, Manchester, 1936.

Studd, J. R. 'The Lord Edward's Lordship of Chester, 1254–72', *T.H.S.L.C.*, 128 (1979), pp. 1–25.

Sylvester, Dorothy, 'A Note on Medieval Three-course Arable Systems in Cheshire', *T.H.S.L.C.*, 110 (1958), pp. 183–6.

— and Nulty, G., *Historical Atlas of Cheshire*, revised edition, 1958.

Terrett, I. B., 'Cheshire', in *The Domesday Geography of Northern England*, ed. H. C. Darby and I. S. Maxwell, Cambridge, 1962.

Victoria History of Cheshire, The, ed. B. E. Harris, II, 1979.

2. Other secondary sources

Altschul, M., *A Baronial Family in Medieval England: the Clares, 1217–1314*, Baltimore, 1965.

Baldwin, J. F. 'The Household Administration of Henry Lacy and Thomas of Lancaster', *E.H.R.*, XLII (1927), pp. 180–200.

— *The King's Council in England during the Middle Ages*, Oxford, 1913.

Barnes, Sir Joshua, *The History . . . of Edward IIId . . . together with that of . . . Edward . . . the Black Prince*, Cambridge, 1688.

Barrow, G. W. S., *Robert Bruce and the Community of the Realm of Scotland*, 1965.

Bean, J. M. W., 'Plague, Population and Economic Decline in the Later Middle Ages', *Ec.H.R.*, Second Series, XV (1962–3), pp. 423–37.

— *The Estates of the Percy Family, 1416–1537*, Oxford, 1958.

Bridbury, A. R., 'Before the Black Death', *Ec.H.R.*, XXX (1977), pp. 393–410.

— *Economic Growth: England in the Later Middle Ages*, 1962.

— 'The Black Death', *Ec.H.R.*, XXVI (1973), pp. 577–92.

— 'The Farming out of Manors', *Ec.H.R.*, XXXI (1978), pp. 503–25.

— 'The Hundred Years' War: Costs and Profits', in *Trade, Government and Economy in Pre-industrial England: Essays presented to F. J. Fisher*, ed. D. C. Coleman and A. H. John (1976).

Britnell, R. H., 'Production for the market on a small fourteenth century estate', *Ec.H.R.*, Second Series, XIX (1966), pp. 380–7.

Broome, D. M., 'An Exchequer Statement of Receipts and Issues: 1339–40', *E.H.R.*, LVIII (1943), pp. 210–16.

— 'The Auditors of the Foreign Accounts at the Exchequer', *E.H.R.*, XXXVIII (1923), pp. 63–71.

Brown, A. L., 'The Authorization of Letters under the Great Seal', *B.I.H.R.*, XXXVII (1964), pp. 125—56.

— 'The Commons and the Council in the reign of Henry IV', *E.H.R.*, LXXIX (1964), pp. 1–30.

— 'The King's Councillors in Fifteenth Century England', *T.R.H.S.*, Fifth Series, 19 (1969), pp. 95–118.

Brown, R. A., Colvin, H. M., and Taylor, A. J., *The History of the King's Works*, 2 vols., 1963.

Bryant, W. N., 'The Financial Dealings of Edward III with the County Communities, 1330–1360', *E.H.R.*, LXXXIII (1968), pp. 760–71.

Cam, Helen M., *Liberties and Communities in Medieval England*, Cambridge, 1944.

— *Studies in the Hundred Rolls*, 1921.

Chaplais, Pierre, 'The Chancery of Guyenne, 1289–1453', in *Studies presented to Sir Hilary Jenkinson*, ed. J. Conway Davies, Oxford, 1957.

Chrimes, S. B., *An Introduction to the Administrative History of Medieval England*, third edition, Oxford, 1966.

Cole, E. J., 'Maelienydd, 30–31 Edward III', *Transactions of the Radnorshire Society*, XXXIV (1964), pp. 31–8.

Coleman, Olive, 'What Figures? Some Thoughts on the Use of Information by Medieval Governments', in *Trade, . . . Essays presented to Fisher*, ed. D. C. Coleman and A. H. John (1976).

Cunningham, W., *The Growth of English Industry and Commerce during the Early and Middle Ages*, fifth edition, I, 1910.

Davenport, F. G., *The Economic Development of a Norfolk Manor, 1086–1565*, Cambridge, 1906.

Davies, J. Conway, *The Baronial Opposition to Edward II*, Cambridge, 1918.

— 'The Memoranda Rolls of the Exchequer to 1307', in *Studies . . . Jenkinson*, ed. J. C. Davies, Oxford, 1957.

Davies, R. R., 'Baronial Accounts, Incomes and Arrears in the Later Middle Ages', *Ec.H.R.*, Second Series, XXI (1968), pp. 211–29.

— 'Kings, Lords and Liberties in the March of Wales, 1066–1272', *T.R.H.S.*, Fifth Series, 29 (1979), pp. 41–61.

— *Lordship and Society in the March of Wales*, Oxford, 1978.

Denholm-Young, N., 'Richard de Bury (1287–1345)', *T.R.H.S.*, Fourth Series, XX (1937), pp. 135–68.

— *Seignorial Administration in England*, Oxford, 1937.

Dobson, R. B., *Durham Priory, 1400–1450*, Cambridge, 1973.

Drew, J. S., 'Manorial Accounts of St. Swithun's Priory, Winchester', *E.H.R.*, LXII (1947), pp. 20–41.

Du Boulay, F. R. H., 'A Rentier Economy in the Later Middle Ages: the Archbishopric of Canterbury', *Ec.H.R.*, Second Series, XVI (1964), pp. 423–35.

— *The Lordship of Canterbury*, 1966.

— 'Who were farming the English demesnes at the end of the Middle Ages?', *Ec.H.R.*, Second Series, XVII (1965), pp. 443–55.

Dyer, C., 'A Redistribution of Incomes in Fifteenth-century England', *Past and Present*, 39 (1968), pp. 11–33.

Edwards, J. G., 'Taxation and Consent in the Court of Common Pleas, 1338', *E.H.R.*, LVII (1942), pp. 473–82.

Elliott, G., 'Field Systems of Northwest England', in *Studies of Field Systems in the British Isles*, ed. A. R. H. Baker and R. A. Butlin, Cambridge, 1973.

Emden, A. B., *A Biographical Register of the University of Cambridge to 1500*, Cambridge, 1963.

— *A Biographical Register of the University of Oxford to 1500*, Oxford, 1958.

Evans, D. L., 'Some Notes on the History of the Principality of Wales in the Time of the Black Prince (1343–1376)', *Transactions of the Honourable Society of Cymmrodorion*, (1927), pp. 25–110.

Finberg, H. P. R., *Tavistock Abbey*, Cambridge, 1951.

Foss, Edward, *The Judges of England*, 9 vols., 1848–64.

Fowler, Kenneth, *The King's Lieutenant: Henry of Grosmont, First Duke of Lancaster, 1310–1361*, 1969.

Fox, Levi, *The Administration of the Honor of Leicester in the Fourteenth Century*, Leicester, 1940.

E. B. Fryde, 'Financial Resources of Edward I in the Netherlands, 1294–8: Main Problems and some Comparisons with Edward III in 1337–40', and 'Financial Resources of Edward III in the Netherlands, 1337–40', *Revue Belge de Philologie et d'Histoire*, XL, XLV (1962, 1967), pp. 1168–87 and 1142–93.

— 'Materials for the study of Edward III's credit operations, 1327–48', Parts I–III, *B.I.H.R.*, XXII, XXIII (1949–50), pp. 105–38, 1–30.

— 'Parliament and the French War', in *Essays in Medieval History presented to Bertie Wilkinson*, ed. T. A. Sandquist and M. R. Powicke (1969).

— (ed.), *The Book of Prests of the King's Wardrobe for 1294–5*, Oxford, 1962.

Fryde, Natalie M., 'Edward's III's Removal of his Ministers and Judges, 1340–1', *B.I.H.R.*, XLVIII (1975), pp. 149–61.

Gras, N. S. B. and E. C., *The Economic and Social History of an English Village, 909–1928*, Cambridge, Mass., 1930.

Griffiths, R. A., and Thomas, Roger S. (eds.), *The Principality of Wales in the Later Middle Ages: the Structure and Personnel of Government*, I, Cardiff, 1972.

Griffiths, R. A., 'The Revolt of Rhys ap Maredudd, 1287–8', *Welsh History Review*, 3 (1966–7), pp. 121–43.

Halcrow, E. M., 'The Decline of Demesne Farming on the Estates of Durham Cathedral Priory', *Ec.H.R.*, Second Series, VII (1955), pp. 345–56.

Hall, Hubert, *Introduction to the Study of the Pipe Rolls*, Pipe Roll Society, 1884.

Harris, B. J., 'Landlords and Tenants in England in the Later Middle Ages: the Buckingham Estates', *Past and Present*, 43 (1969), pp. 146–50.

Harriss, G. L., *King, Parliament and Public Finance in Medieval England to 1369*, Oxford, 1975.

— 'Preference at the Medieval Exchequer', *B.I.H.R.*, XXX (1957), pp. 17–40.

Harvey, B. F., 'The Leasing of the Abbot of Westminster's Demesnes in the Later Middle Ages', *Ec.H.R.*, Second Series, XXII (1969), pp. 17–27.

— 'The Population Trend in England between 1300 and 1348', *T.R.H.S.*, Fifth Series, XVI (1966), pp. 23–42.

— *Westminster Abbey and its Estates in the Middle Ages*, Oxford, 1977.

Harvey, P. D. A., *A Medieval Oxfordshire Village: Cuxham, 1240 to 1400*, Oxford, 1965.

Hatcher, J., *Plague, Population and the English Economy, 1348–1530*, 1977.

— *Rural Economy and Society in the Duchy of Cornwall, 1300–1500*, 1970.

Hewitt, H. J., *The Black Prince's Expedition of 1355–1357*, Manchester, 1958.

Hilton, R. H., *A Medieval Society: the West Midlands at the End of the Thirteenth Century*, 1966.

— 'Lord and peasant in Staffordshire in the Middle Ages', *North Staffordshire Journal of Field Studies*, 10 (1970), pp. 1–20.

— *The Economic Development of some Leicestershire estates in the 14th and 15th centuries*, Oxford, 1947.

Hockey, S. F., *Quarr Abbey and its Lands, 1132–1631*, Leicester, 1970.

Holdsworth, W. S., *A History of English Law*, 16 vols., 1935–66.

Holmes, G. A., *The Estates of the Higher Nobility in Fourteenth Century England*, Cambridge, 1957.

— *The Good Parliament*, Oxford, 1975.

Hoyt, R. S., *The Royal Demesne in English Constitutional History, 1066–1272*, Ithaca, N.Y., 1950.

Jack, R. I., *Medieval Wales*, 1972.

Jeffrey, A. G., *Records and Accounts for Farm Management*, Ministry of Agriculture, Fisheries and Food Bulletin, 176, 1963.

Jenkinson, H., and Broome, D. M., 'An Exchequer Statement of Receipts and Issues', *E.H.R.*, LVIII (1943), pp. 210–16.

Johnson, Charles, 'The System of Account in the Wardrobe of Edward I', *T.R.H.S.*, Fourth Series, VI (1923), pp. 50–72.

Johnson, J. H., 'The System of Account in the Wardrobe of Edward II', *T.R.H.S.*, Fourth Series, XII (1929), pp. 75–104.

Johnstone, Hilda, *Edward of Carnarvon, 1284–1307*, Manchester, 1946.

— 'The Queen's Exchequer under the Three Edwards', in *Historical Essays in Honour of James Tait*, ed. J. G. Edwards, V. H. Galbraith and E. F. Jacob, Manchester, 1933.

— 'The Wardrobe and Household Accounts of the Sons of Edward I', *B.I.H.R.*, II (1925), pp. 37–45.

Kaeuper, Richard W., 'Royal Finance and the Crisis of 1297', in *Order and Innovation in the Middle Ages: Essays in Honor of Joseph R. Strayer*, ed. W. C. Jordan et al., Princeton, N.J., 1976.

Keen, M. H., *England in the Later Middle Ages*, 1973.

Kershaw, I., *Bolton Priory: the economy of a northern monastery*, Oxford, 1973.

— 'The Great Famine and Agrarian Crisis in England, 1315–22', *Past and Present*, LIX (1973), pp. 3–50.

Kirby, J. L., 'Councils and Councillors of Henry IV, 1399–1413', *T.R.H.S.*, Fifth Series, 14 (1964), pp. 35–65.

Lapsley, G. T., *The County Palatine of Durham*, Cambridge, Mass., 1924.

Lennard, Reginald, *Rural England, 1086–1135*, Oxford, 1959.

— 'What is a Manorial Extent?', *E.H.R.*, XLIV (1929), pp. 256–63.

Le Patourel, J. H., *The Medieval Administration of the Channel Islands, 1199–1399*, Oxford, 1937.

Levett, A. E., *The Black Death on the Estates of the See of Winchester*, Oxford, 1916.

— 'The Financial Organization of the Manor', *Ec.H.R.*, I (1927–8), pp. 65–86.

Lewis, N. B., 'A Certificate of the Earl of Lancaster's Auditors, 1341', *E.H.R.*, LV (1940), pp. 99–103.

— 'The Organization of Indentured Retinues in Fourteenth-century England', *T.R.H.S.*, XXVII (1945), pp. 29–39.

Lipsey, Richard G., *An Introduction to Positive Economics*, 1966.

Lloyd, T. H., *The English Wool Trade in the Middle Ages*, Cambridge, 1977.

McFarlane, K. B., 'Bastard Feudalism', *B.I.H.R.*, XX (1945), pp. 161–80.

— *The Nobility of Later Medieval England*, Oxford, 1973.

— 'War, the Economy and Social Change', *Past and Present*, XXII (1962), pp. 3–13.

McKisack, May, *The Fourteenth Century, 1307–99*, Oxford History of England, 1959.

Maddicott, J. R., 'The County Community and the Making of Public Opinion in Fourteenth-century England', *T.R.H.S.*, Fifth Series, 28 (1978), pp. 27–43.

— *The English Peasantry and the Demands of the Crown, 1294–1341*, Past and Present Supplement 1, Oxford, 1975.

— 'Thomas of Lancaster and Sir Robert Holland: a study in noble patronage', *E.H.R.*, LXXXVI (1971), pp. 449–72.

— *Thomas of Lancaster, 1307–1322*, Oxford, 1970.

Madox, Thomas, *The History and Antiquities of the Exchequer*, second edition, 1769.

Maitland, F. W., 'The History of a Cambridgeshire Manor', *E.H.R.*, XXXV (1894), pp. 417–39.

Maxwell-Lyte, H., *Historical Notes on the use of the Great Seal in England*, 1926.

Miller, Edward, 'England in the Twelfth and Thirteenth Centuries: an Economic Contrast?', *Ec.H.R.*, Second Series, XXIV (1971), pp. 1–14.

— 'Farming in Northern England during the Twelfth and Thirteenth Centuries', *Northern History*, XI (1975), pp. 1–16.

— *The Abbey and Bishopric of Ely*, Cambridge, 1951.

— 'The English Economy in the Thirteenth Century', *Past and Present*, 28 (1964), pp. 21–40.

— 'War, taxation and the English economy', in *War and economic development: Essays in memory of David Joslin*, ed. J. M. Winter, Cambridge (1975).

Miller, Edward, and Hatcher, John, *Medieval England: Rural society and economic change, 1086–1348*, 1978.

Mills, Mabel, 'Exchequer Agenda and Estimate of Revenue, Easter Term, 1284', *E.H.R.*, XL (1925), pp. 229–34.

— 'Experiments in Exchequer Procedure, 1200–1232' *T.R.H.S.*, Fourth Series, VIII (1925), pp. 151–70.

— 'The Reforms at the Exchequer (1232–42)', *T.R.H.S.*, Fourth Series, X (1927), pp. 111–33.

Moor, C., *The Knights of Edward I*, Harleian Society, 80–4, 1929–32.

Morgan, Marjorie, *The English Lands of the Abbey of Bec*, Oxford, 1946.

Morris J. E., *The Welsh Wars of Edward I*, Oxford, 1901.

Myers, A. R., *England in the Late Middle Ages*, 1952.

Oschinsky, Dorothea, 'Notes on the Editing and Interpretation of Estate Accounts', *Archives*, IX (1969–70), pp. 84–9, 142–52.

— *Walter of Henley and other Treatises on Estate Management and Accounting*, Oxford, 1971.

Otway-Ruthven, A. J., 'The Constitutional Position of the Lordships of South Wales' *T.R.H.S.*, Fifth Series, 8 (1958), pp. 1–20.

Page, F. M., *The Estates of Crowland Abbey*, Cambridge, 1934.

Parsons, J. C., *The Court and Household of Eleanor of Castile in 1290*, Toronto, 1977.

Phillips, J. R. S., *Aymer de Valence, Earl of Pembroke, 1307–14*, Oxford, 1972.

Pollard, Sidney, and Crossley, David W., *The Wealth of Britain, 1085–1966*, 1968.

Postan, M. M., 'A Note on the Farming out of Manors', *Ec.H.R.*, XXXI (1978), pp. 521–5.

— 'Some Economic Evidence of Declining Population', *Ec.H.R.*, Second Series, II (1950), pp. 221–46.

— (ed.), *The Cambridge Economic History of Europe*, I, second edition, Cambridge, 1966.

— and Rich, E. E. (eds), *The Cambridge Economic History of Europe*, II, Cambridge, 1952.

—, — and Miller, Edward (eds), *The Cambridge Economic History of Europe*, III, Cambridge, 1965.

— *The Medieval Economy and Society*, 1972.

Postles, David, 'Problems in the administration of small manors: three Oxfordshire glebe-demesnes, 1278–1345', *Midland History*, IV (1977), pp. 1–14.

Powicke, F. M., *King Henry III and the Lord Edward*, Oxford, 1947.

188   LIST OF SOURCES

Powicke, F. M., *The Thirteenth Century, 1216–1307*, Oxford History of England, second edition, 1962.

Prestwich, Michael, 'Exchequer and Wardrobe in the Later Years of Edward I', *B.I.H.R.*, XLVI (1973), pp. 1–10.

— *War, Politics and Finance under Edward I*, 1972.

Pugh, T. B. (ed.), *Glamorgan County History, III (The Marcher Lordships of Glamorgan and Morgannwg and Gower and Kilvey...)*, Cardiff, 1971.

Putnam, Bertha, *The Place in Legal History of Sir William Shareshull*, Cambridge, 1950.

Raban, Sandra, *The Estates of Thorney and Crowland: A Study in Medieval Monastic Land Tenure*, Cambridge, 1977.

Raftis, J. A., *The Estates of Ramsey Abbey*, Toronto, 1957.

Rawcliffe, Carole, *The Staffords, Earls of Stafford and Dukes of Buckingham, 1394–1521*, Cambridge, 1978.

Robinson, W. R. B., 'An Analysis of a Ministers' Account for the Borough of Swansea for 1449', *Bulletin of the Board of Celtic Studies*, XXII (1968), pp. 169–98.

Rosenthal, J. T., 'The Estates and Finances of Richard Duke of York, 1411–60', *Studies in Medieval and Renaissance History*, II (1965), pp. 115–204.

Ross, C. D., and Pugh, T. B., 'Materials for the Study of Baronial Incomes in Fifteenth-century England', *Ec.H.R.*, Second Series, VI (1953), pp. 185–94.

Ross, C. D., *The Estates and Finances of Richard Beauchamp Earl of Warwick*, Dugdale Society Occasional Paper, 12, 1956.

Russell, J. C., *British Medieval Population*, Albuquerque, N.M., 1948.

Scammell, J., 'The Origin and Limitations of the Liberty of Durham', *E.H.R.*, LXXI (1966), pp. 449–73.

Searle, Eleanor, *Lordship and Community: Battle Abbey and its Banlieu, 1066–1538*, Toronto, 1974.

Sharp, Margaret, 'The Administrative Chancery of the Black Prince before 1362', in *Essays in Medieval History presented to T. F. Tout*, ed. A. G. Little and F. M. Powicke (1925).

Sherbourne, J. W., 'The Cost of English Warfare with France in the Later Fourteenth Century', *B.I.H.R.*, L (1977), pp. 135–50.

Slicher van Bath, B. H. *The Agrarian History of Western Europe, 500–1800*, 1963.

Smith, J. Beverley, 'Edward II and the Allegiance of Wales', *Welsh History Review*, 8 (1976–7), pp. 139–71.

Smith, Llinos Beverley, 'The Arundel Charters to the Lordship of Chirk in the Fourteenth Century', *Bulletin of the Board of Celtic Studies*, 23 (1968–70), pp. 153–66.

Smith, R. A. L., *Canterbury Cathedral Priory*, Cambridge, 1943.

Somerville, R., *History of the Duchy of Lancaster*, I (1265–1603), 1953.

— 'The Duchy of Lancaster Council and Court of Duchy Chamber', *T.R.H.S.*, Fourth Series, XXIII (1941), pp. 159–77.

Steel, A. B., 'The Present State of Studies on the English Exchequer in the Middle Ages', *American Historical Review*, XXXIV (1928–9), pp. 485–512.

— *The Receipt of the Exchequer, 1377–1485*, Cambridge, 1954.

Stone, E., 'Profit and Loss Accountancy at Norwich Cathedral Priory', *T.R.H.S.*, Fifth Series, XII (1962), pp. 25–48.

Strayer, Joseph R., and Rudishill, George, junior, 'Taxation and Community in Wales and Ireland, 1272–1327', *Speculum*, XXIX (1954), pp. 410–16.

Tait, James, 'The *Firma Burgi* and the Commune in England, 1066–1191', *E.H.R.*, XLII (1927), pp. 321–60.

— *The Medieval English Borough*, Manchester, 1936.

Titow, J. Z., *English Rural Society, 1200–1350*, 1969.

Tout, T. F., and Broome, D. M., 'A National Balance Sheet for 1362–3, with documents subsidiary thereto', *E.H.R.*, XXXIX (1924), pp. 404–19.

— *Chapters in the Administrative History of Medieval England: the Wardrobe, the Chamber and the Small Seals*, I–VI, Manchester, 1920–33.

— 'Flintshire: its History and Records', in *Collected Papers*, II, 1934, pp. 21–44.

— *The Place of the Reign of Edward II in English History*, Second Edition (revised by Hilda Johnstone), Manchester, 1936.

Unwin, George (ed.), *Finance and Trade under Edward III*, Manchester, 1918.

Usher, G. A., 'The Black Prince's Quo Warranto (1348)', *Welsh History Review*, 7 (1974–5), pp. 1–12.

Virgoe, R., 'The Composition of the King's Council, 1437–61', *B.I.H.R.*, XLIII (1970), pp. 134–60.

Waters, W. H., *The Edwardian Settlement of North Wales in its Administrative and Legal Aspects*, Cardiff, 1935.

Watts, D. G., 'A Model for the Early Fourteenth Century', *Ec.H.R.*, XX (1967), pp. 543–7.

Wilkinson, B., 'The Authorisation of Chancery Writs under Edward III', *Bulletin of the John Rylands Library*, 8 (1924), pp. 107–39.

— *The Chancery under Edward III*, Manchester, 1929.

Willard, J. F., and Morris, W. A. (eds), *The English Government at Work, 1327–36*, 3 vols., Cambridge, Mass., 1940–50.

— 'An Exchequer Reform under Edward I' in *The Crusades and other Historical Essays presented to Dana C. Munro . . .*, ed. L. J. Paetow, 1928.

— 'Edward III's Negotiations for a Grant in 1337', *E.H.R.*, XXI (1906), pp. 727–31.

— 'Ordinances for the Guidance of a Deputy Treasurer', *E.H.R.*, XLVIII (1933), pp. 84–9.

— *Parliamentary Taxes on Personal Property, 1290 to 1334*, Cambridge, Mass., 1934.

— 'The Memoranda Rolls and the Remembrancers, 1282–1350', in *Essays . . . Tout*, ed. A. G. Little and F. M. Powicke (1925).

— 'The Taxes upon Movables of the Reign of Edward I', *E.H.R.*, XXVIII (1913), pp. 517–21.

— 'The Taxes upon Movables of the Reign of Edward III', *E.H.R.*, XXX (1915), pp. 69–74.

Williams-Jones, Keith (ed.), *The Merioneth Lay Subsidy Roll, 1292–3*,

University of Wales Board of Celtic Studies, History and Law Series, XXIX, 1976.

Wolffe, B. P., *The Crown Lands, 1461 to 1536*, 1970.

— *The Royal Demesne in English History: the crown estate in the governance of the realm from the Conquest to 1509*, 1971.

Wretts-Smith, Mildred, 'Organization of Farming at Croyland Abbey, 1257–1321', *Journal of Economic and Business History*, IV (1932), pp. 168–92.

INDEX

Pearson, John, **22–3**, 24
Peas and other legumes, *see* Agriculture
Peckforton manor, 126, **129**
  Park, 55, 77, 100, 131
Perton, William, 57, 81, 142
Pestilence
  (1349), **2–3**, **88–93**, 96, 100, **127–8**, 129
  (1361), 97
Philippa, Queen, 7
Pirie, John, 26, 46, 154
Pleas, serjeant of, earl's, 55
Plumber, master, earl's, 55
Plymouth, 38, 49
Plympton, 131
Poitiers, battle and expedition of, 65, 75, 77, 84, 94, 101, **103**, 114, **123**,
     129, **131**, **135**, 139–40
Poker, *see* Macclesfield, Hundred
Poker, Ellen, 114
Poker, Thomas, 114
Poker, William, 102
Pole, John, 66
Population and settlement, **1–3**, 90–1, 137
Postan, M. M., 91
Pott Shrigley, 88, 98, 103, 112
Praers, William, **53**
Prestbury 95
Prices, 65, 95–6
Princes Risborough, 77, **175**
Principality of Chester, 8
Prises, 65
  Sea coal, 47
  Wine, 69
  Wood, 47
Privileges, *see* Liberties
Profit, *see* Administration
Public order, 50, 146
Public Record Office, **11–13**, 43
Purveyance, **5–6**, 10, 13, 43, 78, 81
Puture 80
Pynnok, Nicholas, 26, 46

Quo Warranto (action), 6, 134

Raftis, J. A., 24
Rainow, 98, 103, 112
Ravensmoor, 144
Reapers, 114
Records, 133 (*see also* Accounts)
  Central
    Earls of Chester, **13–14**, 38, 43, **62**, 71–3, 84, 91: Inquisitions post